CHICANA

TRADITIONS

CHICANA
TRADITIONS

CONTINUITY AND CHANGE

EDITED BY NORMA E. CANTÚ

AND OLGA NÁJERA-RAMÍREZ

UNIVERSITY OF ILLINOIS PRESS

Urbana and Chicago

Library of Congress Cataloging-in-Publication Data
Chicana traditions : continuity and change / edited by
Norma E. Cantú and Olga Nájera-Ramírez.
    p.   cm.
Includes bibliographical references and index.
ISBN 0-252-02701-9 (alk. paper)/ISBN 978-0-252-02701-7
ISBN 0-252-07012-7 (paper : alk. paper)/ISBN 978-0-252-07012-9
1. Mexican American women—Social life and customs.
2. Mexican American women—Intellectual life.
3. Mexican American arts. 4. Mexican American
women—Folklore. 5. Feminism—United States.
I. Cantú, Norma Elia, 1947– . II. Nájera-Ramírez, Olga.
E184.M5C4   2002
305.48'868'72073—dc21   2001002644

We would like to dedicate our book to the many traditional artists and tradition-bearers who have devoted themselves to producing, preserving, and promoting our cultural heritage. We especially dedicate our work to the *pioneras* whose work inspired and moved us. Finally, we dedicate this volume to all of our mothers and foremothers whose love and encouragement serve as a constant source of comfort and inspiration.

CONTENTS

ACKNOWLEDGMENTS

We extend our appreciation to everyone who supported this project. We are grateful to the institutions with which we were affiliated during the course of the project: the University of California at Santa Barbara, the University of California at Santa Cruz, Texas A&M International University in Laredo, and the University of Texas at San Antonio. At the University of California at Santa Cruz we were extremely fortunate to receive the support of the Document Publishing and Editing Center, especially the invaluable assistance of Zoe Sodja. Judy McCulloh deserves special thanks for providing us with constant support and encouragement since the inception of this project. Finally, we thank our family, friends, and colleagues for their understanding and loving kindness.

INTRODUCTION

NORMA E. CANTÚ AND OLGA NÁJERA-RAMÍREZ

Chicana Traditions is the first anthology to focus specifically on the topic of Chicana expressive culture. It also represents the first collection to be written by native scholars, that is, Chicanas, engaged in various and sometimes multiple careers as professors, graduate students, performing artists, public sector folklorists, archivists, museum coordinators, and community activists. Some authors are trained in fields such as folklore, anthropology, ethnomusicology, sociology, cultural studies, Chicana/o studies, art history, and literature, while others are not, yet all these authors bring a variety of theoretical perspectives to their examinations and analyses of Chicana traditions. This collection of essays by scholars who are intimately engaged with the subjects of study offers an original and timely perspective that places questions of the politics of culture at the intersection of folklore, feminism, and Chicana/o studies.

DEFINITIONS

Since its establishment in the late 1800s, the field of folklore has witnessed significant changes and developments that have shaped our understanding regarding what constitutes the "folk" and "folklore." As Bengt Holbeck observed years ago, "our views of folk traditions are formed probably to a much higher degree than we think by the prejudices, experiences, and interests that are characteristic of the class we come from. If the social position of this class changes, or if the recruitment of folklorists changes, then the tacit assumptions in our work change and, along with them, our theories and working hypotheses" (1981:140).

In other words, changes in the social location of folklorists have led to important revisions in the field of folklore. Central to this re-visioning have been critical interventions made by feminists (see Stoeltje 1988b) and ethnic scholars (Paredes 1978). As the first collection of studies in Chicana folklore by Chicana scholars and artists, this book contributes to this re-visioning.

The term *folklore* has sometimes been eschewed by scholars or artists who feel that traditions labeled as folklore are often exoticized or pejoratively perceived. However, we use the term to refer to expressive cultural practices not necessarily exclusive to a particular segment of society. This point is especially important, as it underscores the fact that while some of our traditions may enjoy "official status" in Mexico or within their circumscribed community group, north of the border and within the context of the larger cultural panorama of the United States they are reduced to minority status.[1] Further, we employ the term *Chicanas* to refer to women of Mexican descent who reside in the United States, although some of our contributors have chosen to use other relevant terms such as *Latinas* and *Hispanas* (see Zavella 1991; Melville 1994).

Our collection addresses the problem of identification and accessibility presented by the interdisciplinary nature of our topic. Articles on Chicana folklore may appear in various discipline-specific journals in addition to mainstream folklore journals.[2] Scholarly treatments of Chicana folklore also appear in several anthologies and in special-topic issues of journals.[3] Literary anthologies often include folklore (see Castañeda Shular et al. 1972; Rebolledo 1993). Signficantly, edited collections on women and folklore contain little, if any, material on Chicana traditions.[4] Commenting on this void in their recent collection of feminist folklore, the editors of *Feminist Theory and the Study of Folklore* note:

> In reviewing the papers delivered at the conference, however, we found virtually no mention of feminist approaches to the folklore of women who are often doubly marginalized in our society by virtue of other factors in addition to their gender: these include women of color, lesbians, women with disabilities, and older women, who seldom have been the focus of folklore research. Hoping to address this lacuna, we attempted early in the development of the book to solicit essays that addressed these areas, but we did not have much success probably both because we were *not looking in the right places for work that exists and because not enough has been done in these areas.* (Hollis et al. 1993:x; emphasis added)

While we wholeheartedly agree that work on Chicana folklore is often limited and not easily accessible, such scholarship does exist. Furthermore, the idea of Chicana/Mexicana scholars engaged in the collection and publication of folklore material has important antecedents.

LAS FOLKLORISTAS: AN OVERVIEW

Several important intellectual precursors who documented the cultural expressions of women in the Southwest include Jovita González de Mireles (1930a, 1930b, 1932, 1996, 1997), Soledad Pérez (1951), Fabiola Cabeza de Baca Gilbert (1954), Carmen Gertrudis Espinosa (1970), Adelina (Nina) Otero-Warren (1936), Luisa Espinel (1946), Aurora Lucero-White Lea (1941, 1953), and Cleofas Jaramillo (1939a, 1939b, 1941, 1945). Many writers of fiction in the early 1920s and 1930s also chose Mexican folklore and oral tradition as an underlying theme in their writing.[5]

Texas produced several *pioneras* (pioneers) in the field, some of whom attended the University of Texas at Austin. Soledad Pérez completed a thesis in 1949 entitled "Mexican Folklore from Austin, Texas," which was later published as part of Wilson Mathis Hudson's collection *The Healer of Los Olmos and Other Mexican Lore* (1951). Rogelia O. García (1970), Fermina Guerra (1941, 1967a [1943], 1967b [1941]), and others whose master's theses include descriptions of *pastorelas* (shepherds' plays), *matachines* (traditional religious dance), cultural expressions, and folk life in general recorded and chronicled cultural production in South Texas. Jovita González de Mireles, another of our *pioneras tejanas,* was born into an upper-class Mexican American family in Roma, Texas. She completed a master's degree in history at the University of Texas at Austin in the 1920s, where she met and worked with the Texas folklorist J. Frank Dobie. She joined the Texas Folklore Society and eventually became its president.

Josefina Niggli, born in Monterrey, Mexico, lived in Texas for most of her life. She imbued her creative work with folkloric themes, and her literary production presents a vision of folklife in the south Texas–northeastern Mexico area from the 1930s to the early 1950s. Although she gained national prominence as a playwright, her most successful work was an anthology, *Mexican Village* (1945), that incorporates a great deal of folklore. A few one-book writers exhibit similar inclinations. For example, Elena Zamora O'Shea's *Mesquite* (2000 [1935]) is replete with descriptions of weddings, games, and seasonal rituals. But such writing was not only happening in Texas; women in the southwestern United States have been writing of their culture and customs since the first incursions and settlements by the Spanish into the area.

Written and oral narratives by women in the Southwest constitute a rich source of information on the cultural expressions of women in the region from the early Spanish colonial to the Mexican and finally the post–Guadalupe-Hidalgo Treaty period of the nineteenth century. But it is not until the early twentieth century that such forms of expression were published. New Mexico produced several important female folklore scholars during the 1930s and 1940s. Like Jovita González, these women were fluent in English and Spanish, were college graduates, and were active participants in folklore societies. Cleofas M. Jaramillo, for example, a founding member of the Santa Fe Folklore Society, wrote a collection of fairy tales based on stories told to her as a child (1939a), a collection of Hispanic New Mexican recipes (1939b), and two novels based on her family's history (1941, 1945). With Jaramillo, Aurora Lucero-White Lea helped found the Sociedad Folklórica in Santa Fe and later became a member of the New Mexico Folklore Society. Lucero-White Lea devoted much of her scholarship to the collection and study of New Mexican dances and folk dramas. As the assistant superintendent of instruction for the state department of education, she also integrated folklore into the general curriculum. According to one scholar (Ponce 1992:46), she was the only one of the New Mexican *pioneras* to be formally involved in the Federal Writer's Project during the 1930s, when she collected and classified Hispano regional folklore. Her best-known book is *The Folklore of New Mexico* (1941), and her *Literary Folklore of the Hispanic Southwest* (1953) includes children's rhymes and other gender-based traditions.

Like Jaramillo, Fabiola Cabeza de Baca Gilbert and Adelina (Nina) Otero-Warren integrated regional folklore into their published family histories, *We Fed Them Cactus* (1994 [1954]) and *Old Spain in Our Southwest* (1936), respectively. While Otero-Warren did not pay particular attention to women in her publications, she was extremely active in her community, becoming one of the first Spanish-speaking New Mexican women to hold several important political posts, and she campaigned heavily for women's rights. With an interest in regional history, customs, and cookery, Cabeza de Baca's publications focused more directly on women and their experiences. As the first bilingual agent of the Agricultural Extension Service for the New Mexico Department of Agriculture, she educated rural New Mexican women in food preparation methods and taught in Mexico for one year.

Of the New Mexican *pioneras,* Carmen Gertrudis Espinosa was the only woman who was not from an upper-class family, yet she too received a college education, attending college in the United States, Spain, and Mexico. Her particular focus was on Spanish colonial fashions and jewelry. *Shawls, Crinolines, Filigree* (1970) is her most well-known publication. Another folklorist, Mela Sedillo, an instructor in fine and dramatic arts at the University of New Mexico, published a small collection entitled *Mexican and New Mexican Folk Dances* in 1935, and two years later she published *A Practical Study of the Use of the Natural Vegetable Dyes in New Mexico.*

In the 1930s Luisa Espinel collected Spanish folk songs from southern Arizona from her father, Don Federico Ronstadt y Redondo. According to the folklorist Américo Paredes (1991:140), in the mid-1930s Espinel toured a program of southwestern Mexican songs that she entitled "Songs My Mother Taught Me." Little else is known about her, except that her relative, the popular singer Linda Ronstadt, produced a touring show of her own that included Mexican songs, entitled "Canciones de mi padre." Patricia Preciado Martin has published a collection of oral histories from Arizona that also includes traditional folk tales and customs, entitled *Songs My Mother Sang to Me* (1992).

California had its share of early women writers whose stories and tales can be classified as traditional lore, but we did not find as much coverage on this state. While far from complete, this brief overview of the *pioneras* is intended to encourage further interest in these women scholars as well as scholars in other states to develop a more comprehensive understanding of the intellectual trajectory of the chroniclers of Chicana folklore.

In recent times, it is the women who have worked to keep traditions alive in communities not only in the Southwest but wherever Chicanas reside. The Detroit Chicano community, for example, produced an exhibit and an accompanying book that highlights the contributions by both the artists and those in the community who strive to keep traditional culture alive. Folklorists in the public sector have worked with these communities to document and present their traditional culture in museums in Fresno, California, and in Michigan. In Texas it is often through organizations like the Texas Folklife Resources and *centros culturales* (cultural centers) like the Guadalupe Cultural Arts Center and the Esperanza Peace and Justice Center in San Antonio and the Centro Cultural Narciso Martínez that the women continue to work to sustain traditional culture in a more public arena. In the mid-1980s, the Chicana historian Dolores Bahti worked with the historical museum in Tucson to reenact a shepherds' play that included Yaqui indigenous elements. In the late 1990s, the playwright Rodrigo Duarte Clark worked with the women of the community to write and produce *La Pastorela* in Guadalupe, Arizona. And throughout the United States there are women who work behind the scenes to reenact the Virgen de Guadalupe apparition dramas and to celebrate the *día de los muertos* and other folk liturgical traditions. One cannot ignore the role of women whether in sanctioned Guadalupana societies or in home traditions around the Christmas celebrations of Posadas. For example, Heisley and MacGregor-Villarreal's *More Than a Tradition: Mexican American Nacimientos* (1991) documents the contributions of women in the Los Angeles area. Community scholars have worked with public-sector folklorists in documenting their community's traditional cultural expressions. Eva Castellanoz, for example, has worked with the Oregon Historical Society's Folk Arts Program.

As we gathered the essays for this volume, we found that the Chicana scholar—whether a historian, a literary critic, or an anthropologist—often bridges the academic world and the world of her community. This volume provides new insights into women's experiences within well-established traditions, such as the *mariachi, charrería,* and *santo* carving. We also call attention to the ever-changing nature of traditions such as the *quinceañera* and the development of new traditions such as the *cincuentañera*. Indeed, our title, *Chicana Traditions: Continuity and Change,* addresses the ever-evolving landscape of our field of study, for as we can see in many of these essays, the traditional production has changed and continues to change even as it shapes the ways that Chicanas experience their lives. An important component of the project has been our insistence on expanding the parameters of what we know about Mexican women's folklore by including intimate perspectives along with more formal essays by Chicana scholars. Yolanda Broyles-González, for example, engages in a discussion of her grandmother's legacy and her own role in the perpetuation of her traditional culture. In the same fashion, Cynthia L. Vidaurri, by focusing on a particular woman, posits a lucid view of how the women who are immersed in the Fidencista movement have altered a previously all-male terrain. As Tey Mariana Nunn and Helen R. Lucero illustrate in their pieces on Goldie Garcia and the carvers of *santos,* contemporary artists run the gamut and are willing to take traditional art and shape it to their own ends, thus changing the traditions. Additionally, scholars like Nunn are forging new ground, as they apply their analytical skills to what might be considered popular cultural expressions such as jewelry. It is precisely because we have not adhered to strict boundaries of genre or theory that we have been able to bring together essays that speak to and often resonate with each other.

We organized the chapters into three parts. Part one, "Enduring Traditions," explores long-standing gendered traditions such as the *quinceañera, santo*-making, the *indita* song form, children's games, and the legend of La Llorona. Part two, "Practicing Traditions," ranges from personal narratives to intimate, yet scholarly, reflections by community and academic scholars. Part three, "Transforming Traditions," consists of five analyses of how women continue to invent, reshape, and transcend traditional culture. Additionally, we have included a bibliography of selected materials that are relevant to the study of Chicana feminism and folklore.[6] Although not exhaustive, this list includes materials that were critical in our review of existing Chicana folklore scholarship, many of which influenced our work and have shaped the field in general.

In offering the present anthology we accomplish several goals. First, we make our scholarship readily available to a general audience interested in Latino/a, especially Chicano/a, culture. Second, we showcase the unique perspectives offered by senior and newly trained Chicana scholars and artists. Third, this unique collection, featuring a variety of theoretical approaches and topics, contributes a more nuanced understanding of the lives, experiences, challenges, and perspectives of Chicanas. We hope this anthology will inspire academically trained as well as community scholars to pursue and produce more work on Chicana folklore.

NOTES

1. Américo Paredes makes this important observation in "Folklore, Lo Mexicano, and Proverbs" (1982:1). For examples of the shift in status of Mexican folklore across the U.S.-Mexico border, see Nájera-Ramírez 1989, 1994, and in press.

2. For instance, José Limón's "La Llorona: The Third Legend of Greater Mexico" (1986) appeared in the *Renato Rosaldo Lecture Series Monograph,* while "Tex-Sex-Mex" (1997), on the popular Tejana singer Selena, was published in *American Literary History.* Similarly, María Herrera-Sobek has published extensively on women (including two books on the topic), and her numerous articles have appeared in collections on the U.S.-Mexico border and Mexican immigration, in American folklore journals, and in Spanish-language publications.

3. Our review of special collections on Chicano folklore yielded several articles on Chicana traditions. See, for example, Margarita Melville's *Twice a Minority* (1980), which includes articles by José Limón and Terry Mason. The 1982 special

issue of *Aztlán* features important contributions by Rafaela Castro, Kay Turner, and María Herrera-Sobek.

4. See Farrer 1975, which contains an article by Inéz Cardozo-Freeman, and see Jordan 1985. No articles on Chicana folklore are included in more recent publications (Jackson 1987, Stoeltje 1988a, and Hollis et al. 1993).

5. Elena Zamora O'Shea's *Mesquite* (2000 [1935]) is an excellent example of a fictional novel that incorporates regional folklore. For a discussion of some of these early writers, see Velásquez-Treviño 1985, Ponce 1992, Rebolledo 1987, and Padilla 1991.

6. Michaël Heisley's annotated bibliography (1977) and Tey Diana Rebolledo's work (1987, 1993) have been particularly useful in this regard.

WORKS CITED

Cabeza de Baca Gilbert, Fabiola. 1994 (1954). *We Fed Them Cactus.* Albuquerque: University of New Mexico Press.

Castañeda Shular, Antonia, Tomás Ybarra-Frausto, and Joseph Sommers, comps. 1972. *Literatura Chicana: Texto y Contexto.* Englewood Cliffs, N.J.: Prentice-Hall.

Castellanoz, Eva. 1996. Lecture at the Fife Conference, Utah State University, Ogden.

Castro, Rafaela. 1982. "Mexican Women's Sexual Jokes." *Aztlán* 13 (1–2): 275–93.

Espinel, Luisa. 1946. *Canciones de mi padre: Spanish Folksongs from Southern Arizona.* Tucson: University of Arizona.

Espinosa, Carmen Gertrudis. 1970. *Shawls, Crinolines, Filigree: The Dress and Adornment of Women of New Mexico, 1737–1900.* El Paso: Texas Western Press.

Farrer, Claire, ed. 1975. *Women and Folklore.* Austin: University of Texas Press.

García, Rogelia O. 1970. *Dolores, Revilla, and Laredo (Three Sister Settlements).* Waco, Tex.: Texian Press.

González de Mireles, Jovita. 1930a. "Tales and Songs of the Texas-Mexicans." In *Man, Bird, and Beast.* Ed. J. Frank Dobie. 86–116. Austin: Texas Folklore Society.

———. 1930b. "Social Life in Cameron, Starr, and Zapata Counties." M.A. thesis, University of Texas.

———. 1932. "Among My People." In *Tone the Bell Easy.* Ed. J. Frank Dobie. 99–108. Austin: Texas Folklore Society.

———. 1997. *Dew on the Thorn.* Ed. José E. Limón. Houston, Tex.: Arte Público Press.

González, Jovita, and Eve Raleigh. 1996. *Caballero: A Historical Novel.* Ed. José E. Limón and María Cotera. College Station: Texas A&M University Press.

Guerra, Fermina. 1941. "Mexican and Spanish Folklore and Incidents in Southeast Texas." M.A. thesis, University of Texas.

———. 1967a [1941]. "Rancho Buena Vista: Its Ways of Life and Traditions." In *Texian Stomping Grounds*. Ed. J. Frank Dobie, Mody C. Boatright, and Harry H. Ransom. 59–77. Dallas, Tex.: Southern Methodist University Press.

———. 1967b [1943]. "Mexican Animal Tales." In *Backwoods to Border*. Ed. Mody C. Boatright and Donald Day. 188–94. Dallas, Tex.: Southern Methodist University Press.

Heisley, Michael. 1977. *Chicano Folklore: An Annotated Bibliography of Chicano Folklore of the Southwestern United States*. Los Angeles: Center for the Study of Comparative Folklore and Mythology, University of California.

Heisley, Michael, and Mary MacGregor-Villarreal. 1991. *More Than a Tradition: Mexican American Nacimientos*. Los Angeles: Southwest Museum.

Herrera-Sobek, María. 1982a. "The Acculturation Process of the Chicana in the Corrido." *De Colores* 6 (1–2): 7–16.

———. 1982b. "The Treacherous Woman Archetype: A Structuring Agent in the Corrido." *Aztlán* 13 (1–2): 135–48.

———. 1986. "'La Delgadina': Incest and Patriarchal Structure in a Spanish/Chicano Romance-Corrido." *Studies in Latin American Popular Culture* 5:90–107.

———. 1987. "The Discourse of Love and Despecho: Representations of Women in the Chicano Décima." *Aztlán* 18 (1): 69–82.

———. 1990. *The Mexican Corrido: A Feminist Analysis*. Bloomington: Indiana University Press.

———. 1991. "'Rosita Alvirez': Gender Conflict and the Medieval Exemplum in the Corrido." *Centro de Estudios Puertorriqueños Bulletin* 3 (2): 105–10.

———. 1992. "The Treacherous Woman Archetype: A Structuring Agent in the Corrido." In *Chicano Border Culture and Folklore*. Ed. José Villarino and Arturo Ramírez. 129–43. San Diego, Calif.: Marin Publications.

———. 1993. "The Representation of Mexican Immigrant Women Workers in Ballad and Film: Issues of Ideology and Nationalism." Paper presented at the History of Latina Working Women Conference, George Meany Memorial Archives, Silver Spring, Md.

Holbeck, Bengt. 1981. "Tacit Assumptions." *Folklore Forum* 14 (2): 121–40.

Hollis, Susan Tower, Linda Pershing, and Jane Young. 1993. *Feminist Theory and the Study of Folklore*. Urbana: University of Illinois Press.

Hudson, Wilson Mathis, ed. 1951. *The Healer of Los Olmos and Other Mexican Lore*. Dallas, Tex.: Southern Methodist University Press.

Jackson, Bruce, ed. 1987. *Folklore and Feminism*. Special issue of the *Journal of American Folklore* 100 (398).

Jaramillo, Cleofas M. 1939a. *Cuentos del Hogar* (Spanish fairy stories). El Campo, Tex.: Citizen Press.

———. 1939b. *The Genuine New Mexico Tasty Recipes: Pajajes Sabrosos*. Santa Fe, N.Mex.: Seton Village Press.

————. 1941. *Shadows of the Past/Sombras del Pasado*. Santa Fe, N.Mex.: Seton Village Press.

————. 1945. *Romance of a Little Village Girl*. San Antonio, Tex.: Naylor Co.

Jordan, Rosan A. 1985. "The Vaginal Serpent and Other Themes from Mexican Women's Lore." In *Women's Folklore, Women's Culture*. Ed. Rosan A. Jordan and Susan J. Kalcik. 26–44. Philadelphia: University of Pennsylvania Press.

Limón, José. 1986. "La Llorona—The Third Legend of Greater Mexico: Cultural Symbols, Women, and the Political Unconscious." *Renato Rosaldo Lecture Series Monograph* 2:59–93.

————. 1997. "Tex-Sex-Mex: American Identities, Lone Stars, and the Politics of Racialized Sexuality." *American Literary History* 9 (3): 598–617.

Lucero-White Lea, Aurora. 1941. *The Folklore of New Mexico*. Santa Fe, N.Mex.: Seton Village Press.

————. 1953. *Literary Folklore of the Hispanic Southwest*. San Antonio, Tex.: Naylor Co.

Martin, Patricia Preciado. 1992. *Songs My Mother Sang to Me: An Oral History of Mexican-American Women*. Tucson: University of Arizona Press.

Mason, Terry. 1980. "Symbolic Strategies for Change: A Discussion of the Chicana Women's Movement." In *Twice a Minority: Mexican American Women*. Ed. Margarita Melville. 95–108. St. Louis, Mo.: Mosby.

Melville, Margarita. 1994. "'Hispanic' Ethnicity, Race, and Class." In *Handbook of Hispanic Cultures in the United States*. Ed. Francisco Lomelí and Thomas Weaver. 85–106. Houston, Tex.: Arte Público Press.

————, ed. 1980. *Twice a Minority: Mexican American Women*. St. Louis: Mosby.

Nájera-Ramírez, Olga. 1989. "Social and Political Dimension of Folklorico Dance: The Binational Dialectic of Emergent and Residual." *Western Folklore* 48 (1): 15–33.

————. 1994. "Engendering Nationalism: Identity, Discourse, and the Mexican Charro." *Anthropological Quarterly* 67 (1): 1–14.

————. In press. "Haciendo Patria." In *Transnational Latina/o Communities: Politics, Process, and Cultures*. Ed. Carlos Velez-Ibañez, Anna Simpaio, and Manolo González. Boulder, Colo.: Rowman and Littlefield.

Niggli, Josefina. 1945. *Mexican Village*. Chapel Hill: University of North Carolina Press.

Otero-Warren, Adelina (Nina). 1936. *Old Spain in Our Southwest*. New York: Harcourt Brace and Co.

Padilla, Genaro. 1991. "Imprisoned Narrative? or, Lies, Secrets, Silence in New Mexican Women's Autobiography." In *Criticism in the Borderlands: Studies in Chicano Literature, Culture, and Ideology*. Ed. Hector Calderón and José David Saldívar. 43–60. Durham, N.C.: Duke University Press.

Paredes, Américo. 1978. "On Ethnographic Work among Minorities: A Folklorist's Perspective." In *New Directions in Chicano Scholarship*. Ed. Ricardo Romo and

Raymund Paredes. 1–32. La Jolla: Chicano Studies Center, University of California at San Diego.

———. 1982. "Folklore, Lo Mexicano, and Proverbs." *Aztlán* 13 (1–2): 1–11.

———. 1991. *Between Two Worlds*. Houston, Tex.: Arte Público Press.

Pérez, Soledad. 1951. "Mexican Folklore from Austin, Texas." In *The Healer of Los Olmos and Other Mexican Lore*. Ed. Wilson Mathis Hudson. 71–127. Dallas, Tex.: Southern Methodist University Press.

Ponce, Merrihelen. 1992. *The Lives and Works of Five Hispanic New Mexican Writers, 1878–1991*. Working Paper 119. Albuquerque: Southwest Hispanic Research Institute, University of New Mexico.

Rebolledo, Tey Diana. 1987. "Hispanic Women Writers of the Southwest: Tradition and Innovation." In *Old Southwest/New Southwest: Essays on a Region and Its Literature*. Ed. Judy Nolte Lensink. 49–61. Tucson: University of Arizona Press.

Rebolledo, Tey Diana, and Eliana S. Rivero, eds. 1993. *Infinite Divisions: An Anthology of Chicana Literature*. Tucson: University of Arizona Press.

Sedillo, Mela. 1935. *Mexican and New Mexican Folk Dances*. Albuquerque: University of New Mexico Press.

———. 1937. *A Practical Study of the Use of the Natural Vegetable Dyes in New Mexico*. Albuquerque: University of New Mexico Press.

Stoeltje, Beverly J. 1988a. "Introduction: Feminist Revisions." In *Feminist Revisions in Folklore Studies*. Ed. Beverly J. Stoeltje. 141–53. Special issue of the *Journal of Folklore Research* 25 (3).

———, ed. 1988b. *Feminist Revisions in Folklore Studies*. Special issue of the *Journal of Folklore Research* 25 (3).

Turner, Kay. 1982. "Mexican American Home Altars: Toward Their Interpretation." *Aztlán* 13 (1–2): 309–26.

Velásquez-Treviño, Gloria. 1985. "Cultural Ambivalence in Early Chicana Prose Fiction." Ph.D. dissertation, Stanford University.

Zamora O'Shea, Elena. 2000 [1935]. *El Mesquite: A Story of the Early Spanish Settlements between the Nueces and the Rio Grande as Told by "La Posta del Palo Alto."* College Station: Texas A&M University Press.

Zavella, Patricia. 1991. "Reflections on Diversity among Chicanas." *Frontiers: A Journal of Women's Studies* 12 (2): 73–85.

PART 1

ENDURING TRADITIONS

1

CHICANA LIFE-CYCLE RITUALS

NORMA E. CANTÚ

As girls reach puberty, certain markers signal the expected gender-specific behaviors—religious and otherwise—in Mexican American culture. I have been engaged in a project that explores how these behaviors and events have changed diachronically in Chicano society and how cultural "performances" attest to women's active roles as agents in the ever-evolving socialization process; it is a project that keeps taking me back to my own girlhood. During that girlhood, I obeyed and conformed. As a member of the Teresitas[1] during my childhood years, between first communion and my *quinceañera,* I offered flowers to the Virgin Mary during evening rosaries the whole month of May. But as a teen I rebelled against some of the constraining and what I deemed unfair expectations, even while succumbing to others. For example, unlike some of my sisters I did not join the Hijas de María, to my mother's consternation, for she had belonged to both the Teresitas and the Hijas de María and expected her daughters to follow suit. I don't recall why I didn't join nor why I defied my mother's unspoken expectation. But I did have a *quinceañera,* mainly as a concession to my *mamagrande* (my paternal grandmother) and my mother. My *quinceañera* was indeed a life-cycle marker, for after the fiesta I could wear makeup, wear heels, and go to dances.[2] I have described this event previously, and I only refer to it here to show that I did not adhere to the "traditional" event and changed it as much as I could while still keeping my family happy (Cantú 1999). For my working-class family, who often worked out in the fields, my fiesta entailed a tremendous financial sacrifice, and to this day I cannot understand how my parents were able to pull it off, although I have come to understand why it was so crucial that they do so.

The *fiesta de quince años,* the coming-of-age celebration for young Latinas at age fifteen, baffles outsiders who do not understand the contradictions that it underscores in a community with excessively high dropout rates, high teen pregnancy, double-digit unemployment rates, and high levels of poverty. In this brief analysis, I limit my observations to the signifiers of the feminine found in the celebration and the performance and those that position the honoree as a subject in a ritual with roots in European and indigenous traditions where coming-of-age rituals signal fertility as well as responsibility, the change from childhood to adulthood. My discussion of the *quinceañera* focuses on items worn or received by the young woman and briefly looks at the performance, especially the dance, as a rite of passage whereby the young woman becomes an adult female. Noting the changes that this celebration has undergone, I also explore the celebration for women turning fifty, the *cincuentañera.* I focus on how the *cincuentañera* has evolved as a newly *created* tradition and examine what it signifies. Most traditions created to fulfill needs in communities emerge out of earlier ones. So the *cincuentañera,* although only begun in recent years, has gained popularity; however, it is not as widespread a practice as the *quinceañera.* For the Chicano/*mexicano* community, the *quinceañera* as a festival of cultural affirmation enjoys, on a personal and familial level, the same popularity as secular celebrations, such as Cinco de Mayo and 16 de Septiembre. In *Multicultural Celebrations: Today's Rules of Etiquette for Life's Special Occasions,* the folklorist Norine Dresser describes the *quinceañera* and *cincuentañera* celebrations as they occur in Latino communities in the United States and offers guidance for outsiders who may find themselves invited to such an event (1999:70–73).

In my analysis, I follow Chela Sandoval's theory of how oppressed subjects perform their otherness as they read "the mobile webs of power" and "create [by] changing responses capable of providing strategic counter moves" (1982:27) and her ideas about "differential consciousness," whereby subjects give meaning to their positionality in the body politic (1991:14). The *quinceañera* allows Chicanas to perform their cultural identity outside the realm of mainstream U.S. culture. While it is accepted behavior, it often becomes a subversive performance even within the strict social behavior of the cultural group, as the honoree defies strict codes of conduct. Scott's (1990) patterns of resistance are embedded in the performance of the *quinceañera* even within the very sites of the subject's oppression, the church and the dance hall, symbolic social space that becomes a gendered space, the location where her sexual awakening and her new position in society becomes public. The *cincuentañera* is similarly a rite of passage, a critical life-cycle event, as the women, upon reaching fifty, celebrate having arrived at that which was potential at fifteen. Whereas such an event occurs at retirement for some, Chicanas are marking the transition earlier, not necessarily tied to their identities as producers in economic society but rather to their ethnic and cultural identity. Such a transition, marked by biology, occurs as an informal female life-cycle marker—menopause, or *el cambio de vida* (the change of life), commonly referred to as *el cambio*.

Although there is evidence of *quinceañera* celebrations occurring since the early 1900s in Laredo, Texas, many Chicanas do not recall participating in them and often remark that the celebration was only for the elites who were able to afford the ostentatious display of wealth that a complete *quinceañera* would entail. The advent of the *quinceañera* celebration as a full ritual with extended *madrinas* and *padrinos* seems to have reached a watershed in the late 1940s.[3] Prior to the 1950s, it seems that it was considered a celebration for the daughters of the elites, coming-out balls for the daughters of merchants and land-owners as well as professionals such as lawyers and doctors. But by the 1960s the celebration was common in all sectors of society. Shortly after the late sixties and early seventies, however, many Chicano families put aside *quinceañera* celebrations. Perhaps it was the fact that proms became more common at the junior high school level. By then, the more assimilated daughters of Chicano families attended high school presentation balls, such as those of the Pan American Student Forum or the ROTC, and, of course, the more common high school proms, which provided a different arena for acting grown-up by donning grown-up formal wear. In Laredo, school proms, the Black and White Ball, and particularly the George Washington's Birthday Celebration Ball fulfilled the social need for initiating young women of all classes from the working poor (via the prom) to the social elite, into adult society, where they were expected to wear special attire and perform as adults.[4] Although many middle-income and some working-class Chicanas did participate in such activities, proms and presentation balls were prohibitive for the majority; therefore, it is possible that the *quinceañera* remained as a vehicle for such display in addition to fulfilling a religious and cultural need. But, as far as I can tell, it has never been exclusively the domain of one particular social class; the reality is that families across the social spectrum celebrated and continue to celebrate their daughters' coming-of-age with a mass and a dance.[5] In some instances, the more assimilated families may celebrate with a sweet sixteen party instead of the *quinceañera,* as Dresser points out (1999:70–71). The celebration has also undergone a shift in status in relation to the church, where at one time it was limited to a rosary and not a mass and where it is still a point of contention in individual parishes.[6]

In her valuable article on the subject of *quinceañeras,* the anthropologist Karen Mary Dávalos focuses on "the negotiation and contestation surrounding the event." The women in her study negotiate "between various often conflicting views about women, family, and mexicano culture" (1996:103). Her analysis does not consider the particular material objects or the cultural production of the celebration, yet she underscores the use of the event by the Catholic church as a socializing force and by the community in the creation of an ethnic and gender identity (1996:110–11). The place of the celebration in the formation of a young woman's identity as female and as Mexican is unquestionable.

C. Gilbert Romero concludes that the *quinceañera* ceremony constitutes a revelatory tradition, as the young woman remembers her life experiences (1991:80). The key events in the young woman's life become part of her memory, and the "interaction between memory and its interpretation in tradition can result in a revelatory experience" (1991:80). Romero explains that the ceremony "would be the threshold moment of the rite of passage, enabling her to evaluate her past life and its future directions in light of available options" (1991:80). The event itself, then, to use van Gennep's terms, becomes a "liminal" or "transitory place" (1960:21). My position is that the ceremony, including both religious and secular elements, occurs as a marker of ethnicity and functions as a coming-of-age ritual that offers the young woman a space to perform her emergence into adulthood and to contest and shape the expectations that the symbolic act implies.

Wherever it is celebrated, the *quinceañera* remains a cultural marker for Latinidad and, more specifically, *mexicanidad,* and for the honoree it remains a coming-of-age ritual. In all cases, the celebration signals a change, a transformation; it is therefore loaded with significant ritual behaviors that reflect the transformation. Aside from the obviously sexualized nature of what could be called an initiation rite, there are the concomitant signals of the individual's induction into an adult society.[7] I limit my discussion here to those gender-specific elements that function as racial (or ethnic) and gender markers of the transition. Moreover, since I have elsewhere offered a description and analysis of the different forms of the fiesta along the U.S.-Mexican border (Cantú 1999), I focus on the celebration as it occurs in Laredo, Texas, a border community where *quinceañera* celebrants observe rules of behavior

that include certain essential elements. I begin with an analysis of the socialization of the young women into female Chicano culture through the celebration and of the objects worn and received during the fiesta by the young
honoree that signify female adulthood. The following discussion centers on
these cultural icons: the dress, the diadem, the missal and rosary, the jewelry, the shoes, the last doll, and the performance in the dance. From a feminist perspective, the performance of the ritual is an act of womanist theology and of the necessary rendition of a female ritual in a particular space, at
a particular time in a woman's life. However, one can also argue that in its
socializing fervor the celebration is antifeminist in intent, for instead of ac-
knowledging the young woman's self-determination and potential, it can
become a way of constricting and limiting her choices. Even as she moves
from childhood into womanhood, she remains bound by the expectations
of the church and the community. One church scholar has noted that the
central elements of the ceremony are her "renewal of the baptismal prom-
ises and the commitment to be of service to the community" (Romero
1991:72), and another has seen the occasion as a "teachable moment" (Erevia
1980:5). The areas that I have chosen to focus on for my discussion are contested sites where the potential for socialization arises; yet, because these are
markers of gender and ethnic identity, they can also function as the sites for
cultural and gender affirmation.

The *quinceañera* dress is the young woman's first formal adult attire. Like
the wedding gown, it marks a change in the wearer's status in the community. The wedding gown signals that the woman is joining the ranks of
married women; she becomes a *señora*. The *quinceañera* dress signals that
the young woman is moving from girlhood to her new status as *señorita* and
is available for marriage. Because it is formal, the dress indicates the coming-of-age of the celebrant and is therefore a critical element in the fiesta.

The color and style of the *quinceañera* dress signals ethnic and social status. In my previous work I note that one of the differences between the U.S.
and Mexican celebrations is often the color of the dress (Cantú 1999). In
Mexico, Central America, Cuba, and Puerto Rico the honoree invariably
wears a pink or pastel shade, such as lavender, lime green, pale blue or yel-
low, or salmon. In some areas of Mexico and the United States a white dress
is a must, and it is the *damas,* the fourteen young women who accompany
the honoree, who don the pastel dresses. But sometimes the change occurs
with the *damas,* as exemplified in Brenda de la Rosa's fiesta, where the *damas*
wore burgundy lace over satin bodices and short skirts over which they wore
full-length satin overskirts, which they removed at one point during the

choreographed dance. According to a seamstress in Nuevo Laredo, her clients from Laredo or farther north from the U.S. border, San Antonio or Houston, ask for white dresses, while young women from Nuevo Laredo or farther south from the Mexican border, Sabinas or even Monterrey, wear only pink or pastel colors. Recently a friend told me that her daughter had refused to have a *quinceañera* if her dress could not be red. Of course, the mother protested, but in the end the daughter got her way and walked down the aisle in perhaps the only red *quinceañera* dress ever worn. The young woman's blatant resistance to the expected behavior constitutes an affirmation of her sexuality, whether on a conscious or unconscious level, for white has traditionally signaled virginity. The color is one of the most obvious areas of negotiation between the young woman and her community, and many are choosing to defy expectations and wear dark colors, including black, or even prints. Along with color choice, design is also important. Often the prevailing preference for modesty must be negotiated, especially in the church service. Off-the-shoulder or strapless styles are shunned and, if selected, usually include a shawl or a jacket that is then discarded for the dance presentation.

Along with the dress, which is usually formal length, the honoree wears a special headpiece, a *diadema* or tiara, and carries a matching nosegay, or *ramo*. Prior to the mid 1960s, before Vatican II, women had to have their head covered when inside a church. *Quinceañeras* of that time often wore a plain lace head scarf, similar to what they would have worn for their first communion, topped by a *corona*. Today one frequently sees artificial flowers used on the *diadema* as well as for the *ramo,* and the lace scarf is gone. Traditional artists who make the *arreglos* for weddings and *quinceañeras* use natural flowers dipped in wax to construct the elaborate headpieces and *ramos*. Eva Castellanoz notes that "Fewer young women choose the traditional *diadema*" and prefer to wear tiaras with rhinestones or glass beads for their headpiece (1996). The *damas* often wear similar headpieces. Brenda de la Rosa and her *damas* wore identical headpieces: their hair up in french twists topped by curls, they sported a string of pearls falling onto the forehead suspended from a band of tiny silk flowers. Angela Erevia explains that the *diadema* is "a symbol of [the young woman's] sharing in the mission of Christ as Priest, Prophet and King" (1985:94) and "the victory the young lady has won in trying to live a Christian life in the midst of all the problems and challenges of her environment" (1980:7). So although Catholic church requirements have changed and women must no longer cover their head, the *quinceañera* tradition retains the *diadema* or tiara as a marker of femininity.

Other markers of the female role that the young woman is about to assume include the prayer book, or missal, and rosary, always referred to as the *libro y rosario,* that she carries during the religious ceremony. Brides but not grooms also receive the *libro y rosario.* In the *quinceañera,* the *libro y rosario* signal the coming-of-age of the celebrant, for she no longer receives the child-sized rosary or the first communion missal but adult objects for worshipping as an adult. Through the gift of the *libro y rosario,* the young women are initiated into a gender-specific domain for prayer and religion often seen as the domain of women.[8] One contested element is the substitution of the traditional Spanish-language prayer book with an English-language Bible. In the U.S. Latino community, an increasing number of publications clearly meant for the *quinceañera* have been published in English. This variation from the traditional Spanish-language missal can be seen as a move to affirm and signal the honoree's bilingual cultural experience even as it signals the feminine.

The young woman also receives gifts of jewelry that signify that she is about to join the adult world—the ring, *esclava* (identity bracelet), earrings, and the religious medal, the *medalla de oro,* often of the Virgen de Guadalupe. Erevia mentions that "the medal symbolizes the religious expression of faith" and that the young woman is placed under the protection of the image on the medal (1980:7). Dávalos also notes that the young woman becomes aware of a special connection to the Virgen de Guadalupe (1996:114). Some churches have instituted classes for the young woman and her court of honor, where they receive instruction on the meaning of the celebration. The *quinceañera* is told that she is now avowed to the Virgen de Guadalupe. She recites a prayer during the mass: "Our Lady of Guadalupe, I honor you as the Mother of God. I ask that you guide my steps as I am molded into the image of Jesus, your son. Help me to be faithful to my baptismal promise" (Erevia 1992:106). As an adult, she can now wear the expensive piece of jewelry, the gold medal of the Virgen de Guadalupe. But the medal signals more than her coming-of-age, it also functions as an identity marker that focuses her attention on her cultural heritage and establishes a direct link to her indigenous past; however, in spite of claims by various journalists and other writers, there is no concrete evidence that links the celebration to a specific pre-Columbian or contemporary indigenous celebration.[9]

The medal of the Virgen de Guadalupe, perhaps the most religious of the gifts, assumes an even greater role in so far as it signals a bond with other women. The *madrina de medalla* (sponsor of the medal) is usually a relative—an aunt, grandmother, or older sister—thus reinforcing the importance of this bond. The madrina will place the medal of the Virgen de Guadalupe and the gold chain around the young woman's neck prior to the mass, so it can be blessed during the mass. As evidence of what a strong symbol it is, the honoree will continue to wear it, sometimes for life, to signify her personal vow to the Virgen de Guadalupe.

Briefly, I now turn to other items that establish her as a female member of her community: the ring, the bracelet, and the last doll. The *madrina de anillo* gives the *quinceañera* a birthstone ring. Like the medal, it may be inscribed with the initials and the date. In some cases, when there is no *quinceañera* celebration, the parents or grandparents still give the young woman a ring as a symbol of her coming-of-age. Erevia claims that "The ring symbolizes the tie and the responsibility that the young lady has to the community and to her God" (1980:7).[10] Also, the community and family expect that someday she will replace the *quinceañera* ring with another life-cycle marker, a wedding band or an engagement ring. While children might wear gold bracelets, the *esclava* of the *quinceañera* signifies adulthood and the feminine, although sometimes young boys are also gifted with a similar but more masculine-looking bracelet when they are around the same age.

We have been examining the gifts that the young woman receives to mark her entrance into a community of adults, but other aspects of the celebration are more clearly symbolic of her new status as a woman. Various symbolic acts, such as the first dance and the drinking of alcohol, signal initiation into adulthood for young people in various cultures. The *quinceañera,* however, may feature additional elements that, although not occurring in all celebrations, are nevertheless indicative of the fact that the celebration is a coming-of-age initiation ritual. The *brindis,* or toast, the first waltz often danced with the father, and a number of other aspects of the celebration also occur at weddings, yet there are some ritual actions particular to the *quinceañera.* During the reception, when the emcee announces that the young woman will now change from flats to high heels, or announces that it is time for the *entrega de la última muñeca,* those in attendance clap and gather round for the spectacle. But in some cases it is in an anticlimactic tone that the *madrina de la última muñeca* and *la madrina de zapatos de tacón* present the objects to the honoree. The degree of fanfare surrounding these two actions depends on the overall plan for the fiesta. Usually the young woman and her parents stand together, and the *madrinas* may say a few words, although it is not a scripted *parlamento* (traditional spoken words in rites or rituals). The young woman thanks her *madrinas* with a hug. She puts on the shoes, which in many cases are not really her first pair of heels, and cradles the doll as if it were a baby. This second action perhaps shows that, more than a sign of her last doll, the signifier stands for her new capacity to be a mother. These symbolic acts clearly mark a change in the status of the young woman. As I note in an earlier piece, "the wearing of high heels can be seen as a hardship as well as a sign of the suffering to come for the young women as they enter the world of adults where women must self-torture to fit society's idea of what is beautiful and feminine" (Cantú 1999:89). Mary Daly, the feminist theologian, has noted that "hobbling on spiked heels . . . women feel physically and emotionally unsteady" (1978:146). Footwear is but one area that renders the fiesta a coming-of-age ritual; in many contemporary fiestas the young woman also receives a "last doll," signaling the change as she leaves her childhood behind and is symbolically ready for motherhood. One scholar notes that "on a basic level the creative forces symbolized by the young woman's fertility are celebrated by the community as an affirmation of its own potential for continuity"; "the ritual celebration of her fertile status ensures a right relationship with the creative forces of the cosmos and thus a victory over chaos, not only for the young woman herself, but also for the community" (Romero 1991:72). This victory exists in both secular and religious arenas. The dress, the jewelry, the doll, and the shoes are icons of her new secular status as a woman in society, while the Virgen de Guadalupe medal and the *libro y rosario* signal her new status in a religious sense.[11]

The *quinceañera,* as a religious and secular coming-of-age ritual deployed in the corresponding sites, the church and the *salón,* or dance hall, signals transition. There are other symbols that signal adulthood, but not necessarily her status as a woman. In the Chicano cultural imaginary that she inhabits, she is now a woman and as such can sip alcohol during the *brindis;* she can dance formally with her father and her *chambelán* (escort). The young woman's sexual awakening is also acknowledged by the instruction given in some parishes to prepare the young people involved in the *quinceañera* (Lorch 1996:C4). But the most powerful messages are those transmitted by the event itself, a performance of budding womanhood on at least two levels: religious and social. Such a passage or transition occurs in all cultures and is marked in a unique fashion in each. For Chicanas in the United States, the *quinceañera* affirms a cultural tradition from the root culture even as it may also be a site for increasing assimilation, as Dávalos points out (1996:123).

In looking at rites of passage such as the *quinceañera* and the *cincuentanera,* I have found the work of the folklorist and ethnographer Arnold van

Gennep useful. After observing numerous such rites in a number of cultures, he gleaned a pattern common to all rites of passage. He identifies three common phases in the rites of passage: separation, transition, and incorporation (1960:10–11). The *quinceañera* celebration can be said to adhere to these three phases with the added dimension of bridging the religious and secular aspects of life. And because it occurs in a culture that is at the crossroads of two powerful hegemonic forces—those of Mexico and the United States—the fiesta can also be read as a performance wherein Gennep's phases are integrated and recursive and not necessarily linear. Succinctly put, the separation occurs as the young woman is taken by her parents to the church—usually in a limo—and is physically separated from her peers and the rest of her family and friends. At the church she is the center of attention, as she enters alone or escorted by her parents and followed by her *corte de honor,* her peers. At the conclusion of the religious ceremony she enters the second phase, the transition, and engages in various activities marking her emergence and final incorporation into the adult world: the ritualistic change of shoes, the ritual meal, drink, and dance, as well as the usual entrance into the *salón de baile* through an *arco,* usually decorated to fit the theme of the fiesta, can be read as signs of incorporation from the liminal world between childhood and adulthood that she has occupied from the moment she stepped out of her house until she entered the *salón de baile* (Gennep 1960:24).[12] Although most fiestas include certain common elements, the ritual is not static; it is constantly changing to accommodate the needs and the desires of the participant. The choreographed dance, the addition of sponsors for such things as videotaping, and the new fad of having themes for the fiesta or even events such as a cruise disrupt the established sequence. It is in these permutations and additions and in the negotiation of a variety of elements that we can observe how the hegemonic force of U.S. and Mexican popular culture impels the communities to adapt and shift in a fluid manner. But even so, certain markers remain. For example, most contemporary fiestas include both the choreographed dance with the *corte de honor* and the first waltz. While the choreographed dance is a relatively new addition, it has become an essential part of the fiesta. Yet the older and, to some, more traditional custom would have the honoree dance the first waltz with her father or male elder (grandfather, uncle, brother, or cousin) of the family if the father is not available in these days of divorce and separation.

The recursive nature of the fiesta resists and contests the sequencing of events within the reception. As a performance, the fiesta adheres to its own sense of time and order. For the *quinceañera,* this order is mostly dictated by several older women, usually relatives of the honoree or friends of her family. Often the group includes her sacramental *madrinas,* who plan and execute various stages of the celebration, from the mass to the closing *serenata* by the mariachis at midnight.[13] So although the individual fiestas may not follow the same order, they do follow a general sense of the stages of a rite of passage as outlined by Gennep and described by Turner, who claims that "The dominant genres of performance in societies at all levels of scale and complexity tend to be liminal phenomena . . . performed in privileged spaces and times, set off from the periods and areas reserved for work, food and sleep" (1988:25). Similarly, although not all fiestas include the same symbolic elements, most adhere to the basic elements as described above to signal the feminine. For example, some may choose to forego the changing of the shoes and the giving of the last doll, but few would give up the mass or the first dance.

The fiesta has changed as it evolves in immigrant communities in the United States. These changes are due mostly to the changing mores of the new cultural space where the celebration happens, which blends and accommodates both cultures while maintaining the integrity of a tradition whose function remains one of celebrating life and signaling a transition from childhood into young adulthood. These changes, however, are not confined to the *quinceañera* celebration, but as in other instances where a tradition is duplicated or expanded, this one is in the process of undergoing transformations. It has already spawned a few nontraditional celebrations. One such phenomenon is the introduction of "theme" *quinceañeras,* where the decorations and the honoree's and *damas'* dresses adhere to a specific theme, such as country-western or Cinderella. Another transformation is the birthday celebrations held by Chicanas as they turn fifty.

In a section titled "On Becoming Elders" in *Multicultural Celebrations,* Norine Dresser describes the newly created ceremony whose roots lie in the *quinceañera* celebration, the *cincuentañera* (1999:85–87). A *cincuentañera* follows a similar plan as the *quinceañera,* yet is much more open-ended and does not yet adhere to strict conventions or rituals. In 1996, Judge Hilda Tagle marked her fiftieth birthday with a *cincuentañera* celebration in Corpus Christi, Texas; I subsequently held my *cincuentañera* in 1997 in Laredo, Texas. Other celebrations have occurred in Mexico City; Phoenix, Arizona; El Paso, Texas; Las Cruces, New Mexico; and California.[14] Most of these include similar elements: an invitation to be a *madrina,* a formal invitation to the *cincuentañera,* gifting, a formal fiesta with food and music, and

sometimes a list of *madrinas*. Hilda Tagle, Laura Rendón, and I sent printed preinvitations asking friends to join and become sponsors. Many of the
elements of the traditional *quinceañera* appear, some in jest and others seriously, as the list of the *padrinos* and *madrinas* in the formal invitation to
my fiesta indicates: *madrina de queques, padrinos y madrinas de música,
madrina de AARP, madrina de hierbas y remedios caseros, madrina de recuerdos, madrina de libro y rosario* (sponsor for cake, sponsors for music,
sponsor for AARP, sponsor for herbs and home remedies, sponsor of memories, sponsor of the missal and rosary).[15]

These expressions of celebration and thanksgiving mark the same type of
life-cycle events as the *quinceañera,* yet they celebrate a later period; it is
no longer the initiation into adulthood but the celebration of a full adult
female life, as exemplified in the decoration, music, and attire. The fiesta
itself functions as a passage in a different sense from the *quinceañera.* The
symbolic actions signal the community's welcome to the initiate in the former
and celebration and thanksgiving in the latter. Romero asserts that for the
young woman, the "occasion of the *Quinceañera* ceremony [is] the threshold moment of the rite of passage, enabling her to evaluate her past life and
its future directions in light of available options" (1991:80–81). The same
holds true in terms of the ceremony of the *cincuentañera,* for it allows the
woman at fifty "to evaluate her past life and its future directions in light of
available options." The stages and phases of this recently created celebration, however, adhere to the three phases identified by Gennep as rites of
passage (1960:10–11). The separation phase, in Gennep's terms, is similar
to that of the *quinceañera,* as the woman is usually alone or accompanied
by a small coterie of women—mostly family and close friends—who help
organize and prepare the celebration. In the liminal stage, for the rite of transition, she is in sacred time and space, as she wears special formal attire and
indulges in ritual actions—cutting the cake, dancing, offering a toast, and
gifting her *madrinas* and *padrinos.* She finally emerges into the third, or post-
liminal phase, through the rites of incorporation, as she bids her guests
goodnight and invites a few close friends and family members for a final
nightcap and the opening of the gifts. I begin with a brief description of the
three fiestas and offer some final comments on the changes in coming-of-
age traditions among Chicanas in the United States. I focus on three celebrations: Hilda Tagle's (in December 1996), my own (January 1997), and
Laura Rendón's (in Phoenix, Arizona, July 1998).

"Judge Hilda Tagle Celebrates 50th Birthday with a Bang: *Cincuentañera*
the First of Its Kind in City," a Corpus Christi, Texas, publication reported

(Rivera 1997:11). Accompanying the text are a series of photos showing Tagle escorted by her ex-husband dressed as a *charro,* several of her *madrinas,* and other guests. Many of those in attendance dressed in vintage dresses and danced to music from the forties and fifties: *boleros, danzones,* and recordings of singers such as Lydia Mendoza and Isidro López. The Galván Ballroom was decorated with symbols that had special significance to the honoree, such as old albums and balloons from her political campaign. "I used everything that's made me what I am," Tagle explained. "This was for those who wanted a *quinceañera* and never had one or a big wedding or the one who always wanted to be prom queen" (Rivera 1997:11). She claims that the fiesta was to celebrate who she is and her accomplishments. At age fifty, Tagle had been nominated by President Clinton to fill a new judgeship in Brownsville, Texas, thus becoming the first Chicana federal judge in Texas. She still held the position in 1999. Although croning ceremonies occur at no specific age, *cincuentañeras* are particular to the fiftieth birthday. Both traditions, however, exist in opposition to a general "over-the-hill attitude," as older women develop "new traditions to honor rather than to disparage age," as Dresser notes in her discussion of the ceremonies (1999:85).

My own celebration adhered to the *quinceañera* ritual, but only on the structural level. The elements were all there, but the signifiers were different and signaled a coming-of-age at midlife rather than the onset of adulthood. A mass, held on my birthday, where friends and family gathered, began the two-day celebration. At the conclusion of the service, the priest called the family to receive a blessing, and everyone in attendance—friends, family, and parishioners—clapped and celebrated. That evening, after the mass, there was an informal family gathering at home, attended by a few close friends and family; the major reception at the Woodmen of the World *salón de fiestas* followed the next day. Like Tagle's, the event included numerous sponsors, including the *madrina de queque* (cake sponsor). But unlike Tagle's, the *madrinas* were all female and were asked to wear *rebozos* (traditional Mexican shawls). The celebration included the traditional cake, a *brindis,* and traditional celebratory foods. The decorations also signaled significant life events, such as graduations or publications.

Laura Rendón's celebration in Phoenix, like mine and Tagle's, included live music, *madrinas* and *padrinos,* and generally followed the traditional pattern. At the reception there was an entrance, in which the honoree, escorted by two friends, entered the ballroom of the hotel to the music of mariachis. At one point there was a toast and the cutting and distributing of the cake by the *madrina de queque.* A live dance band provided music for the dancing that followed the meal. As in my celebration, the guests were invited to take the mementos at the table and were asked to write *recuerdos* and good wishes to the honoree in the *libro de recuerdos*. The *madrinas de recuerdos* also placed disposable cameras at each table, and guests were invited to photographically record the event. At the end of the evening the *madrinas* took the cameras, and the photos were developed and placed in a photo album that was given to the honoree.

As these three cases indicate, the *cincuentañera* is about remembering, offering thanks, and celebrating the honoree's achievements. Romero's analysis of the *quinceañera* is applicable to the *cincuentañera,* for it is a discourse of celebration that remembers the past and looks to the future: "The faith discourse becomes revelatory when members of the faith-community of family, plus friends and parishioners, interpret as relevant for themselves the meaning of any life traditions of the young woman, her sense of personal cumulative history, or the symbols of the ceremony itself" (1991:80). This same faith discourse characterizes the *cincuentañera,* as the woman and her family, friends, and, when it includes a religious service, parishioners see the meaning of the tradition as a celebration of her personal cumulative history as well as a significant event for the whole group. The inclusion of friends and family through the sponsorships provides an affirmation of bonds of family and friendship as well as a cultural affirmation in the space where we live our lives and where our communities celebrate life-cycle markers. We reclaimed that space in ritual where we can celebrate our femaleness and collectively draw the community of friends and family into a liminal space. Performances of rites of passage in contemporary Chicano society, such as the *quinceañera* and the *cincuentañera,* become cultural rituals whereby the whole group undergoes a transformation. Gennep's three phases are clearly marked in these rituals, and the liminal moment is the axis upon which the wheel of transformation turns, especially for the young woman being initiated into adulthood. Furthermore, the *quinceañera* ceremony could be the beginning of a long-standing and in some cases permanent condition of transformation, as the young woman enters a stage between childhood and full adulthood and, in terms of sexuality and fertility, after puberty and before marriage and/or motherhood. Still to come is the rite of matrimony, which the *quinceañera* anticipates, and future rites for motherhood and menopause.

I mentioned earlier that as a child I had defied my mother's expectations by not following her example and joining the Hijas de María. I am still defying the expected patterns, and I have not joined the Guadalupana society that women my age join in many Catholic parishes. My drifting away from the church and my independence worry and intrigue my mother; she often remarks that some Guadalupanas who went to school with me send their greetings. At my *cincuentañera*, she and my father emotionally wished me a happy birthday, and I offered a toast to them for their support throughout my life. They joined me in celebrating my life. Celebrations for those who defy the patterns as set forth by society require affirmation. The *quinceañera* is currently in a process of transformation, but it remains necessary as a coming-of-age event in a young woman's life. The *cincuentañera* has been created to fulfill a need in the lives of women as they age and pass through menopause.

As Solon T. Kimball writes in the introduction to Gennep's text, "There is no evidence that a secularized urban world has lessened the need for ritualized expression of an individual's transition from one status to another" (1960:xvii). Perhaps it is this need for ritualized expression along with the need to affirm cultural values that has popularized the *quinceañera* and given birth to the *cincuentañera*. As Kimball notes, "The critical problems of becoming male and female, of relations within the family and of passing into old age are directly related to the devices which the society offers the individual to help achieve the new adjustment. . . . somehow we seem to have forgotten this—or perhaps the ritual has become so completely individualistic that it is now found for many only in the privacy of the psychoanalyst's couch" (1960:xvii). Because "one dimension of mental illness may arise because an increasing number of individuals are forced to accomplish their transitions alone and with private symbols" (Kimball 1960:xvii–xviii), it might be useful to conclude with a turn to social psychologists who study the ways that subaltern subjects negotiate their reality and survive. The issue of how cultural expression by subordinated groups in a capitalist society determines that group's identity arises from theories of social psychology that explain how power relations are negotiated and how violence is averted. Erika Apfelbaum has noted two processes whereby subordinated groups can achieve what she calls "re-grouping and rediscovery of their identity" (1979:203).[16] The first entails examining "peculiarities and characteristics" that may have caused the exclusion, and the second entails the subordinated group rediscovering its "own cultural roots and historical background." Her analysis applies to my discussion of *quinceañeras* and *cincuentañeras* in Chicano communities, for the two celebrations exist as both a reclaiming of cultural roots and an acknowledgment of our cultural historical background. Participating in them is an examination as well as a contestation of mainstream celebrations such as proms. I concur with Aída Hurtado, who claims that the community will often "focus on interpersonal relationships as a source of nurturance and validation of personhood" (1996:75). Such a focus, according to Hurtado, is a result of the colonization of Chicanos, which results in "the devaluation of the work performed outside the home." Furthermore, "Social events such as *bailes, bautismos, loteria, bar-b-ques, fiestas de cumpleaños, misa, posadas, quinceñeras* [sic], *velorios* (dances, baptisms, Mexican bingo, barbecues, birthday parties, mass, Christmas celebrations, fifteen-year-old birthdays for young women, funerals) all become central to Chicano men and women in valuing themselves as human beings because of the enormous economic and social constraints they faced as a result of white racism" (1996:75). I would add that although these social events take place within such a milieu, they also occur in U.S. Latino and Mexican culture and fulfill a perhaps even wider function, becoming, in a more anthropological sense, the social glue that marks the celebrant and the community engaged in the celebration ethnically as Mexican or Latina and, in the case of *quinceañera* and *cincuentañera* celebrations, the honoree as female.

Cincuentañeras and *quinceañeras* affirm cultural tradition and then celebrate the individual's history within the context of the group. Both help the individual undergoing the transition to cope, to achieve the transition, but not alone, incorporating symbols that have cultural meaning on personal and communal levels. When the *madrinas* in the *quinceañera* celebration enter the church holding the symbols of the sacraments—baptism, confirmation, first communion—that the young woman has already passed through, she and the community are reminded of all she has achieved and of the sacraments still to come. When the *cincuentañera's* cake is decorated with symbols from her life, a *quinceañera* doll, a graduation cap, a baby carriage, or a miniature replica of a publication, she and her community are reminded of the significant passages in her life, and she is reminded of the passages still to come. Both celebrations honor and remember a past comprised of what Romero would call negative and positive life experiences (1991:80). Young girls, young women, brides, mothers, single women, and older women all encounter passages along their path.

Since I began my work on *quinceañeras,* the younger sisters of Brenda de la Rosa and others whose fiestas have become the focus of my study have celebrated their own *quinceañeras,* their own initiation ritual, attesting to the fact that these fiestas are ongoing and that they will continue to be celebrated in our communities. Birthdays are to be celebrated, and the fiftieth, because of its significance, has given rise to the *cincuentañera* celebrations that are quickly becoming a tradition. Both have also recently been taken up by boys and men who are in need of marking life-cycle changes. The social pages of the newspapers in Nuevo Laredo, Tamaulipas, México, and Laredo, Texas, often feature boys' *quinceañeros*, and I know of at least two men's *cincuentañeros* in the last two years. The markers are for masculine culture, and although they include the same elements—a mass, a reception with sponsors for cake, and music—they do not include the last doll or the change of shoes, clear feminine markers. Such changes in the tradition signal that the fiesta is indeed fulfilling a need in our communities and that they will continue to flourish.

NOTES

1. The Teresitas, a Catholic girls' sodality, teach young girls proper behavior; they wear dresses that resemble the brown habit worn by St. Therese of the Little Flower. The Hijas de María is a sodality of young women who wear white dresses and a blue sash and are devoted to the Virgin Mary; when one of their members marries, at the end of the wedding mass the bride's friends, members of the sodality, line the aisle as she leaves the altar with the groom. As elders, many women join the Guadalupanas, a group devoted to the Virgen de Guadalupe that is in charge of various parish events, including the December 12 feast day celebration.

2. Along with restrictions on food, such as *aguacate* (avocado), limes, lemons, and sometimes Cokes, and certain behavior during menstruation, girls were prohibited from certain actions, such as riding a bicycle.

3. Nutini and Bell note that in the rural community of Belén, in Tlaxcala, the acquiring of sponsors to cover the costs of the fiesta, the institution of *compadrazgo*, for *quinceañeras* didn't begin until 1948 (1980:138).

4. Black and White presentation balls exist in numerous Latino communities for the eighteen-year-old daughters of members of the social organization. Senior high school daughters of members of the George Washington Birthday Association and representatives from the local high schools are presented in an elaborate pageant that includes a dramatized script set in U.S. colonial times.

5. Nutini and Bell claim that the practice is "widespread throughout Mexico in both urban and rural areas and across all social strata" (1980:138). They also classify the *quinceañera compadrazgo* system as primarily nonsacramental and therefore not as strong as the sacramental *compadrazgo* bonds. I would add that the celebration is equally endemic in Latino communities in the United States. While Williams (1990) notes a decline in the *compadrazgo* system in U.S. Latino commu-

nities, even as it serves to lend social stability and as a buffer to outside forces the ritual kinship appears to be still operative, albeit to a much lesser degree than sacramental *compadrazgo* bonds.

6. See Romero's discussion of the pastoral implications of the fiesta. He calls for the pastoral agent "to be transformed culturally" (1991:81–82). Also, see Icaza's work apparently addressing a non-Latino audience about the rite of passage that, for the sake of discussion, she groups with the sacraments (1992:147).

7. I distinguish a puberty rite from a coming-of-age ritual in the same sense that Gennep distinguishes between physical and social puberty (1960:68).

8. Loya explores the critical role of Latinas in creating "a Hispanic feminist theology" and cautions that women's roles as "promoters of Hispanic spirituality . . . will be increasingly eroded by North American secularization" (1992:131).

9. A search for origins of the celebration has not resulted in any conclusive evidence. See Rodríguez, Beard, and Conway, qtd. in Dávalos 1996:112–13, Erevia 1980, and Cantú 1999.

10. The teenager will wear the ring on her left hand, according to the folk belief that requires one to wear a birthstone ring on the hand leading to the heart.

11. Erevia's popular guides help both religious and secular celebrants understand the various elements (1985, 1992). See Cantú 1999 and Dresser 1999 for a description of the fiesta and its various elements.

12. For a discussion of liminality based on Gennep, see Turner 1969, 1988.

13. It is common to see the women—the mother, sisters, aunts, and grandmothers as well as the *madrinas*—assume responsibility for the execution of all action and behavior during the celebration, from the sequence of the presentation to the cutting and distribution of the cake. As one father informed me, "I just pay the bills."

14. In addition to the three under discussion, I have been aware of other celebrations of the fiftieth birthday. Among these are celebrations for Margarita Zires, Yvonne Yarbro Bejarano, Denise Chávez, María Hernández, and Yolanda Broyles-González. Some but not all of these women held *quinceañera*-like celebrations, yet all marked their fiftieth birthday in a special fashion, celebrating life.

15. The sponsors who provide financial support as well as ritual gifting are an essential part of the fiesta. See Cantú 1999 for a discussion of the role of *madrinas* and *padrinos* in *quinceañera* celebrations in Chicano communities, and Nutini and Bell 1980:138–42 for the same role in a Tlaxcaltecan community.

16. I thank Aida Hurtado for making me aware of Apfelbaum's work.

WORKS CITED

Apfelbaum, Erika. 1979. "Relations of Domination and Movements for Liberation: An Analysis of Power between Groups." In *The Social Psychology of Intergroup Relations*. Ed. W. G. Austin and S. Worchel. 188–204. Belmont, Calif.: Wadsworth.

Cantú, Norma Elia. 1999. "La Quinceañera: Towards an Analysis of a Life Cycle Ritual." *Southern Folklore* 56 (1): 73–101.

Castellanoz, Eva. 1996. Lecture at the Fife Conference, Utah State University, Ogden.

Daly, Mary. 1978. *Gyn/Ecology: The Metaethics of a Radical Feminism.* Boston: Beacon Press.

Dávalos, Karen Mary. 1996. "*La Quinceañera*: Making Gender and Ethnic Identities." *Frontiers: A Journal of Women Studies* 16 (2–3): 101–27.

Dresser, Norine. 1999. *Multicultural Celebrations: Today's Rules of Etiquette for Life's Special Occasions.* New York: Three Rivers Press.

Erevia, Angela, M.C.D.P. 1980. *Quince Años: Celebrating a Tradition.* San Antonio, Tex.: Mexican American Cultural Center.

———. 1985. *Quince Años: Celebrating a Tradition.* San Antonio, Tex.: Missionary Catechists of Divine Providence.

———. 1992. *A Remembrance of My Quince Años.* San Antonio, Tex.: Missionary Catechists of Divine Providence.

Gennep, Arnold van. 1960. *Rites of Passage.* Trans. Monika B. Vizedom and Gabrielle L. Caffee. Chicago: University of Chicago Press.

Hurtado, Aída. 1996. *The Color of Privilege: Three Blasphemies on Race and Feminism.* Ann Arbor: University of Michigan Press.

Icaza, Rosa María, C.C.V.I. 1992. "Prayer, Worship, and Liturgy in a United States Hispanic Key." In *Frontiers of Hispanic Theology in the United States.* Ed. Alan Figueroa Deck, S.J. 134–53. Maryknoll, N.Y.: Orbis Books.

Kimball, Solon T. 1960. "Introduction." In *Rites of Passage,* by Arnold van Gennep. Trans. Monika B. Vizedom and Gabrielle L. Caffee. v–xix. Chicago: University of Chicago Press.

Lorch, Donatella. 1996. "Quinceañera: A Girl Grows Up." *New York Times,* February 1, C1, C4.

Loya, Gloria Inés, P.B.V.M. 1992. "The Hispanic Woman: *Pasionaria* and *Pastora* of the Hispanic Community." In *Frontiers of Hispanic Theology in the United States.* Ed. Alan Figueroa Deck, S.J. 134–53. Maryknoll, N.Y.: Orbis Books.

Nutini, Hugo G., and Betty Bell. 1980. *Ritual Kinship: The Structure and Historical Development of the Compadrazgo System in Rural Tlaxcala.* Princeton, N.J.: Princeton University Press.

Rivera, Anissa. 1997. "Judge Hilda Tagle Celebrates 50th Birthday With a Bang." *La Onda,* January, 11.

Romero, C. Gilbert. 1991. *Hispanic Devotional Piety: Tracing the Biblical Roots.* Maryknoll, N.Y.: Orbis Books.

Sandoval, Chela. 1982. *The Struggle Within: Women Respond to Racism.* New York: Center for Third World Organizing.

———. 1991. "U.S. Third World Feminism: The Theory and Method of Oppositional Consciousness in the Postmodern World." *Genders* 10 (Spring 1991): 1–24.

Scott, James C. 1990. *Domination and the Arts of Resistance: Hidden Transcripts.* New Haven, Conn.: Yale University Press.

Turner, Victor. 1969. *The Ritual Process: Structure and Anti- Structure.* Chicago: Aldine.

———. *The Anthropology of Performance.* New York: Performance Arts Journal Publications.

Williams, Norma. 1990. *The Mexican American Family: Tradition and Change.* Dix Hills, N.Y.: General Hall, Inc.

2

ART OF THE SANTERA

HELEN R. LUCERO

In New Mexico, Hispanic women have long been "the keepers of the Roman Catholic faith." They have been responsible for cleaning the churches and stitching and laundering the garments worn by the saints' images. They have cared for the church altars and embroidered the *colchas* that sometimes decorate church and home altars. And they have prepared the food for countless religious holidays.

While it has only been since the 1970s that Hispanic women have become *santeras,* as part of an overall revival in Hispanic arts, this new role may be viewed as a logical extension of their caretaker role, as another expression of their faith and devotion.

Historically, the word *santero* refers to men who produce religious images in the form of *bultos* (carved wooden figures in the round) or *retablos* (paintings on wood panels). During the Spanish colonial period, Hispanic men were the ones who interacted with the public and who consequently received credit for the production of religious art. Anglo men were the first to write about the New Mexican carvings and paintings, and they may have perpetuated their own biased notion that only Hispanic men produced religious images.

There is no documentation that Hispanic women created holy images during the Spanish colonial period, or even that they assisted men in the production of *bultos* and *retablos*. However, it is known that Hispanic women "helped out" with most other tasks, such as weaving and farming; it would therefore stand to reason that they also "lent a hand" in the production of religious images. Additional research may someday reveal a woman's hand in the works that are not currently attributable to any known *santeros.*

When the Spaniards first settled New Mexico in 1598, they brought with them several Franciscan friars. These friars used hide paintings with images of saints as tools for converting the indigenous peoples. Hide paintings, *bultos,* and *retablos* were used as vehicles of devotion and instruction for Spaniards and Indians alike. Lithographic prints, imported from Europe and later from the eastern United States, were also used as instructional texts and were copied by *santeros* in the production of their own work.

ART OF THE SANTERA EXHIBITION

As the curator of contemporary New Mexican Hispanic crafts and textiles for nine years at the Museum of International Folk Art in Santa Fe, this author curated the traveling exhibition, *Art of the Santera,* which premiered in the Hispanic Heritage Wing of the museum from July 1993 to January 1994. Following its inaugural showing, TREX (the Traveling Exhibition Service of the Museum of New Mexico) toured the exhibition to the following five venues: (1) the Biblical Art Center, Dallas, Texas, in 1994, (2) the Nora Eccles Harrison Museum, Utah State University, Logan, in 1994, (3) the Mexican Museum, San Francisco, California, in 1995, (4) the University Museum, New Mexico State University, Las Cruces, in 1995, and (5) the Old Jail Art Center, Albany, Texas, in 1995.

The exhibition was partially conceived as an attempt to determine whether Hispanic women had produced some of the older religious images. The proliferation of *santeras* in New Mexico during the previous ten years merited further research. Questions posed included looking at how women's work differed from that produced by men, especially regarding potential elemental differences such as delicate versus bold style, small versus large scale, and a preference for female versus male saints. There was also a desire to find out what motivated women to become *santeras.* Was it artistic inspiration, economics, or spirituality? These, and several other questions, led the author to embark on this project.

Twenty-six *santeras,* represented by forty images, were selected for inclusion in the exhibition. As would be expected in a group this size, the women differed in many ways, including artistic ability, age, and spiritual and philosophical outlook. In an attempt to learn more about their similarities and differences, a questionnaire was sent to each *santera,* asking, "Why did you become a *santera?*" "What motivates you to create holy images?" and

Twelve of the twenty-six *santeras* who participated in the Museum of International Folk Art's *Art of the Santera* exhibit gathered for a group photo in July 1993. Top row, left to right: Mónica Sosaya Halford, Guadalupita Ortiz, Donna Wright de Romero, Anita Romero Jones, Marie Romero Cash, Zoraida Ortega, and Sabinita López Ortiz. Bottom row, left to right: Tomasita Rodríguez, Paula Rodríguez, María Hesch, Eppie Archuleta, and Irene Martínez Yates. Photo by Blair Clark.

"How do you feel about creating holy images that may be sold to 'nonbelievers'?" The data gathered from these questionnaires, along with several interviews, provided the basis for the exhibition. Some of the women's answers were integrated into the exhibit label text so that museum visitors could "hear" the *santeras'* own voices. Four *santeras*—Marie Romero Cash, Gloria López Córdova, Mónica Sosaya Halford, and Guadalupita Ortiz— were also videotaped working in their homes or studios. The fifteen-minute video provided viewers with wonderful personal insights into their work.

PROTOTYPES

Today, *santeros* and *santeras* alike use Spanish colonial images from the eighteenth and nineteenth centuries as prototypes for their work or as inspiration for their contemporary pieces. For example, about 150 years separate Marie Romero Cash from the *santero* José Rafael Aragón, yet she

Marie Romero Cash, *Our Lady of Mount Carmel*, 1993, 36 × 24 × 1 in., *retablo*, wood and paint. The scapulars visible in Marie's *retablo* help the viewer identify this particular depiction of the Virgin Mary and Child as Our Lady of Mount Carmel. Collection of Marie and Don Cash. Photo by Blair Clark.

consciously copied the Spanish colonial *santero's* work in producing her own *Santo Niño,* or Christ Child. Altar screens, such as those from Córdova, New Mexico, dating from the mid-nineteenth century, also have served as inspiration for Marie's own altar screens. One of her most significant altar screens graces the Marian Shrine in Santa Fe's newest Catholic church, Santa María de la Paz.

Marie Romero Cash and her sister, Anita Romero Jones, are perhaps the best-known *santeras* working in New Mexico today. They are the daughters of Emilio and Senaida Romero, noted tin workers. Marie and Anita regularly incorporate tin work into their pieces, showing a willingness to experiment and innovate not evident in the Spanish colonial *bultos* and *retablos.* Marie's philosophical approach to her work is also quite different from that of her *santero* ancestors. When questioned about the sale of holy images to nonbelievers, she replied: "I consider the whole *santero* product as a folk art and, therefore, feel it is removed from a 'holy' or 'Catholic' status. This allows the buyer to use it for whatever purpose. If they want to set it on an altar and pray before it, or in a center surrounded by other art objects, it is their choice."[1]

HUSBAND AND WIFE COLLABORATION

Marie Romero Cash, like many other *santeras,* has collaborated with her husband in the production of *bultos* and *retablos.* She and her former husband, Don Cash, created and signed many of their pieces together. Husbands and wives often divide the labor according to physical difficulty: the men will "block out" the sculptural images or boards with power tools, while the women do the sculptural finishing and painting.

Eulogio and Zoraida Ortega are another couple who work together to produce religious images. Zoraida did not publicly acknowledge her part in painting the couple's *bultos* for several years. She had this to say regarding their collaboration: "After my husband and I retired, I went back to school and learned to weave, which fascinated me and which I enjoyed. My husband is color blind, so I began to help him with the painting. I found the process exciting and fascinating, so I began to paint *retablos* and help with the *bultos.* My greatest happiness is to help people who want a certain *santo.* Painting *santos* is a form of meditation, prayer, and relaxation which gives me a great sense of accomplishment."[2]

It is interesting to note that Zoraida, who was born in 1918, is typical of women of her generation; she chose to remain anonymous while promoting

Zoraida and Eulogio Ortega, *San Antonio Milagroso,* 1988, 24 × 10 × 11 in., *bulto,* wood and paint. This *bulto* is an excellent example of collaboration between husband and wife in the creation of a saint's image: Eulogio carved and Zoraida painted this San Antonio *bulto.* Collection of Zoraida and Eulogio Ortega. Photo by Blair Clark.

her husband's work. This was not done with any attempt to deceive; she did this in a spirit of cooperation with her husband and in her role as the supportive member of the family. However, she did not have any difficulty promoting herself as a weaver, a traditionally female occupation.

In the spirit of La Sagrada Familia, or Holy Family, entire families are often involved with a *santera's* occupation. The home is the center of family life in New Mexican Hispanic families, and the mother and father follow the model of Mary and Joseph. Often the family is extended in time, with several generations living together. The elders in the family teach the children about the saints, the elements of faith, and virtues such as respect, generosity, and obedience. *Santeras* also teach their children how to create images of the saints. Gloria López Córdova exemplifies the manner in which a *santera's* artistic tradition is transmitted within a family over several generations.

CÓRDOVA WOODCARVERS

Gloria López Córdova is a fourth-generation woodcarver. Her grandfather, José Dolores López, is credited with starting the Córdova style of unpainted, chip-carved religious and secular woodcarvings made of aspen or cottonwood. Anglo artists and writers who moved to New Mexico in the 1920s "discovered" López and encouraged him to carve images of saints. However, the outsiders imposed their own aesthetic sensibilities by providing him with carvings to copy. Doors, chests, numerous whimsical animals, and a lazy Susan produced by López all bear the stamp of this outside influence. The well-meaning Anglos also discouraged López from painting his religious images.

The men in Gloria's family, especially her uncle, George López, perfected what became known as the Córdova style of woodcarving, which today is considered a legitimate variation of the older *santero* tradition. Regarding her own work, Gloria said: "My parents' *santos* were my inspiration and they encouraged me and taught me what I know. Looking at the work of my grandfather, José Dolores López, and great-grandfather, Nasario López, inspired me, too. But the *santos* I make are my own ideas. I carve them the way I feel it should be and the detail work is all mine. I like it that way; it has to come out of your own head."[3]

Another Córdova carver is Sabinita López Ortiz, Gloria's cousin. Like her grandfather, she was inspired to carve an image of "Our Lady of Light." Regarding her work, Sabinita says, "every time I carve a *santo,* I feel holy in

Mónica Sosaya Halford, *Santa Librada,* 1993, 24 × 15 × 2 in., *bulto,* wood and paint. Santa Librada is dressed in the Basque costume of Mónica's ancestors. Museum of New Mexico Collections, Museum of International Folk Art, Santa Fe, N.Mex. FA.1993.42-1. Photo by Blair Clark.

my heart, and it feels like I am talking to the *santo* I am working on because it is a gift from God to us through my grandfather José Dolores López."[4]

Sabinita's mother, the late Benita Reynolds López, is probably the first documented *santera*. She married Ricardo López and became integrally involved with the family's production of woodcarvings starting in the 1920s. However, the couple's images of saints were originally marketed under Benita's name because Ricardo thought it was "wrong to sell the saints to the tourists."[5] It is interesting to note that the first Hispanic *santera* had an Anglo maiden name (Reynolds) and that she gained public recognition because her husband chose to conceal his identity by using her name to sign their religious items. Ricardo's discomfort with signing his own name to religious images produced for sale has bothered more than one *santero* or *santera*; most deal with this discomfort by saying that the images are not holy until they are blessed by a priest.

Today, the Córdova style of carving is in its fifth generation and has had many practitioners. Ironically, Sabinita's son, Lawrence Andrew Ortíz, and her nieces, Trina and Pamela Martínez, have begun to paint some of their chip-carved images, thereby returning to a painted element that previously had been discarded in this eighty-year-old traditional art form.

SAINTS AND ICONS

Mónica Sosaya Halford's childhood was rooted in the Catholic faith and devotion to the saints. "We grew up with the *santos*," she remembers. "They were like part of the family. My favorite saints are the Virgin Mother, in all forms, and San Antonio. My mother always prayed to him. So now I do. I'm always misplacing things and, besides misplacing things, I'm always asking him for everything else. When things go right, I thank him and give to his poor. I feel very close to him. I even get angry at him. I wouldn't dare get angry at the Virgin, but San Antonio and I go round and round. I'm sure he gets angry at me, too."[6]

Older Hispanic Catholics in New Mexico have a close relationship with their *santos*, not unlike that described by Mónica. Different saints have the power to grant different requests. God the Father, Jesus, and the many forms of the Virgin Mary are in a category above that of the saints. All are prayed to as intercessors, but God and members of La Sagrada Familia are in a superior position that commands more respect.

All saints are identified by their attributes, the objects that are included in their depictions. These attributes are also known as the iconography of a work of art, as the set of symbolic forms that bear the meaning of the work, and they help tell the story of a given saint. For example, St. Joseph became the husband of Mary and the foster father of Jesus after the High Priest of Judea assembled all the widowers of the land and asked each of them to put a staff upon the altar of the temple. When Joseph, a carpenter, placed his staff on the altar, it miraculously bloomed, indicating that he was divinely chosen to be the husband of Mary. Thus, Joseph is recognized by the flowering staff that he holds in one hand, while he holds the Christ Child on the other arm. He is usually bearded and crowned. As the father of Jesus, St. Joseph is asked to intercede on behalf of families. He is also the patron saint of persons seeking to buy or sell houses, and he provides supplicants with a good death.

SANTA LIBRADA

Santa Librada is a female religious personage who became very important in Spanish colonial New Mexico. This apocryphal saint dates from the third century, and according to legend, her father, the pagan king of Portugal, wanted her to marry the king of Sicily. Librada, who had become a Christian, did not want to get married. She prayed that God would make her ugly, and overnight she grew a mustache and beard. The royal suitor withdrew his request, and Librada's father, enraged, accused her of witchcraft and had her crucified. Her witnessing from the cross converted many of those present to Christianity, including her father. Santa Librada is the only female saint who is depicted in a crucified position.

During the Spanish colonial period, Hispanics relied heavily on the intercession of saints to help them during times of need. This female martyr (who was never depicted with a mustache or beard in New Mexico) was especially important, because Catholics believed strongly in the sanctity of marriage and did not have the option of obtaining divorces. As a result, Santa Librada gained wide popularity as the saint to whom women prayed when they needed help with troublesome husbands.

Today, Santa Librada might serve as the icon for the women's movement, and especially for *santeras*. This "liberated" saint could be called upon to intercede on behalf of women who are still suffering at the hands of difficult males, whether at home or at work.

Gloria López Córdova, *Our Lady of Sorrows,* 1990, 23 × 13½ × 8 in., *bulto,* unpainted wood. The chip-carving characteristic of the Córdova style is readily evident in this *bulto.* International Folk Art Foundation Collections, Museum of International Folk Art, Santa Fe, N.Mex. FA.1990.37-1. Photo by Blair Clark.

OUR LADY/THE VIRGIN MARY

Guadalupita Ortíz has a special affinity for the Blessed Mother. She was born on the feast day of Our Lady of Guadalupe (December 12) and was given her name by the nuns at St. Vincent's Hospital in Santa Fe. In recalling who introduced her to Our Lady and influenced her to become a *santera*, "Pita" reminisced:

> I would say that the one person who was an influence on my becoming a *santera* was my Aunt Cleotilde, my father's sister. She was always praying the rosary. In the 50s, she would listen to KDCE, a Spanish radio station that would broadcast religious stories about apparitions. She knew the biographies of many saints and loved to go to the Carmelite Monastery in Santa Fe. She had a statue of the Blessed Virgin Mary as a child. I will never forget the statue because the face was so beautiful and had an expression of gentleness. It had small glass eyes that looked life-like. For Aunt Cleotilde, religion wasn't ever a facade. She was humble and very generous and really believed in the power of prayer and the intercession of the Blessed Mother and other saints.[7]

Anita Romero Jones is another *santera* who has carved and painted countless images of the Virgin Mary in her many guises, especially as Our Lady of Guadalupe. La Guadalupana, as she also is called by Hispanics, is an image of the Virgin Mary as the Immaculate Conception. The Virgin appeared to an Indian named Juan Diego in 1531 on a hillside at Tepeyac, outside Mexico City. She asked that a chapel be built in her honor on that very spot. Juan Diego went to the Bishop in Mexico City, who said that a chapel could not be built unless Juan Diego could bring him some proof of his vision. He returned to the hillside, and the Virgin appeared to him again. When he told her of his dilemma, she instructed him to fill his cape with roses and take it to the bishop. He did as he was instructed, and when he opened his cape before the bishop, the roses fell out, revealing an image of the Virgin. She stood on a half-moon and was clothed in a blue mantle emblazoned with stars; she wore a crown on her head and was surrounded by the rays of the sun.

The Virgin of Guadalupe is easy to recognize because all depictions of her are based on the image imprinted on Juan Diego's cape. Like that of the Indian to whom she appeared, La Guadalupana's skin is sometimes shown as tan or brown. Because the Virgin of Guadalupe was one of the first apparitions of the Virgin in the New World, and, more specifically because she appeared to a native, she became the patron saint of New Spain. Her image is widespread throughout Mexico and New Mexico.

DOÑA SEBASTIANA

The figure of death is known in Spain, Mexico, and New Mexico by two names, both of which are feminine: Doña Sebastiana and La Muerte. This figure traditionally has been used in New Mexican Hispanic culture as a reminder of human mortality and of Christ's triumph over death. During Holy Week, the members of a lay religious order, the Penitente Brotherhood, would do penance by placing an image of death on a cart filled with stones and pulling it in a reenactment of the procession to Calvary.

Death was usually portrayed as a skeletal figure. In New Mexico, this figure was sometimes dressed, and a member of a Penitente's family would contribute hair for her head. Like other religious images, Doña Sebastiana carries an array of objects, including a scythe, hatchet, knife, or bow and arrows. The arrows may be a tribute to the martyrdom of Saint Sebastian, who was killed by arrows. They also may have a more local meaning derived from the Spaniards' fear of Indian attacks. In Hispanic culture, *santeras* have an intimate association with death, which most see as only the beginning of a new life. Women are also the ones who take care of the sick and dying. It is therefore not surprising that some *santeras,* like Gloria López Córdova, feel comfortable enough to dress, and even carve, images of Doña Sebastiana, the woman who will come calling at the completion of everyone's life.

ARTISTIC STYLES AND THE TRANSMISSION OF TRADITION

Ellen Chávez de Leitner is one of the *santeras* whose work fits the stereotype of femininity; she paints in a sweet and delicate style. She says that one of her favorite saints is St. Therese of the Little Flower, because "she is so simple, sweet, and ardent." Ellen, a musician, played with the Graz Philharmonic Orchestra in Austria for two years. Regarding her various creative activities, she says, "I have always felt called to serve Our Lord, and I hope that I have done so, and continue to do so, in various ways—through my music as a violinist, as a wife and mother, and also through my art as a *santera*. I enjoy re-creating the direct simplicity and appealing designs and colors of *santeros* such as Molleno, José Aragón, and Rafael Aragón, who expressed so well the personalities and virtues of the saints."[8]

Tomasita Rodríguez, like Ellen Chávez de Leitner, has taken advantage of her place in twentieth-century America to explore different avenues. She has worked in various styles and media and in both miniature and large scale.

Regarding her philosophy, Tomasita said: "I am not traditional, and my work usually represents a 'different viewpoint.' I try to bring together the dynamism of the Renaissance with the austerity of the New Mexican *santos*. I want to interpret the expressions of the kind of people the saints might have been. I'm trying to portray that fine line of transition from human to saint, and I want to bring out the emotion of that moment—indecision, tranquillity, and strength."[9]

Tomasita also has strong opinions regarding the production of *santos* during the nineteenth century:

> I don't wholly believe the saints' images were produced by men, although they have received the credit. In Europe, the masters often took credit for pupils' work, so individual works became attributed to certain well-known *santeros*. There are many cases of *santos* which don't fit the prescribed artist's style. Those often are finer, more delicate of hand. Also, since many *santeros* unconsciously copy their own faces onto their *santos*, such finesse and delicacy of features suggest, to me, a woman's hand.[10]

Ellen Chávez de Leitner's and Tomasita Rodríguez's artistic styles reflect the fact that all *santeras'* work cannot be classified as sweet or delicate; Ellen's work fits the sweet, feminine stereotype, but Tomasita's work can be delicate at times and bold at others. The two women are similar in another way: they both are educated and very articulate. Their sophistication is at odds with their classification as folk artists, since folk artists are sometimes considered to be indigenous peoples or just plain "quaint folk." Another departure from the folk art stereotype is the method by which these women learned their craft: they did not learn it from their families but are, instead, self-taught. Many *santeras* today are learning their craft as apprentices, in classes, or from museum-sponsored workshops.

Rosina López de Short came to her work as a *santera* through her public school teaching. Her interest in *bultos* and *retablos* developed largely through her "desire to re-awaken in her students a knowledge and pride in the old art of the *santeros*."[11] She says,

> When I was an art and history teacher in the mid-70s, I wanted to find an art project for my art students that pertained to the history and culture of northern New Mexico. In the course of working with the mid school and high school students, I just naturally fell into this art form. Becoming a *santera* myself means that I have been able to grow and realize my Hispanic heritage more fully. Having the artistic ability to express my history and culture in this way gives me great satisfaction. I do feel "in touch" with those early settlers of

northern New Mexico, and my study of the saints and their lives only adds to my Catholic faith.[12]

Art educators know the value of teaching different subject matter through art. In Rosina's case, she taught herself and her students about Hispanic history, culture, and religion through the vehicle of *bultos* and *retablos*.

Irene Martínez Yates concurs with Rosina López de Short about the value of teaching, this time to an older age group: "Teaching is sharing, and teaching is also learning. I believe all art is an expression of love. I have been fortunate enough to teach at the Senior Citizen Center in Santa Fe, where I have learned from my students as much as they have learned from me. Yes, I feel it is very important to teach and share any knowledge we are blessed with."[13]

Irene has specialized in miniature re-creations of church altar screens. However, like many other *santeras,* she earns a living as an artist by painting anything that will sell, whether it is furniture, walls, or clothing. She says, "I am a self-supporting artist by profession. I need to create art or starve."[14]

FINANCIAL CONCERNS

Monetary remuneration is of great importance to the majority of the *santeras.* Their work is viewed as a profession, and their product is often driven by sales principles. Many of them live in small communities where outside employment is not readily available, and they often need to find a way to earn a living or to augment their husbands' salaries. Creating holy images for sale in Santa Fe, one of the major art markets in the United States, is seen as a viable and sometimes even lucrative way to earn money.

A *santera's* fame and the complexity of a particular religious image generally determines the amount of money for which a *bulto* or *retablo* is sold. However, other factors sometimes guide the *santeras* in pricing their work. Marie Romero Cash, perhaps the best-known *santera,* produces work for three different markets with three different sets of prices: (1) serious collectors and museums, (2) the Spanish Market, and (3) the local population. In 1997, Romero Cash generally sold a 14" × 10" *retablo* to the latter two markets for between seventy-five and one hundred dollars, because she wanted to "make her work accessible to more people." Lesser-known *santeras* charged about the same amount of money for comparably sized *retablos; bultos* usually sold for a higher price. Today, a few large-scale *bultos* and altar screens produced by *santeras* sell for thousands of dollars. Unfortunately, the women's religious images generally sell for less than those produced by their male counterparts.

Teresa Vigil Montoya, who owns her own art gallery, listed "financial reward" as one of her reasons for producing holy images. She is in an especially unusual situation as a *santera* because she is not a Roman Catholic; she is a Mormon. Her interest in painting *retablos* is not grounded in the doctrine of her church but originates instead from a sincere desire to connect with her Hispanic heritage and from a monetary interest: "Before I started painting *retablos* I always thought it was something of the past, something we could never capture in the present. I feel it is a great honor to reproduce something that was done so long ago by my ancestors."[15]

She believes it is right to create holy images that may be sold to nonbelievers, because "*santos* are also interpreted as folk art." When asked how she felt about producing the holy images, Teresa said, "spiritually, I get a warm and comforting feeling from seeing the images come to life."[16] Her daughter, Melissa Montoya, has followed in her mother's footsteps by painting *retablos;* she generally sells out at the annual Spanish Market in Santa Fe, where she has won numerous awards.

Yet another interesting connection to Mormons in New Mexico is the case of the late *colcha* embroiderer Frances Varos Graves. Her story reads like a fairy tale. During the 1930s, two Catholic Hispanic sisters, Frances and Sophie, married two Mormon Anglo brothers, Richard and Frank, in the Mormon community of Carson, New Mexico. Because of financial difficulties brought on by the Depression, the brothers and their brother-in-law, Elmer Shupe, would ask Frances and Sophie to mend Spanish colonial blankets and *colchas,* which the Mormon men then sold to tourists and collectors. From this experience, Frances learned how to do the *colcha* stitch, so she began to create her own pieces from recycled yarns salvaged from old blankets. Frances also taught the *colcha* stitch to the other women in Carson, which led to a thriving cottage industry where Hispanic and Anglo women produced what have come to be known as Carson *colchas.*

An interesting side note to this story is that, in New Mexico, *colcha* embroidery had traditionally been nonfigurative. Saints' images first appeared on *colcha* embroideries in Carson, New Mexico, during the 1930s and were introduced by the Graves brothers—that is, by Mormons, not Catholics—who initially drew the saints' figures for their women. They capitalized on making the women's work more marketable by incorporating Hispanic and Native American subject matter. They also "passed off" some of the *colchas* as being much older than they really were; this was possible because the Carson *colchas* were, after all, made with old materials. Today, the Carson *colchas* are seen as an interesting blend of cultures (Anglo, Hispanic, and Native American) and religions (Mormon and Roman Catholic).

In 1994 Frances Varos Graves received a National Heritage Fellowship Award for her role in preserving the folk art of *colcha* embroidery in New Mexico. Her work has inspired many other women, such as Victoria López, from Española, who thinks it is perfectly normal for her to draw and embroider her own images of saints.

NEW DIRECTIONS

Although the word *santera* traditionally has referred to Hispanic women, women from other ethnic groups have become increasingly involved with the production of *bultos* and *retablos*. One of the ways in which this involvement is most readily apparent is through interethnic marriages. Almost half of the women in the *Art of the Santera* exhibit were married to non-Hispanics, as is evident by reviewing their surnames (see the appendix). Anglo husbands are usually supportive of their wives' work; they enjoy learning about the religious images of a different culture and appreciate the supplementary income.

The motivation behind producing religious images that are not part of an individual's cultural heritage is quite complex. Some women do so because of an affinity for the Hispanic culture or the Catholic church; others are motivated primarily by monetary interest. Still others, such as E. Boyd, the first Spanish Colonial curator at the Museum of New Mexico, drew religious images for documentary reasons. She produced several watercolors of saints during the Depression years as part of a portfolio that recorded the Hispanic folk arts of New Mexico.

More recently, Linda Daboub, an Anglo, was commissioned to produce an image of a Black saint, San Martín de Porres, and Maxine Toya, a Native American, was commissioned to sculpt the Indian saint Kateri Tekakwitha for a Catholic church in Santa Fe. The parishioners wanted artists and saints reflective of the ethnic diversity of their congregation, which includes Anglos, Hispanics, African Americans, and Native Americans. In addition to being non-Hispanic, Linda and Maxine introduced yet another new element to the art of the santera; they used an art medium, clay, which has been employed only recently in the creation of *bultos*.

Other artists also have begun to experiment with media not traditionally employed in the manufacture of *santos*. Straw appliqué was used extensively during the Spanish colonial period. However, the work produced was always nonfigurative. Eliseo Rodríguez revived this dying art form in the 1930s, and he and his wife, Paula, went on to become masters of straw appliqué. Paula's figurative work, like that of her husband, consists of tiny blades of straw that are slit, flattened, cut, and arranged to form biblical scenes. They also produce nonfigurative designs.

Weaving is another art form that has a long and important tradition in New Mexico. During the early nineteenth century, weaving was a major export item to Mexico. However, as was the case with straw appliqué, weaving began to be used as an art medium to create figurative images only recently. For the exhibition, Epifania (Eppie) Archuleta wove an image of Our Lady and Irene E. López contributed a large tapestry of Nuestro Señor de Esquipulas, based on the main altar screen at the Santuario de Chimayó.

Paula Rodríguez, *Saint Francis,* 1986, straw appliqué, wood, and paint. Paula's images are made with painstaking care, as each piece of straw is slit, flattened, and pasted to form religious and secular images. Museum of Spanish Colonial Art, Spanish Colonial Arts Society, Inc., Santa Fe, N.Mex. L.5.86.5. Photo by Blair Clark.

Like religious paintings on wood panels, paintings on copper or tin are called *retablos;* they are also sometimes referred to as *láminas. Láminas* have a long history in Mexico and Latin America but not in New Mexico. However, one New Mexican *santera,* Guadalupita Ortiz, sometimes uses copper or tin as a base for her paintings.

Hide paintings also date back to the early colonization of the Americas. Anita Romero Jones is one of a handful of *santeras* who have used hides as canvases for their work. She was also the only woman selected to participate in another project, at the University of New Mexico's renowned Tamarind Institute. While working there, she and five *santeros* each produced two color lithographs depicting holy images. The lithographs were shown in 1990 at the Museum of International Folk Art in the exhibition *Tamarind Invites: Lithographs by New Mexican Santeros.*

Anita's case is a good example of the degree to which *santeras* are taking advantage of different media and different opportunities. Most are willing to experiment and remain open to projects that will increase their visibility and sales. Anita's work usually sells out at Spanish Market during the first hour. Her fame, however, like that of the other *santeras,* has not come without its price. Most *santeras* have to choose their commissions carefully because of mounting back orders. It is also not unusual to see Anita and other *santeras* with bandaged fingers and arms in slings, reminders of the dangers of their profession.

CONCLUSION

This project examined various issues concerning the *santeras* and their work. Several of the questions posed were answered, while others probably always will remain a mystery. Perhaps the most surprising finding was the *santeras'* overwhelming belief in the power of the holy images. Again and again, they spoke of a spiritual connection in their lives and of their gratitude for a God-given talent. New Mexican *santeras* can rightfully claim that they are no longer just the Catholic church's caretakers of holy images. They have discovered another vehicle by which to express their faith and devotion directly, through the holy images that they create.

APPENDIX

Following is a list of the twenty-six New Mexican *santeras* who were included in the *Art of the Santera* exhibition.

1. Epifania (Eppie) Archuleta (b. 1922)—weaving
2. Rosa María Calles (b. 1949)—ceramics
3. Marie Romero Cash (b. 1942)—*bultos* and *retablos*
4. Gloria López Córdova (b. 1942)—*bultos*
5. Corine Mora Fernández (b. 1940)—*bultos*
6. Frances Varos Graves (b. 1910)—*colcha* embroidery
7. María Fernández Graves (b. 1945)—*colcha* embroidery
8. Mónica Sosaya Halford (b. 1931)—*bultos* and *retablos*
9. María Hesch (b. 1909)—*colcha* embroidery
10. Anita Romero Jones (b. 1930)—*bultos* and *retablos*
11. Ellen Chávez de Leitner (b. 1951)—*retablos*
12. Benita Reynolds López (1918–77)—*bultos*
13. Irene E. López (b. 1949)—weaving
14. Victoria López (b. 1927)—*colcha* embroidery
15. Teresa Vigil Montoya (b. 1951)—*retablos*
16. Zoraida Ortega (b. 1918)—*bultos* and *retablos*
17. Guadalupita (Pita) Ortiz (b. 1950)—*retablos*
18. Sabinita López Ortiz (b. 1938)—*bultos*
19. Linda Martínez de Pedro (b. 1946)—*retablos*
20. Paula Rodríguez (b. 1915)—straw appliqué
21. Tomasita (Toma) Rodríguez (b. 1956)—*bultos*
22. Donna Wright de Romero (b. 1953)—*colcha* embroidery
23. Rosina López de Short (b. 1936)—*retablos*
24. Carmelita Laura Valdez (b. 1940)—*retablos*
25. María Vergara-Wilson (b. 1943)—embroidery
26. Irene Martínez Yates (b. 1940)—*bultos* and *retablos*

NOTES

1. Marie Romero Cash, questionnaire administered by the author at the Museum of International Folk Art, Santa Fe, N.Mex., spring 1983.

2. Zoraida Ortega, questionnaire administered by the author at the Museum of International Folk Art, Santa Fe, N.Mex., spring 1983.

3. Gloria López Córdova, questionnaire administered by the author at the Museum of International Folk Art, Santa Fe, N.Mex., spring 1983.

4. Sabinita López Ortíz, questionnaire administered by the author at the Museum of International Folk Art, Santa Fe, N.Mex., spring 1983.

5. Ibid.

6. Mónica Sosaya Halford, questionnaire administered by the author at the Museum of International Folk Art, Santa Fe, N.Mex., spring 1983.

7. Guadalupita Ortíz, questionnaire administered by the author at the Museum of International Folk Art, Santa Fe, N.Mex., spring 1983.

8. Ellen Chávez de Leitner, questionnaire administered by the author at the Museum of International Folk Art, Santa Fe, N.Mex., spring 1983.

9. Tomasita Rodríguez, questionnaire administered by the author at the Museum of International Folk Art, Santa Fe, N.Mex., spring 1983.

10. Ibid.

11. Rosina López de Short, questionnaire administered by the author at the Museum of International Folk Art, Santa Fe, N.Mex., spring 1983.

12. Ibid.

13. Irene Martínez Yates, questionnaire administered by the author at the Museum of International Folk Art, Santa Fe, N.Mex., spring 1983.

14. Ibid.

15. Teresa Vigil Montoya, questionnaire administered by the author at the Museum of International Folk Art, Santa Fe, N.Mex., spring 1983.

16. Ibid.

SELECTED BIBLIOGRAPHY

Briggs, Charles L. 1980. *The Woodcarvers of Córdova, New Mexico: Social Dimensions of an Artistic "Revival."* Knoxville: University of Tennessee Press.

Deutsch, Sarah. 1987. *No Separate Refuge: Culture, Class, and Gender on an Anglo-Hispanic Frontier in the American Southwest, 1880–1940.* New York: Oxford University Press.

Forrest, Suzanne. 1989. *The Preservation of the Village: New Mexico's Hispanics and the New Deal.* Albuquerque: University of New Mexico Press.

Jensen, Joan M., and Darlis A. Miller, eds. 1986. *New Mexico Women: Intercultural Perspectives.* Albuquerque: University of New Mexico Press.

Lecompte, Janet. 1981. "The Independent Women of Hispanic New Mexico, 1821–1846." *Western Historical Quarterly* 12: 17–35.

Norwood, Vera, and Janice Monk, eds. 1987. *The Desert Is No Lady: Southwestern Landscapes in Women's Writing and Art, 1880–1980.* New Haven, Conn.: Yale University Press.

Pierce, Donna, and Marta Weigle, eds. 1996. *Spanish New Mexico: The Spanish Colonial Arts Society Collection.* Santa Fe: Museum of New Mexico Press.

Rebolledo, Tey Diana, ed., with Erlinda Gonzáles-Berry and Millie Santillanes. 1992. *Nuestras Mujeres: Hispanas of New Mexico—Their Image and Their Lives, 1582–1992.* Albuquerque: El Norte Publications/Academia.

Stoller, Marianne L. 1986. "The Hispanic Women Artists of New Mexico: Present and Past." *El Palacio* 92 (1): 21–25.

Weigle, Marta, ed., with Claudia Larcombe and Samuel Larcombe. 1983. *Hispanic Arts and Ethnohistory in the Southwest.* Santa Fe: Ancient City Press, and Albuquerque: University of New Mexico Press.

Wroth, William. 1982. *Christian Images in Hispanic New Mexico.* Colorado Springs: The Taylor Museum of the Colorado Springs Fine Arts Center.

THE INDITA GENRE OF NEW MEXICO

GENDER AND CULTURAL IDENTIFICATION

BRENDA M. ROMERO

The *indita* has recently captured the attention of folklorists, ethnomusicologists, and historians in New Mexico[1] because of its association with the underresearched subject of *genízaro*[2] culture and miscegenation in general in colonial New Mexico (see Córdova 1979, Gutiérrez 1991, Koegel 1997, Lamadrid 1993, and Romero 1997). While there is some evidence that many Pueblo Indians were also *genízaros,* the term is usually applied to Catholicized and missionized non-Pueblo Indians, baptized with Christian names and assigned Spanish surnames, who spoke Spanish along with their Indian languages. Some *genízaros* were former Indian slaves or their descendants; some were mixed and others were full-blood Indians. For many generations (and long before New Mexico became a state in 1912), Spanish Mexicans of this region denied and suppressed direct acknowledgment of the mixing of Comanche, Diné (Navajo and Apache), Ute, and Pueblo Indians with Españoles (Spaniards) or Hispanos (Spanish acculturated mestizos).[3] People were often secretive about their Indian relatives, and the imposition of Spanish surnames obscured indigenous ancestries, aiding the process of suppression. The *indita* may well be the only form in which this history can still be perceived; thus it serves as a unique window through which we can begin to understand the rich complexity of ethnicity and expressive culture among Indo-Hispanos in New Mexico, among them the contemporary descendants of *genízaros.*

The *indita* is a song genre that originated in Mexico and was diffused as far north as present-day New Mexico, where elements of the Mexican *indita's* character manifested themselves in different song forms and subsequently formed a regional *indita* genre. In 1980 John Donald Robb published *Hispanic Folk Music of New Mexico and the Southwest,* a comprehensive book of songs he had collected in the Southwest, with the greater part from New Mexico. He was assisted in the enormous task of classifying the songs by the Mexican musicologist Vicente Mendoza, who came to New Mexico for nine months in 1946 at Robb's invitation. Mendoza's own *Estudio y clasificación de la música tradicional hispánica de Nuevo México,* written while he was in New Mexico, was published posthumously in 1986. In these and other works, Mendoza and Robb classified songs as *inditas* according to a set of disparate yet fascinating characteristics, sometimes expanding on the already confusing New Mexican categories by including songs these scholars felt belonged there. In our collaborative study of the *indita,* the literary folklorist Enrique Lamadrid and I have further expanded the genre by including ceremonial music and dance genres such as the Matachines and the Comanchitos in the *indita* category. Whereas musical genres are usually distinguished from one another by their formal structures, by the ways they are used, by the instruments used, or by features of the performance (Kaemmer 1993:5), the all-encompassing nature of the *indita's* regional classification poses problems in studies of the genre. Each type of *indita* could seemingly define its own genre, and this has led me to explore ideas that extend the traditional boundaries of genre classifications. In this essay, however, I explore various cultural and musical assumptions that appear to operate as the basis for the *indita's* classification.

The *indita,* by virtue of crossing the border and being found both in Mexico and in New Mexico (part of the northern frontier of Mexico for 250 years and now a U.S. state bordering El Paso, Texas, and Juarez, Mexico), brings into relief New Mexico's border status, binding this discussion to a contemporary scholarly emphasis on the nature of borderlands. Seen as places of power and violence, where multiple modernities and traditions subsist side by side,[4] the borderlands are a place where things don't fit and where social identities change as quickly as one can cross over. As Alicia Arrizón remarks with regard to Milcha Sánchez Scott's performance piece *Latina,* "The barbed wire fence is the 'object' through which the subject's venture is dramatically transformed: the act of crossing the border requires that the subject surrender her identity" (1999:103). Consider also the quote from Carlos Fuentes's *The Old Gringo,* which José Limón uses as the frontispiece for his book, *American Encounters* (1998): "Each of us carries his Mexico and his United States within him, / a dark and bloody frontier we dare to cross only at night."

Social categories are constantly being constructed on the border, and the *indita* emerges as an aspect of expressive culture that reflects this process of social construction in the nineteenth century and continues to do so today.

By being called *indita,* the diminutive form of *india* (indigenous woman), the genre is also female-gendered and indigenous. When examined in the light of recent writings by Chicana feminist scholars as well as recent Chicano scholarship on the erotics of culture (see Limón 1998; Arrizón 1999), the *indita* song and dance genre appears to be informed by hidden and not-so-hidden cultural conceptions, some mythical, of what it means to be an Indian woman and, by extension, a *mexicana* in New Mexico and Mexico. The first part of this essay reveals an implicit cultural paradigm underlying the nineteenth-century *indita* that is not new: the colonial model, with its stereotypical attitudes about indigenous women as sexual objects and as the subjects of coarse, crude humor.

The second part delineates the need to move away from this model, as we arrive at the contradictions inherent in it that allow us, as mestizos and mestizas, to see the New Mexican *indita* as a way of coming to terms with our indigenous mother. This is delineated in part through the Chicana feminist literary conception of an abstract metaphorical feminine borderland that represents the paradoxical inner space occupied by those of us who identify as Chicana/o and Mexican across borders. This seems an appropriate construction through which to examine a form of expressive culture that connotes the essences of multiple identities and gives voice to the conflicts created by colonization and miscegenation. The *indita* emerges as a vehicle of liminality,[5] negotiating a wide variety of gendered cultural meanings in this metaphorical borderland, the formative space between cultures and identities. I examine its various musical and cultural characterizations, speculating on their historical and social significance in Mexico, and particularly in New Mexico.

Because the *indita* originated and is still found in Mexico, the Mexican *indita* serves as a point of reference for evaluating the multiple ways that the Indian woman is perceived in deeper cultural layers across borders. Examining the Mexican *indita* also helps us to see more clearly how the performance of *inditas* in New Mexico has helped to define and continues to reinforce a regional Indo-Hispano identity.[6] I suspect that *inditas* not only reflect cultural attitudes but also demonstrate a syncretism of the high literary arts of Aztec and other New World indigenous cultures with those of the Spanish, to exploit metaphor and double meaning whenever possible.

GENERAL CHARACTERISTICS OF INDITAS

According to Mendoza (1986), the first *inditas* were Indian songs adapted as *sones* for Spanish musical and theatrical presentations called *tonadillas* in the Coliseo de la Ciudad de México (Coliseum of Mexico City), starting in the seventeenth century. The *tonadilla* incorporated also the indigenous *tocotín* dances, performed to bilingual songs, as well as *villancicos* (secular songs in the vernacular, such as those composed by Sor Juana, often juxtaposing Spanish and Nahuatl, the classic Aztec language) (Contreras Arias 1999; Lamadrid 1999).[7] The Coliseo thus offered ample opportunities for the mixing of European and indigenous music and dance forms as well as African music and dance traits (brought by slaves) that were absorbed by the mainstream. This led to the formation of syncretisms, new forms reflecting characteristics of the three musical cultures. *Son* is a highly syncretized song style (often accompanied by dance) that tends to conform to the regional characteristics of predominating music cultures.[8] Over time, the Mexican *son* incorporated indigenous languages, images, and song styles; European literary forms, melodies, and rhythmic organization (Mendoza 1986:466); fast, African-influenced tempos and percussive and syncopated rhythmic styles of playing the string instruments (Contreras Arias 1998). Both African and Spanish gypsy influence is felt in the use of cross-rhythm (in general, a fast 6/8 time in alternation or together with 3/4 time) as a basis for more complicated rhythmic elaboration (often supplied by the dancers). Mendoza attributed the dance style ("estilo y caracter . . . de los ritmos bailables") to the Indians and the dance rhythms ("el ritmo del baile") to the Spanish, although the vigorous and defined rhythms of the footwork called *zapateado* noted by Mendoza (1986:466) probably derived from the gypsies rather than from mainstream Spanish culture. (One recalls the improvisatory nature of rhythmically complicated hand-clapping and foot-stamping in gypsy flamenco when one sees *zapateado* in Mexico today.)

The most important of the early *inditas* was based on an elegant old Aztec song called "Xochipitzahuatl," "Flor menudita," or "Little Flower," which is still popular today (see *Ofrenda de flores* 1998). "Una indita en su chinampa" (an Indian maiden in her floating garden), as a *son*, appeared in a *tonadilla* called *La indita*. *Inditas* spread to all parts of Mexico after this, entering its northern periphery (what is now Texas and New Mexico) in the early part of the nineteenth century (Mendoza 1986:465). Certain textual aspects of some of the Mexican *inditas* identified many of the New Mexican *inditas* as well, including the use of the line "Indita, indita, indita" to

begin a verse or refrain, as heard in "Indita tapatía," a popular Mexican
mariachi standard until recently:

> Indita, indita, indita,
> indita me decías
> ya las horas del día,
> a esas horas dormías
> Dale, que dale el sí,
> dale, que dale el no,
> viendo que su marido,
> que de viejo se murió. (*Bailes folklóricos de México* n.d.)

> [Indita, indita, indita,
> indita, you used to tell me
> the hours of the day when you slept.
> You say yes,
> you say no,
> seeing that your husband,
> was so old when he died.] (my translation)

In New Mexico, it was equally common to sing "Indita, indita mía" (indita, my indita) as a first line, perhaps the influence of another popular old
Mexican folk song called "Indita mía." Similar to the use of "sí" and "no"
in the refrain of "Indita tapatía" (and in many other old Mexican folk songs),
the refrain "Indita que sí, Indita que no" appears in "El indio Vitorio" (the
Indian Vitorio), an *indita* collected by Robb in Albuquerque, New Mexico,
in 1971 (Robb 1980:431), but in few *indita* texts from this area.

Many of the New Mexican *inditas* that were recorded by collectors conform to an early *corrido* format, which gives the date, place, exposition,
development, and farewell (*despedida*). The texts place these surviving *inditas* at the turn of the twentieth century. I refer to them as *indita corridos,*
classifying them as early New Mexican *corridos,* which have been seemingly
absent from this region (Garcia 1996). In these, the term *indita* might only
appear in the title, where it signifies a tragic ballad, as does the term "corrido" today (making the term "indita corrido" a tautology). Alternatively,
the term "indita" might appear both in the title and as the first line of the
refrain. Some *inditas* that are similar to the *corrido* types only use "indita"
in the first line of the refrain. Examples of these are provided in the discussion of the New Mexican *indita* below.

In characterizing the New Mexican *indita,* Robb seemed unaware of the
Mexican *son,* believing the Indian-influenced melody to be the *indita's* char-

acteristic feature (Robb 1980:418). This is not surprising, as melody was the most significant Western musical element for many collectors of Robb's era, who were not sensitized to non-Western rhythmic developments nor to the process of cultural syncretism, although Robb was aware of its implications: "I am inclined to think that the origin of the *indita* is as natural as the mixture of Spanish and Indian blood by intermarriage" (1980:419). Also, by the time he collected the New Mexican *inditas,* primarily in the 1940s and 1950s, they were fragmented and usually collected without instrumental accompaniment.

What is now New Mexico was in the past a Spanish outpost. Following the signing of the Treaty of Guadalupe Hidalgo in 1848, there existed *mexicanos* of the same *español* mentality that had provoked rebellion after Mexico gained its independence from Spain, a rebellion that led to the assassination of the Mexican governor, Albino Pérez, in 1837. This faction, which included many of the most privileged landowners and their *genízaros,* now emphasized a romanticized Spanish identity, encouraged by Anglo elites, many of whom resisted statehood because the lawlessness of territorial government facilitated land grabbing from the Spanish Mexicans (Sena 1999). For them, such romanticization may have been desirable as a way of pacifying the Spanish Mexicans. For those tired of waiting for statehood, such romanticization may have seemed to attract statehood.[9] Many of the privileged Spanish Mexicans thus distanced themselves as far as possible from Mexican "bastardized" identity, to use David Montejano's term to describe a general attitude—probably deriving from the Spanish *casta* system, in which European racial purity was the key to privilege and status (1998). Many who identified strongly with the old Spanish culture preserved the old pan-European dances, such as the vals, the polka, the chótis, and the varsoviana. The *son* that was preserved in the religious Matachines repertoires still performed in New Mexico had probably arrived in the region long before the *son* underwent its transformation in Mexico and does not typically exhibit the syncretic qualities listed above.[10] The New Mexican *indita* sometimes incorporated some of the fast rhythmic vitality of the syncretic Mexican *son*-based *indita,* but in general New Mexican *inditas* seem to have been reinterpreted to conform to European folk styles that were inherently simpler than the rhythmically complicated Mexican *sones.* Many songs thus retained the name "indita" but assumed the character of various local genres, suggesting that the important signifier was not generic musical form but the strength of the symbol or embodiment of the Indian woman or maiden.

THE INDITA IN MEXICO

In Mexico, *inditas* typically alluded to love and eroticism, often using double entendres to evoke the erotic. Many were burlesques of the Indians, male and female, although the Indian woman in particular was the object of demeaning texts. There were many degrees of eroticism and/or burlesque in the Mexican *inditas*. Take, for instance, the text to "Indita tapatía" above, with its suggestion that her aged husband, now dead, could not have satisfied her, yet she waffles between saying yes and no to his advances.

A classic example of the Mexican *indita* is the famous "Una indita en su chinampa," in which the double meanings begin with the first verse:

> Una indita en su chinampa
> cortaba diversas flores,
> y un indito cuatro orejas
> gozaba de sus favores. (Mendoza and Mendoza 1991:135)

> [An indita at her chinampa
> cut diverse flowers,
> and an indito greatly
> enjoyed her favors.] (my translation)

The metaphor of the cut flowers requires no explanation. The term "cortar una oreja, dos orejas" translates as "being awarded an ear, two ears" as a reward for a good performance, and in this case it is four ears, metaphorically implying that she is particularly pleased. The portrayal of the Indian maiden as seductress is poetically but clearly established. A similar *son,* called "El indito," collected by Mendoza in the area of Central Puebla, uses the verse above as the basis for its first *copla,* then exemplifies the *indita's* use of Indian refrains, in this case probably in the Mixtec language of the region[11]:

> Tarimbé shímata percas,
> tarimbé shíshiri yuca
> papatí shuca shashi comá
> agua dipé, shíshiri yú quiri shiadi. (Mendoza and Mendoza
>   1991:136)

The incorporation of Indian words and images was probably as natural as the marriage between cultures noted by Robb (1980) and was no doubt especially useful in bringing larger audiences to the Coliseo, where the *inditas* were first featured in Mexico. While the context of this song is love between two Indians, the *indita* is romanticized into an enticer. This image helps in erasing the traces of the violence with which the Spanish "conquered" the Indian women in the early colonial period. This and other Mexican *inditas* that used Indian refrains could also be interpreted as burlesques of Indian eroticism, with the "four ears" as a form of ridicule. For instance, "El indio de Colima" (*Bailes folklóricos de México*) refers to an old metaphor, *estar en el guayabo,* which means to make love. The text implies that the *india,* having eaten unripe guavas, has had premarital sex.[12] A *saltillo* (literally a short jump or leap) is a watery area, like a gully, where guavas might grow, although here it implies marriage. This song is similar in construction to "Una indita en su chinampa." The refrain is more of a soundplay and is less likely to have lexical meaning than the Indian refrain cited above.

> El indio le dijo a la india,
> "¿Porqué estas tan amarilla
> de comer guayabas verdes
> sin pasear en el saltillo?"
> De Salaytica, de Chichirimeca,
> de Salayti, de Quiquirigui. (*Bailes folklóricos de México* n.d.)

> [The Indian man said to the Indian woman,
> "Why are you so yellow
> from eating green guavas
> without passing through the saltillo?"
> From Salaytica, from Chichirimeca,
> from Salayti, from Quiquirigui.] (my translation)

"El indio de Colima" is similar to another Mexican *indita* type in which older Spanish texts were transformed into *inditas* for dances, with the addition of ta-ra syllables, or refrains (Mendoza 1986:465) that used such syllables entirely. One example is "Las inditas," which uses this technique, as well as grammatical mistakes, to burlesque the broken Spanish spoken by the Indians (Contreras Arias 1999).

> Somos indita-ra-ras, Michoacanita-ra-ras
> que ando paseando-ro-ro por lo portal
> vendiendo guaje-re-res, y jicari-ta-ra-ras
> y floreci-ta-ra-ras del temporal.
> Pero aunque trove la guarecita,
> pero aseadita del delantal. (*Tarascan and Other Music of Mexico* 1958)

[We are inditas, from Michoacán
and I am walking through the porch
selling gourds and chocolate cups
and flowers of the season.
But even if this Purepecha maiden sings,
Always her apron is very clean.] (my translation)

In other contexts, the *indita* in Mexico became a vehicle for the Spanish song contest tradition to continue in the New World, as it did through other genres such as the *décima* and the *copla*. According to Guillermo Contreras Arias, in the *cuenca* regions of the Rio Balsas of Mexico, including the Región Planeca in Michoacán and the Región Calentana in Guerrero, in the state of Mexico, and in parts of Michoacán, the now-declining *indita* genre is the basis for song contests in which improvisation is the rule, and the literary texts are often clever double entendres. A careful assessment of skills in musical, literary, and cultural arenas determines a contest winner.[13] *Inditas* flourished in the gulf area of Veracruz, including the Región Jarocha, Oaxaca, Tarasco, Puebla, and in the Región Tuxtleca. The erotic double entendres could be explicitly sexual, dominating late-night male bar scenes. In Tuxtleca, these late-night song contests eventually became identified with homosexuals (Contreras Arias 1998, 1999).

Later *inditas* and those sung in polite company did not emphasize erotic and burlesque content but focused more on romance (Contreras Arias 1999), as in "Indita mía," which begins thus: "Indita mía, si no me quieres, / si no me quieres ten compasión" (*Los Alegres de Terán* 1970; my indita, if you don't love me, / if you don't love me have compasión [my translation]). Many *inditas* from the Calentana, Planeca, Montaña, and Costa Chica regions similarly focused on more poetic images of romantic love:

India del alma,
ya supe tu bajadero
donde te vas a bañar.
Allá mandaré un jilguero
que te valla acompañar,
blanca rosa de castilla,
acabada de cortar. (Contreras Arias 1999)

[India of my soul
I've learned the descent you take
to the place where you bathe.

I will send a linnet there
to accompany you,
white Castillian rose,
freshly cut (young and fresh).] (my translation)

Since improvisation was common, many versions are still heard; an alternative ending to this verse is: "porque deveras te quiero, / me he empezado a enamorar" (Contreras Arias 1999; because I truly love you, / I have begun to fall in love with you [my translation]).

THE NEW MEXICAN INDITA

While the Mexican *indita* focuses on erotic images and love, the New Mexican *indita* is more typically a lament. One of the functions of the early New Mexican *indita* was to relate accounts of Hispano captives taken by the Indians (Mendoza 1986:465), primarily the Navajo and the Comanche. The heartbreak of captivity is commemorated in "La cautiva Marcelina," the lament of a woman being taken captive, as she witnesses the deaths of those close to her, including her father and her children. The theme of rape is just below the surface, since the implications are that her captors are men. Musically, this *indita*[14] is very interesting, combining aspects of European and indigenous musics and creating a soundscape in which Spanish words and musical elements are juxtaposed with indigenous rhythmic motifs. Rubén Cobos collected an early version of this song in 1945, and Mendoza transcribed it using alternating 3/4 and 2/4 meters in the first half of the verse (a typical *son* characteristic that recalls the days when Mexican cultural forms circulated freely in what is now New Mexico).

   The following analysis is based on my own performance, a stylized version of Jack Loeffler's field recording of Virginia Bernal in Colorado in the 1970s (Lamadrid, Loeffler, and Gandert 1994). While Bernal also alternated between 3/4 and 2/4, her rather complicated and inconsistent folk guitar performance does not lend itself to a detailed analysis. My version of this *indita* does not seek to duplicate her performance, but rather the style. I alternate a 3/4 waltz rhythm, reinforced by the guitar, with *indio*-style "isorhythm," in which every syllable has its own beat, and some phrases where the language and melody dictate the duple division of beats. This is only one possibility for how the guitar and textual accents correspond in this style, a true challenge for the transcriber. The numbers represent the rhythms:

```
1 2   3  1231  2  3 1231 123 1  1 1 1 1    1
La cau-ti - va  Mar-ce-li - na,  ya se va, ya se la lle-van,

1 1 1   1 1 1 1 2312  3   1 2   1 2 1   2   1 2 1 2
ya se va, ya se la lle - va - n, par' e-sas tier - ras men-ta - das

1 2  1   1 1 1 1  1  1 1 1  1  1 1 1 1 2 3  1 2 3
a co-mer car-ne de ye-gua, a co-mer car-ne de ye - gua,    Por

1 2 1 2   1  2  1   2   1   2  1 2 1 23 1 2 3
es-o ya no quier - ro'en el mun-do más a-ma - r,     De

1   1  1 1  1 1 1   1   1  1 1 1 1 23 1 2 3
mi que-ri-da pa - tria me van a re-ti-ra – r –
```

La cautiva Marcelina,
ya se va, ya se la llevan,
ya se va, ya se la llevan
par' esas tierras mentadas,
a comer carne de yegua,
a comer carne de yegua.
Por eso ya no quiero en el mundo más amar
de mi querida patria me van a retirar. (Lamadrid, Loeffler, and
    Gandert 1994:28–29)

[The captive Marcelina,
she is going, they are taking her,
she is going, they are taking her
to those infamous lands,
to eat mare's meat,
to eat mare's meat.
That's why I no longer want to love in this world,
from my beloved homeland they are taking me away.]
    (translation by Lamadrid)

Evidence that "La cautiva Marcelina" is probably an Hispano *indita* is seen
in the line about eating mare's meat, a typical Hispano stereotype about wild
Indians. Contemporary awareness of *genízaro* culture in colonial New
Mexico, however, reinforces textual evidence that some *inditas* were composed by Indians who spoke Spanish. Among them were many about important *indios* (Indian men), and typically these *inditas* revolve around tragic
circumstances but do not fit the *corrido* format. These include "La indita
de Manuelito" and "El indio Vitorio," names easily associated with famous

Navajo and Apache leaders, respectively. The presence of Anglo names and terms suggest that these *inditas* date back to the period after 1848, when the territory was taken over by the United States. "La indita de Manuelito" is related by Mariano, the brother of Manuelito:

> Indita, indita, indita,
> ¡con qué sentimiento estás!
> que en el ojo de la gallina
> te dieron muerte de paz.

> No te mataron peliando,
> ni tampoco bien a bien,
> te mataron a traición
> Charles y Capitán Grey.

> Yo soy el indio Manuel,
> hermanito del Mariano,
> que con mi flecha en la mano
> empalmo de dos a tres.

> [Indita, indita, indita,
> what grief you must feel
> that at Gallina Springs
> they dealt you the peace of death.

> They didn't kill you fighting
> nor did you want to die.
> They killed you by treachery,
> Charles and Captain Grey.

> I am the Indian Manuel,
> little brother of Mariano,
> who with my arrow in hand
> pierce two or three at once.] (Robb 1980:434)[15]

Many lyrical songs without dance accompaniment, similar to "La cautiva Marcelina" and "La indita de Manuelito," continued to be sung in New Mexico throughout the first half of the twentieth century. While some of these clearly depart from the Mexican models seen previously, others do not. For example, "El comanchito" (The little Comanche)[16] demonstrates the use of Indian words or Indian-sounding syllables. As in Mexico, early *inditas* of this type are typically burlesques of the Indians:

Allí vienen los indios,
por el chaparral,
Aye nanita, aye nanita
me van a matar.
¡Jeya, jeya, jeya,
jeya, jeya, jeya,
jeya, jeya, jeyaaaaah!
Baila el comanchito,
toca el tambor;
baila por buñuelos,
baila por licor.

[There come the Indians,
through the chaparral,
O grandmother, o grandmother,
they're going to kill me.
Heya, heya, heya,
heya, heya, heya,
heya, heya, heyaaaaah!
The little Comanche dances,
he plays the drum;
he dances for fritters,
he dances for liquor.] (Robb 1980:419)

Lamadrid (1993:159) proposes that this type of burlesque reflects the process of softening and transforming the "dangerous" Indian into the "ridiculous" Indian.[17]

While there is insufficient information to be certain, we can speculate that perhaps the erotic, burlesque, and romantic connotations of the Mexican *indita* may all account for the popular use of the term to denote a ballad in late nineteenth-century New Mexico. The fact that the content of these ballads departs so clearly from the Mexican models leads me to speculate instead that perhaps *indita* ballad types were so called because they were about or composed by *genízaros*. These *inditas* often begin with the phrase "Aye, indita," signaling the aforementioned ballad in the *corrido* style (Mendoza 1986:465). A clever double entendre operates here, for the refrain personifies the *indita,* while the titles of these *corrido* types characterize the *indita* as a ballad. The use of *indita* in titles further expands the range of potential meanings. For instance, "La indita de Amarante Martínez" implies a ballad but translates literally as "The Indian woman [Indian slave?

maid?] of Amarante Martínez," although the text does not support such a scenario. "La indita del Río Grande" and "La indita del 1884" literally describe where and when she is from, respectively. In a version of "La indita de Manuelito," which uses the title as the first line of one verse, Robb's translation is "Indian Wife of Manuelito," but this confuses the text, sounding in one verse as if she was killed and focusing on his death in the next verse (Robb 1980:432). This instance does, however, make evident the potential double meanings inherent in this use of the term "indita," and a more detailed inspection of texts may be particularly revealing. Since these ballads are on tragic subjects, they may imply some kind of loyal subject in the Indian woman, to whom one might address such sad sentiments.

Analyzing what makes the *corrido* types *inditas* is also complicated. The only orally documented distinction between the *indita* and the *corrido* came from Celestino Segura, who told Robb (probably in 1949) that the *indita* was performed "softly, with feeling," and "a *corrido* you can sing loud" (Robb 1980:418). Robb's own comparison of the *indita* and *corrido* indicates that while the *corrido* is typically in a major tonality, the *indita* is more often modal. While he did not interpret his findings, according to Western musical conventions this implies that the *indita* uses older melodies and introspective, if not sad, subject matter. The differences between the *indita* and *corrido* described by Segura suggest that the personified *indita* imbued the ballad with feminine qualities absent in the *corrido* (a male-gendered term), which developed in Mexico not long after the *indita* arrived in the southwestern United States.

The refrain of the *indita corridos* is typically a lament directed at an Indian woman, but it is as if the *indita* somehow is the spirit of the earth itself. A good example is the "Indita del 1884," about the flooding of the *genízaro* village of Tomé, New Mexico: "¡Ay! indita del Río Grande, / ¡Ay! que ingrata te estas mostrando" (Koegel 1997:180; Ay! indita of the Río Grande, / Ay! how ungrateful you are showing yourself to be [my translation]). Another of these ballads, "Me quemaron el rancho" (They burned my ranch), is about *la gringada* with *guangoches* (gunny sacks) over their heads, or white vigilantes, trying to burn out the *mexicanos*. The term "indita" appears only in the first line of the refrain: "Ay indita, y eso no, / en el rincón Colorado, / la quemazón me rodió" (Robb 1980:449; Ay! indita, not that, / in Red Rock Canyon / the fire surrounded me [translation by Lamadrid]).

THE INDITA AND THE BORDERLANDS

Integrating the viewpoints of contemporary feminist Chicana and Chicano writers (including Gloria Anzaldúa, Sandra Cisneros, Norma Cantú, and Luis Alberto Urrea), Nohemy Solórzano sums up various literary ideas that feminize the border and of the borderlands. She ties to this phenomenon a liberating influence from traditional patterns of male dominance for many contemporary Mexican women, because they go to the border to work and escape gender abuse (1997). I like this idea primarily because it incorporates the indigenous concept of the land as feminine and nurturing, but this idea in itself is not new. As Antonia I. Castañeda notes, Spanish colonial litera-ture has often equated women with land: "Much has been written about women as a metaphor and emblem for land, as well as for nation. Both women and land are conquered, tamed, husbanded and seeded" (1993:266).

Solórzano goes on to note that border literature often asks "What does it mean to belong to a place?" and "What does it mean to be Chicano?" (1997:4). She refers to a geographical space that is correlated with an ab-stract metaphorical borderland, and it is in this metaphorical borderland that the *indita* finds cultural perspective.

The metaphorical space can be said to be that border identified by Luis Alberto Urrea as running "down the middle of our hearts" (1996:4)—the hearts of Chicanos, Chicanas, Mexicans, and others identified with the cul-ture across borders. The daily contradictions of living in this metaphorical borderland become the reality of our lives. In half of one's heart *la india* personifies the beloved dark-skinned Indian mother and the tenderness of the earth and its rich sustenance. She is the landscape personified; she is the Aztec earth mother Tonántzin and La Virgen de Guadalupe at one and the same time. In New Mexico she is the pure, young, and chaste Malinche, the first Christian convert or a spirit guide, depending on whether you are His-panic and Catholic or indigenous and traditional. She is the *indita*, in the diminutive, connoting the affection in which she is held.

In the other half of one's heart are the hegemonic male voices that exploit-ed *la india,* the erotic Indian woman, free for the taking, and at the same time a symbol of the collective melancholy of a people whose ancestry is both rape victim and perpetrator. She is La Malinche, to whom contemporary Mexi-can masculine elites attribute the selling out of indigenous culture, in spite of the fact that she was only one of thousands of indigenous people who assist-ed the Spanish, only too happy to rise up against their imperialist Aztec land-lords. Syncretized with the biblical Eve, *la india* is *la hija perdida,* the lost woman, upon whose shoulders lies the burden of the sin of rape that leads to the *mestizaje*.[18] To *la india* are attributed all the negative aspects of the personality in this patriarchal system, the shadow self in the Jungian sense.

"DOWN THE MIDDLE OF OUR HEARTS . . ."

While New Mexico is a borderland area, extending informally to the immigration port of Juarez, it has long been a stronghold of male dominance. Yet the Spanish were defeated by the Pueblo Indians during the Pueblo Revolt of 1680 and remained subdued for twelve years before they made it back. The borderlands are thus not only feminized but also indigenized, in contrast to the male mainstream influences coming from the north and south.[19] All New Mexican folk songs on Indian topics are grouped as *inditas,* reflecting the metaphorical borderlands where the *indio* is a feminine aspect of *mexicano* identity.

The New Mexican *indita* genre reinforces the idea of the feminine personification of the land, much in the way that Indian cosmologies personify it. Examples of this are seen in "La indita del Río Grande," "Me quemaron el rancho," and the "Indita del 1884," among others. After the genre ceased to relate the sad incidents of captivity, the qualities of the *indita* continued to be called upon in more abstract ways to define the early New Mexican *corrido*. The textual images always return to "her," the *indita*, in the refrain, as a point of reference, with convention dictating an unaggressive style of performance, compared to that of the masculine-gendered *corridos*. Was there perhaps something of the feminine borderlands' liberating influence, mentioned above, in the *indita* as well?

In a sense, we all live on *la frontera*, the "crossing of different identifying elements: cultures, politics, genders and agendas. It is the meeting place of all these paths and the creation of a broadly encompassing space that attempts to reconcile different worlds" (Solórzano 1997:1). Recurring approaches to the border, Solórzano suggests, often see it "as a feminine space that welcomes the crosser with open arms, inviting him/her to cross over to *el otro lado*" (1997:2), and "crossing over acquires a sexualized quality" (1997:3). The *indita* sits squarely within the metaphorical borderland area, where the genre's ambiguous and liminal connotations grant permission for other culturally defined shadow identities, as in the Mexican Tuxleca contexts, to "cross over." An important shadow identity is the *india* who was raped and became our ancestor. In the New Mexican *inditas* we began to acknowledge her indirectly, as the sacred power of this mother-land.

In the metaphorical borderland *la indita* is personified, sacred, fertile land-scape. Oral narratives of contemporary New Mexicans indicate that a clear Indian influence on the local culture is the belief in the concept of *tierra sagrada* (sacred earth). Yearly pilgrimages are made to the Santuario at Chimayo, where pilgrims take a little of the miraculous, healing, sacred earth reputed to replenish itself daily. By extension, through the Mexican association of La Virgen de Guadalupe with Tonántzin, the Aztec earth mother, and because Guadalupe is an Indian Virgen, she is often referred to intimately as *morenita* (the dark-skinned maiden, synonymous in this case with *indita*)—so the laments in the New Mexican *inditas* may be sub-consciously, if not consciously, directed at her, the Virgen of this land. In the New Mexican lament style, eroticism is effectively transformed into mysticism, and women are at least ideologically protected from the violence of rape and exploitation. The shift to a lament style is not surprising, giv-en the influential role that the Penitente sects played in colonial New Mex-ico, helping to define a local religious and cultural aesthetic (Romero 1993; Lamadrid 1997).

THE CONTEMPORARY NEW MEXICAN INDITA

The only recently composed *inditas* that I know of further reinforce the belief in *tierra sagrada,* describing aspects of New Mexican landscape, foods, and people. "Enaje yo, indita del Rio Grande" was written by Benito Flores and edited and performed throughout New Mexico and Colorado by Jesús "Chuy" Martínez in the last few years. Cleofes Vigil's "El himno al pueblo de las Montañas de la Sangre de Cristo" (anthem for the people of the Blood of Christ Mountains), uses both isorhythm and Indian vocables (nonlexi-cal syllables), praising the "beautiful *inditas*" from whom we descended and focusing closely on the sacred land (Lamadrid, Loeffler, and Gandert 1994).

As mentioned at the outset, the past ten years have seen the tendency to designate as *inditas* all Indo-Hispano genres, in particular the ancient, resil-ient pantomime "Los matachines" and "Los comanches" (which might in-clude *cautivas,* enactments of captivity, as in Abiquiu), and these are relevant to the discussion of a regional gendered cultural identification. During this time also, the term "Indo-Hispano" has emerged to more accurately reflect the ancestry and culture of most of the Hispano population that lives in New Mexico. The association of the New Mexican *indita* with Indo-Hispanos, among them the contemporary descendants of *genízaros,* brings into relief the complexity of Hispano cultural identification in New Mexico.

While much is known and written about the Matachines, suddenly, it seems, Comanche ceremonials in former *genízaro* villages in rural New Mexico are being "discovered," having been preserved for an unknown length of time by particular families who identified with their Indian ancestry and were not ashamed to preserve their heritage through yearly performances of songs and dances. That this *indita* song and dance ceremonial genre still exists in New Mexico is in itself a subject of much interest. In spite of prevailing hegemonic attitudes, or perhaps because of them, some New Mexican families and villages identified with Indian musical contexts. Interactions between the Hispanos and *indios* of New Mexico seem to have been fairly complicated and not always unfriendly. Evidence that Pueblo Indians were being empowered in local affairs is seen in documents showing them winning cases in the local courts by 1820 (see Schroeder 1972) and even earlier through the Protector de Indios, a government office that looked after Indian affairs. Indios and Hispanos also frequently shared religious and secular contexts after the early colonial struggles. While the Matachines Danza was the only Catholic-sanctioned music and dance genre, at least unofficially,[20] other ceremonial contexts featuring Plains, and more specifically Comanche, dress style reflect the identification of many Indo-Hispanos with their *genízaro* ancestors.

The contemporary *indita* genres include the dances still enacted at Abiquiu, once designated a *genízaro* village. In 1997 I conducted fieldwork in Abiquiu for the Feast of Santo Tomás, the village saint. The feast is always celebrated on the weekend following Thanksgiving, when many family members who no longer live there are likely to be visiting. Before the mass, a small troupe of young girls dressed in Plains-style dress (but in solid red, which the Plains groups do not wear), were led dancing from the *morada*[21] to the church by a man in a similar style of dress, wearing a feather headdress, playing a Pueblo drum, and singing in Indian vocables. The red outfits are probably a Mexican Chichimeca influence, although the influence may have gone the other way a long time ago.[22] These "indios" sang and danced into the church and in front of the church after the mass. During this time people also visited with each other. While I am not related directly to anyone in Abiquiu, we all recognized each other as possible or probable kin, and everywhere I was treated as a neighbor, as were my mother and my niece.

After the mass, the community reconvened at the houses of the two couples of *mayordomos* (stewards) for the fiesta. At both houses elements of burlesque were hinted at, along with a genuine affection for things *indio*. For instance, I was warned that "only *biscochitos*[23] and whiskey" would

be served at the fiesta, obviously a stereotyped image. (Actually, there was
a wide variety of sweets as well as drinks served, from soft drinks to Crown
Regal whiskey and much in between.)

Among the dances they enacted was El Coyote. They offered to teach me
what this was about. Before I knew it, I was taken to dance a kind of grace-
ful two-step to the *indio* singing and drumming. Since couple dancing was
introduced by the Europeans to the New World, this part is from the Hispano *baile* (dance tradition). Suddenly the music stopped, and the one dressed
indio and one of two men now singing yelled out to the crowd: "¿Quién la
conoce?" (who knows her?). I looked out to see if my mother was still
around . . . no mom. Luckily, my colleague and collaborator on the *indita*
project, Enrique Lamadrid, who was there videotaping, paid the ransom to
buy my freedom. The money went to the musicians. While lighthearted in true
indio style, where humor is valued as a necessary aspect of ritual (Romero
1997:163), the enactment at Abiquiu commemorates the captive status that
genízaros, and particularly young girls and women, often suffered.

Descendants of *genízaros* in the town of Abiquiú, New Mexico, in a circle dance
accompanied by Indian-style singing and drumming for the patronal feast of Santo
Tomás. Photograph by Brenda M. Romero.

Equally interesting are the ways in which Comanche genres that have survived in other New Mexican villages celebrate cultural mixing in a style derived from the Mexican burlesque *indita,* reinterpreted as a religious expression without the burlesque. "Los Comanches Guadalupanos" and "Los Comanchitos," both collected by Lamadrid, are *inditas* that are sung in Spanish *coplas* with Indian vocable refrains, either for the feast day of La Virgen de Guadalupe or for the Christ child instead of Posadas at Christmas.[24] As in Abiquiu, the dancers in some of these villages, who sing as well, wear Plains-style red-accented Indian dress and play Pueblo Indian-style rattles and drums. Each line of the vocable refrain is repeated (vocables are not translated, since they are nonlexical), as in "Los Comanchitos":

> Ana jeyana, jeyana heyo
> ana jeyana, jeyana heyo
> ana yana yo-o, ana yana yo
> ana yana yo-o, ana yana yo
> ana jeyana, jeyana heyo
> ana jeyana, jeyana heyo. (*Music of New Mexico* 1992)

In the metaphorical borderland, the Comanche and Comanchito *indita* genres are in the mystical space occupied by *la morenita,* our Lady of Guadalupe.

CONCLUSION

The various manifestations of *inditas* across borders derived historically from conflicting underlying cultural assumptions and subject positions of Indian women. Because the Indian woman has been at once maligned, eroticized, beloved, and mysticized, different *inditas* have reflected different subject positions. In New Mexico the musical and many of the cultural elements that typically defined the Mexican *indita* genre were reinterpreted to reflect different dynamics of cultural interaction between the Pueblos and the *mexicanos.* Also, many *inditas* appear to have been composed by *genízaros.* Because the *indita* crosses borders, I have attempted to understand the various subject positions as a continuum across borders. What I took to be hidden conceptions of the *indita* are sometimes obscured, rather than hidden, in New Mexico, where the thread of historical commonalities with Mexico was severed in the mid-nineteenth century. Not so hidden is the recasting of the colonial relationship between the Indian woman and the Spanish conqueror in the subsequent contexts of the Chicana and the Anglo colonizer, "not only in what later became the Southwest but in Mexico as well, especially northern Mexico, where such domination often extended. By this reading, casting Mexican women in particular as sexually promiscuous made them sexually available within a prevailing code of racism, even as it ratified and extended the right of Anglo conquest to the realm of the sexual" (Limón 1998:130).

The New Mexican *inditas* lost the erotic contexts and meanings of the Mexican ones, replacing these elements with a lament style, signifying the *indita* as a personification and feminization of the land, with associated implications of an indigenous conceptualization of the land and culture. The idea of a metaphorical borderland is liberating because it points to a new notion of an unfixed border where one can move freely to create one's own identity. The path "down the middle of our hearts" is not a straight path, but it takes us here and there as we struggle to recover and own our heritage, all of it.

NOTES

Versions of this essay were delivered at the National Association of Chicana/Chicano Studies Conference held in June 1999 in Mexico City; the Eighth University of New Mexico Conference on Ibero-American Culture and Society, held in February 1999 at the University of New Mexico, Albuquerque; the Society for Ethnomusicology's Regional Meeting held in April 1999 at Colorado College, Colorado Springs; and the College Music Society Annual Conference, held in October 1999 in Denver, Colorado.

I would like to acknowledge my ongoing collaboration on the "Indita Project" with Enrique Lamadrid, a literary folklorist at the University of New Mexico, Albuquerque, with whom I have shared discussions, field trips, and performances on the subject of the *indita*. His expertise and encouragement have always nurtured my work on this topic. I would also like to thank Charles L. Briggs, an anthropologist and professor of ethnic studies at the University of California at San Diego, for his suggestions about the nature of borderlands that informs the *indita,* and Roberta Maldonado, a doctoral student in education at the University of Colorado, Boulder, for her insightful editorial comments and suggestions.

1. Although New Mexico did not become a state until 1912, the term "New Mexico" is used throughout to refer to the general region encompassed by present-day New Mexico and southern Colorado.

2. Literally: "begotten by parents of different nations" (Velázquez de la Cadena et al. 1964).

3. The process of miscegenation between Europeans and New World indigenous peoples that produced mestizo cultures began early in the colonial period, particularly in what is now Mexico and further south to Latin America. Many of the immigrants who came north from Mexico to settle in what is now the southwestern United States during the colonial and postcolonial periods were officially identified as mestizos to maintain the Spanish hierarchy that privileged only Europeans born in Europe and their children.

4. Charles L. Briggs, personal communications with author, Boulder, Colo., 1999.

5. Liminality is a concept developed by Victor Turner.

6. I would like to thank Maestro Guillermo Contreras Arias, professor of ethnomusicology at Universidad Autónoma de México and researcher at Centro Nacional de Investigación, Documentación e Información Musical Carlos Chávez del Instituto Nacional de Bellas Artes for information on the contemporary Mexican *inditas*.

7. Enrique Lamadrid, personal communications with author, Albuquerque, N.Mex., 1999. For a historical description of the *tocotín*, see Stevenson (1980:165). The term "tocotín" derives from the onomatopoeic syllables used to signify the rhythms and pitches of the two-toned *teponaztli* (slit drum).

8. This is in contrast to the *son* of the Caribbean area, which is associated with a particular instrumentation and musical sound.

9. In both cases romanticization was probably seen by elites as a possible commodity.

10. Rural Hispanos and Pueblo Indians continue to pantomime (enacting the story without texts and with instrumental music only) the Matachines dance drama on the feast day of Our Lady of Guadalupe, during the Christmas season, and on other important feast days, such as San Antonio and San Lorenzo.

11. This is an example of how Indian words are often used. It appears to be Mixtec or a dialect of it.

12. Nicolás Moreno, personal communication with the author, 2001. Nicolás Moreno is a well-known painter of Mexican landscapes and has had a long association with Mexican folklore and music.

13. In Spain the song contest tradition still survives among the Basques.

14. I have also heard this type of *indita* referred to as a *cautiva*.

15. The texts in Robb's book, *Hispanic Folksongs of New Mexico and the Southwest* (1980), were translated by quite a few people and individuals are not credited in the book itself.

16. "El Comanchito" survives as a children's song in Texas, where it is called "El indito" (Paredes 1995:21).

17. The Indians had burlesques of the Spanish as well, which they called "sneak ups" (Wapp 1998).

18. The idea of the lost woman is intimately tied into the Christian narrative, and it is no surprise that it was Octavio Paz and other masculine elites who promulgated the image of La Malinche as traitoress in Mexico.

19. Recent fieldwork that I have conducted on *danza* in Juarez and southern New Mexico supports this view.

20. Lamadrid 1999 reports that "a controversy is brewing in Tijeras, New Mexico, because the parish priest has called them [the Matachines dances] 'demonic.'"

21. The *morada* is a designation for the small, austere prayer chapel of the penitent sect.

22. The ethnomusicologist Stephen Duncan told me an interesting story about how the Kiowa used to employ Mexican scouts to lead them into foreign territories. They dressed the Mexican scout in red, so that raiding parties might spot and kill him first, thus giving the Kiowa advance warning (Duncan 1997). If this is a legitimate connection, then the fact that the Chichimecas wear red as well as Plains-style headdresses suggests that for the Mexican groups it may have been an honor to serve the wild and resilient Plains Indians, a test of courage worthy of their northern neighbors.

23. *Biscochitos* are a traditional holiday sugar cookie.

24. See "Los Comanchitos" in *Music of New Mexico* 1992. See also Lamadrid et al. (2000).

WORKS CITED

Arrizón, Alicia. 1999. *Latina Performance: Traversing the Stage*. Bloomington: Indiana University Press.

Bailes Folklóricos de Mexico. n.d. Performed by Mariachi México de Pepe Villa. Peerless 1097.

Briggs, Charles L. 1999. Personal communications.

Castañeda, Antonia I. 1993. "Memory, Language, and Voice of Mestiza Women on the Northern Frontier: Historical Documents as Literary Text." In *Recovering the U.S. Hispanic Literary Heritage*. Ed. Ramón Gutierrez and Genaro Padilla. 265–77. Houston, Tex.: Arte Público Press.

Contreras Arias, Guillermo. 1998, 1999. Personal communications.

Córdova, Gilberto Benito. 1979. "Missionization and Hispanicization of Santo Thomas Apostol de Abiquiu, 1750–1770." M.A. thesis, University of New Mexico.

Duncan, Stephen. 1997. Personal communications.

Garcia, Peter J. 1996. "The New Mexican Early Ballad Tradition: Reconsidering the New Mexican Folklorists' Contribution to Songs of Intercultural Conflict." *Latin American Music Review* 17 (2): 150–71.

Gutiérrez, Ramón A. 1991. *When Jesus Came the Corn Mothers Went Away*. Stanford, Calif.: Stanford University Press.

Kaemmer, John E. 1993. *Music in Human Life*. Austin: University of Texas Press.

Koegel, John. 1997. "Village Musical Life along the Río Grande: Tomé, New Mexico, since 1739." *Latin American Music Review* 18 (2): 173–251.

Lamadrid, Enrique R. 1993. "Entre Cíbolos Criado: Images of Native Americans in the Popular Culture of Colonial New Mexico." In *Reconstructing a Chicano/a Literary Heritage*. Ed. María Herrera-Sobek. 158–200. Tucson: University of Arizona Press.

———. 1997. "'El Sentimiento trágico de la vida': Notes on Regional Styles in Nuevo Mexicano Ballads." *Aztlán* 22 (1):27–47.

———. 1999. Personal communications.

Lamadrid, Enrique R., Jack Loeffler, and Miguel Gandert. 1994. *Tesoros del Espíritu: A Portrait in Sound of Hispanic New Mexico*. Embudo, N.Mex.: El Norte/Academia Publications.

Lamadrid, Enrique R., Ramón Guitiérrez, Lucy Lippard, and Chris Wilson. Miguel Gandert, photographs. 2000. *Nuevo Mexico Profundo: Rituals of an Indo-Hispano Homeland*. Santa Fe: Museum of New Mexico Press.

Limón, José E. 1998. *American Encounters, Greater Mexico, the United States, and the Erotics of Culture*. Boston: Beacon Press.

Los Alegres de Terán: Mi Canción de Navidad. 1970. Falcon Records FLP-2066.

Mendoza, Vicente T. 1986. *Estudio y Clasificación de la Música Tradicional Hispánica de Nuevo México*. México, D.F.: Universidad Nacional Autónoma de México.

Mendoza, Vicente T., and Virginia R. R. de Mendoza. 1991. *Folklore de la Región Central de Puebla*. México, D.F.: Centro Nacional de Investigación, Documentación e Información Musical Carlos Chávez.

Montejano, David. 1998. Personal communications.

Moreno, Nicolás. 2001. Personal communication.

Music of New Mexico, Hispanic Traditions. 1992. Smithsonian Folkways SF 40409.

Ofrenda de flores, taller de música tradicional indígena de México. 1998. Compact disc with notes by Juan Guillermo Contreras. Consejo Nacional para la Cultura y las Artes. Culturas Populares, México, D.F.: Programa de Apoyo Cultural a Municipios y Comunidades.

Paredes, Américo. 1995. *A Texas-Mexican Cancionero: Folksongs of the Lower Border*. Austin: University of Texas Press.

Robb, John Donald. 1980. *Hispanic Folksongs of New Mexico and the Southwest*. Norman: University of Oklahoma Press.

Romero, Brenda M. 1993. "The Matachines Music and Dance in San Juan Pueblo and Alcalde, New Mexico: Contexts and Meanings." Ph.D. dissertation, University of California at Los Angeles.

———. 1997. "Cultural Interaction in New Mexico as Illustrated in the Matachines Dance." In *Musics of Multicultural America: A Study of Twelve Musical Communities*. Ed. Kip Lornell and Anne Rasmussen. 155–85. New York: Schirmer Books.

Schroeder, Albert H. 1972. "Rio Grande Ethnohistory." In *New Perspectives on the Pueblos*. Ed. Alfonso Ortiz. 41–70. Albuquerque: University of New Mexico Press.

Sena, Val. 1999. Personal communications.

Solórzano, Nohemy. 1997. "*Testimonios* from *la Frontera*: Narrative on the Edge;

Border Writings and Feminine Perspectives on *la Frontera,* the Border and the Borderlands." Paper delivered at the Chicano Literary Conference, University of Colorado, Boulder.

Stevenson, Robert. 1980. *Music in Aztec and Inca Territory.* Berkeley: University of California Press.

Tarascan and Other Music of Mexico: Songs and Dances of the Mexican Plateau. 1958. Recordings and notes by Charles M. Bogert and Martha R. Bogert. Folkways 8867.

Urréa, Luis Alberto. 1996. *By the Lake of Sleeping Children: The Secret Life of the Mexican Border.* New York: Anchor-Doubleday.

Velázquez de la Cadena, Mariano, Edward Gray, and Juan L. Iribus. 1964. *Velázquez Spanish and English Dictionary.* Newly revised by Ida Navarro Hinojosa and Manuel Blanco-González. Chicago: Follett Pub. Co.

Wapp, Ed. 1998. Personal communications.

DANGER! CHILDREN AT PLAY

PATRIARCHAL IDEOLOGY AND THE CONSTRUCTION OF GENDER IN SPANISH-LANGUAGE HISPANIC/ CHICANO CHILDREN'S SONGS AND GAMES

MARÍA HERRERA-SOBEK

> Jugar es un acto político. . . . El juego es un recurso de la domi-
> nación. (To play is a political act. . . . Games are one of the stra-
> tegic devices [the hegemonic classes] use to dominate.)
> —Aída Reboredo, *Jugar es un acto político* (my translation)

The games children play are not the innocent activities they appear to be. In fact, children's ludic activities are impregnated with political and ideological content codified within the verbal and/or physical system of communication inherent in play activities. Many songs and games children use for supposedly innocent entertainment have been constructed within the sociohistoric space and political economy of a culture and therefore reproduce the ideological discourse within which they are inscribed. In this study I analyze children's songs and games that involve singing in their performance. I center my analysis on the construction of gender by examining the various discursive strategies appearing in Hispanic/Chicano children's lore. I use the term "Hispanic" because most of these songs and games are found throughout Spain, Latin America, and the American Southwest. The construction of gender in children's songs and games encompasses constructions of motherhood, including the paradigmatic perfect mother, the Virgin Mary, and associated roles of the married woman or housewife, the girlfriend or lover, and elderly women. All of these constructions are part of the ideological structures of patriarchy as they relate to women and are closely associated with the political, religious, and social ideology espoused by Western civilization in general and Hispanic culture in particular.

Aída Reboredo has written an extensive critique regarding the damage done to Third World countries via the use of toys imported from industrialized nations such as the United States. In *Jugar es un acto político* (1983), she demonstrates how ludic activities are in fact abstract communications full of signification. Although she zeroes in on industrial toys, and her analysis neglects to take into consideration the important question of gender and the construction of gender in social relations, her insights into the ideological formations in Third World children's mental structures via the use of industrial toys in ludic activities can nevertheless contribute to an analysis of traditional children's songs and games for their patriarchal ideological content. In the present study I posit that patriarchal dictums are inscribed in children's songs and games and that careful analysis demonstrates how this ideological content aids in the construction of gender formation in boys and girls.

Ludic activities repeated through the centuries and reenacted by individuals throughout their childhood, as in the case of Hispanic songs and games, serve as an ideological instrument of socialization used by patriarchal institutions to reproduce the status quo. Heterosexual relations as well as the sexual division of labor are inscribed in the games and songs children sing and play. These songs and games are part of the hegemonic patriarchal system's arsenal of strategies for imposing and retaining social cohesion and reproducing social patterns that ensure its continued domination and control. As the Hunter College Women's Studies Collective underscores:

> The consequences of such definitions of women affect our daily lives. They undergird the legal system we live in and the public policy that affects our control over our bodies in matters of contraception and abortion, and they shape our society's approaches to women's physical and mental health and occupational opportunities. They mold our self-esteem from childhood to old age. What is more, the act of defining what a woman is also tells women what they *should* be. In the process of socialization, these definitions of woman communicate to us what we should aspire to. In this way, definitions also provide a framework within which to censor women who do not, or will not, conform to them. (1983:20)

Reboredo writes that "los juegos son espejo de la sociedad. De aquí se desprende que cada colectividad produce los juguetes que le permite y le impone su espacio cultural: se puede hablar de jueguetes feudales, renacentistas, facistas, imperialistas" (1983:22; games mirror society. The collectivity produces toys that permit it to impose its own cultural space: one can speak of feudal toys, renaissance toys, fascist toys, imperialist toys [my translation]). Games and toys are indeed a "cultural reflection" of the people that produce them (1983:29). She is correct in asserting that "El juego es un recurso de la dominación" (Games are one of the strategic devices [the hegemonic classes] use to dominate) since they are "organizadora(s) y directora(s) de estructuras mentales . . . al discurso ideológico" (1983:30; they organize and direct mental structures [within the parameters of a specific] ideological discourse [my translation]). We know that playing involves the development of cognition and affective structures and is significant in the development of a child's mental abilities. Playing develops motor, verbal, mental, affective, and social skills. It is, in fact, a "mimesis de las relaciones sociales y productivas de las sociedades altamente industrializadas" (1983:19; mimetic activity of social and production relations of highly industrialized societies [my translation]) and reproduces the philosophy, ethics, customs, and other types of social and political relations of a people (1983:19). Reboredo amplifies:

> Por otra parte, los juegos se caracterizan por reproducir, con modificaciones pertinentes al sistema imaginario, lo real inmediato: los ritos de interacción, los sueños y temores de la época, las dinámicas institucionales. Por ejemplo, cuando los niños juegan al médico, la enfermera y el paciente, cristalizan elementos de interrelación tales como jerarquías, dependencias, autoridad, poder, que aparecen al efectuar un análisis de la instituticón médica tal y cual existe en la realidad. (1983:22)

> [On the other hand, games have the characteristic of reproducing with pertinent modifications the imaginary system, immediate reality, rites of interaction, the dreams and fears of the period, and the dynamics of institutions. For example, when children play at being doctor, nurse, and patient, they crystallize the elements of social relations such as hierarchical relations, dependencies, authority, and power that are evident upon analyzing the medical profession as it exists in reality.] (my translation)

It should not surprise us that Hispanic children's songs and games reflect the predominant ideology of the society in which they live. Ideology entails that system of beliefs, values, and attitudes embraced and advocated by a class or a group. Since cultural concepts encompassed by the group's ideological system are perceived as important for the continuation and propagation of that system, socialization and enculturation of these concepts begins early in the life of each individual. Thus the Hunter College Women's Studies Collective points out how "Definitions [of women] are communicated in direct as well as subtle ways in all cultures. They are communicated in social roles; in myths, rituals, and folklore; in the symbols of a culture; and in the language used to express ideas. Inevitably, those described are pressured to fit the symbols and definitions used to describe them, thereby lending support to the original definitions" (1983:20).

The anthropologist Sandra McCosker writes that the lullaby serves as a vehicle for communicating the cultural values of the San Blas Cuna Indian community to the child: "Cuna mothers use these lullabies as an effective tool for enculturation. They prepare the children for the different stages of their lives by describing how their daily activities and responsibilities will relate to their family and tribe" (1976:29).

Similarly, although in a more formalized and structured manner, children's songs and games in Hispanic culture provide children with a system of symbolic features that represent the cultural role or roles they will play as they become incorporated into society. This enculturation process is of course not perceived by most individuals as such. As the historian Vern L. Bullough comments,

> Ordinary people do not think through their reasons for adopting an attitude or even critically survey the attitudes they hold. They acquire their attitudes in the socialization process, most of which occurs in childhood years. This means that those who rear the young hold great power over attitudes, and since women have always had some hand in this activity they turn out to be an effective force in creating negative stereotypes about themselves. Children acquire an image of themselves in their early years and usually well before the age of five they have a clear idea of their sexual identity, as well as some idea about their social status in the society. This self-image includes not only the facts about who they are, but the evaluative overtones of that identity. (1974:131)

Thus we find embedded within the innocent rhymes of lullabies and later in the songs and games of the more mature child a progression of female representations: some of these representations were created by males; others, no doubt, were propagated by women, since these images reflect the low status of women in society and the marginal roles they have played therein.

The games I have selected for my study specifically involve singing; that is to say, there is a literary text involved in the performance of the games. For reasons of space I have left out other categories such as riddles (another folklore genre) and other types of games that involve basically physical activity (such as hide-and-seek, catch, and more contemporary sports such as baseball, basketball, soccer, and volleyball). I am interested in examining those literary texts related to games, and I view them as important documents that can yield insights into the socialization of women. E. Ann Kaplan points out how mothers and mothering have not been studied in their full dimensions: "We have little evidence about the actual nature of mothering work in any historical period, or about the quality of mother-child relations, or how historical mothers 'managed' their institutionally assigned roles. Historians continue to seek such evidence, but much more research is required in this area" (1992:18). Many children's songs and games provide us with a means through which we can theorize about mother-child relations. My thesis is that since children's songs and games are literary texts, they form part of the mother discourse and national imaginary à la Benedict Anderson's formulations in his book *Imagined Communities: Reflections on the Origins and Spread of Nationalism* (1983). As such, these literary texts are important elements that aid in the configuration of a national cultural landscape. In the construction of a nation, women play an important role as mothers or prospective mothers. Thus a nation configured within a patriarchal paradigm will promote the construction of gender within certain parameters. These parameters often involve a strong nuclear family with the father at the helm and the mother in a subservient position as caretaker of the house and children. The reproduction of this paradigm is of paramount importance, and various strategies are committed to its successful promotion and implementation. The literary imaginary is one such strategy, and children's songs as well as games that involve singing form part of this national imaginary.

SOCIAL CONTEXT IN WHICH GAMES ARE PLAYED

Henrietta Yurchenco, in *A Fiesta of Folk Songs from Spain and Latin America* (1967), lists many songs popular with Hispanic/Latin American/Chicano children. Some of these include "Don Gato," "La calandria," "El pollo," "Los diez perritos," and "Mi abuela tenía un huerto." Under the category of singing games and dances, she includes: "A la víbora," "El vito," "Arroz con leche," "Doña Blanca," "Las horas del reloj," "Naranja dulce," "Matarile, rile, ro," "El patio de mi casa," "La viudita del Conde Laurel," "Riquirrán," and "Quisiera ser tan alta como la luna." Her fieldwork was undertaken in Spain, Latin America, and Mexico (1967:iv). Yurchenco sum-

marizes some of the themes in Hispanic children's songs and games and
details the social context in which they appear:

> There was the lark in her golden cage struggling to get free; there was elegant
> Don Gato on his throne wearing silk stockings and white shoes, and the Zum-
> ming Bumblebee hotly pursuing poor Doña Blanca. Was it really going to take
> place—that wedding between the flea and the louse? Near the house was Doña
> María grumbling as usual about the chickens eating all the bread dough, and
> how she couldn't leave the house, not for a minute!
>
> Whether the characters are real or imagined, the children of Latin America
> and Spain treasure these songs. They sing them during the long winter months,
> seated in front of wide-open fireplaces, sipping cups of foamy hot chocolate.
> During the summer they play ring games in the dusty village streets or in the
> plazas of cities, far into the cool night, as their parents look on approvingly.
> (1967:2)

José-Luis Orozco, in a recent edition of his collection *"De colores": And
other Latin-American Folk Songs for Children* (1994), prefaces the volume
with these words:

> This rich collection of children's music from the Spanish-speaking world rep-
> resents the contributions of many people from cultures in Europe, Africa, and
> the Americas who have handed down songs from one generation to the next—
> songs for special occasions and for every day, songs for learning, for singing
> in a family or group, and songs just for fun.
>
> Many of these pieces I learned as a child from my grandmother, mother, or
> friends in the barrio of Peralvillo in Mexico City. Others I heard from the
> families with whom I lived as I traveled through North, Central, and South
> America, the Caribbean, and Spain during a three-year journey with the
> Mexico City Children's Choir. More recently, some have come from my fre-
> quent tours to Mexico, and to Spanish-speaking communities in the United
> States. (1994:5)

Orozco includes such songs as "Buenos días" (also known as "Martinillo,"
"Fray Felipe," and "Bartolito"), "El barquito" (Uruguay); "Al tambor"
(Panamá); "Vamos a la mar" (Guatemala); "La granja" (also known as "Mi
rancho"—Latin America); "De colores" (Spain, United States); "Naranja
dulce" (Latin America), and others. These two collections demonstrate the
popularity of children's games and songs throughout Latin America and the
Spanish-speaking population of the United States.

Chicano children continue to play Spanish-language games in spite of the
pervasive influence of English-language games and the new industrial-type

toys continuously introduced in the marketplace. Although the more acculturated and assimilated monolingual Chicano children do not play Spanish-language games, many first-generation Chicano and immigrant children
do play these games. (See, for example, McDowell 1979). At the University of California at Irvine (where I taught from 1975 through 1996), I frequently taught a course titled "Folklore in the Southwest," in which students were asked to collect all genres of folklore, including children's songs
and games. They were able to collect a great number of traditional songs
and games in the Orange County, California, area. Children played the
games at school during recess, at home, at parties, and at any gathering of
children. With the advent of bilingual education in the 1960s, elementary
school teachers included many of the Spanish-language traditional games
in their curriculum either for cultural development or for cognitive instruction. I played many of the games cited in this study as a child growing up in
the borderlands of Texas and Mexico. The songs and games sung in Spanish were mostly played in Reynosa, Tamaulipas, in the late 1940s and early
1950s. We played in the daytime and early evening in the neighborhood
streets or nearby empty lots. On the American side we played mostly jump
rope, hopscotch, baseball, and tag.

Undoubtedly, traditional Hispanic songs and games are rapidly disappearing in the United States and are more slowly disappearing in Spain and other
Latin American countries. Nevertheless, they are present today and will
continue to exert their influence in the near future. The study of these games
and songs aids us in understanding gender construction in the past and in
the future.

GENDER CONSTRUCTION: THE MOTHER

Kaplan's book includes a chapter on "Motherhood as Institution and Social Discourse," wherein she posits that there were

> three historical eruptions producing the early modern, high-modernist and
> postmodern mothers. These mother-related discourses may be described as
> first, Rousseaunian discourses (produced along with the early modern moth-
> er institution); second, Darwinian/Marxist/Freudian discourses (produced
> along with First World War and high-modernist challenges to the family); and
> finally, recent, postmodern mother discourses (produced along with even more
> drastic challenges to the family through the electronic revolution and its im-
> pact on corporate capitalism). (1992:19–20)

According to Kaplan, Rousseau's focus on the importance of raising and educating the child in his enormously popular book *Emile* (1762) was a revolutionary breakthrough on child-rearing practices that influenced North America. It also influenced Latin America, as is evident in the writings of José Joaquín Fernández de Lizardi (such as *El periquillo sarniento* [1816]). Rousseau was widely read in Latin America for his political ideas as well as his philosophy on education and his theories on the "natural man." Kaplan claims that Rousseau's child-rearing theories were of great importance in the formation of future mother discourses and the construction of early-modern mother paradigms that are still evident today (1992:20). "The early-modern-mother paradigm, indeed, turns out be the one most difficult to dislodge largely because of its close links to nineteenth-century religious ideologies and authorities. Its traces *still* influence struggles on the discursive level today" (1992:20).

Basically, Rousseau's philosophy of child-rearing involves the parents' complete attention to the child. The child becomes the focus of the home, and all attention is given to the child's needs, particularly to boys: "For Rousseau, the girl's biological processes shape her to be a mother, and thus require an attention that has no parallel for the boy. The very survival of the human race depends, for Rousseau, on the woman's function in cementing the family through her skills in emotions and relationships" (Kaplan 1992:20). Kaplan perceives a link between the rise of the bourgeoisie in the eighteenth century and the need for an educated "man"/citizen for the state and for the development of modern capitalism (1992:21). As industrial societies developed in the nineteenth century, the split between the public and the private helped solidify the sexual division of labor. The female was expected to stay at home, and the male was expected to be in the public sphere of the labor force. Capitalism promoted women's place in the home as the consumers of the products it produced (1992:21).

In the high-modernist period (the mid-nineteenth century and the first half of the twentieth century), Darwin's theories on evolution also crystallized the need for women to take care of children. In the postmodern (post–World War II) era the mother discourse paradigm has been challenged, particularly by feminist scholars. The present study follows the methods of feminist scholars who, through discourse analysis, challenge and deconstruct centuries-old paradigms regarding women's role in society.

As might be expected, the mother figure is found throughout children's lore. From lullabies to more developed and dramatic games, the figure of the mother appears performing various functions depending on the type of song or game. Frances Toor, in her collection of Mexican folklore *A Treasury of Mexican Folkways* (first published in 1947 and reprinted for many decades, into the 1980s), asserts that women, for the most part, were the ones that played with children and sang them traditional songs (1987 [1947]: 262–73).

In the more elementary though exquisite "canciones de cuna" (lullabies) we encounter the figure of the devoted, dutiful mother rocking her infant to sleep. These delicate rhymes structured in hexasyllabic quatrains delineate important constructions of women as mothers often in terms of the image these women have of themselves. I suggest that these lyrical "coplas" were probably authored by mothers themselves, since cultural custom dictated that rocking a baby to sleep was not a proper masculine activity. The male, when mentioned within the song, generally appears as a secondary character in the small drama enacted between mother and child. The presence of the mother, deeply stenciled in the lyrics of these musical compositions, provides us with a portrait of a tender, loving woman preoccupied with the humble tasks of housework. Speaking in the first-person singular, she engages in a simple but charming dialogue with her infant. The popular "Canción de cuna" provides a fine example:

> Duerme, muchachito
> que tengo que hacer;
> lavar tus pañales
> ponerme a coser. (Garrido de Boggs 1955:42)

> [Sleep my baby
> For I have work to do;
> To wash your diapers
> And to sew.] (my translation)

And a more Mexican version:

> Duérmete mi lindo
> que tengo que hacer
> hechar las tortillas
> ponerme a moler. (personal collection)

> [Sleep my precious
> For I have to work,
> Make tortillas
> And grind the corn.] (my translation)

An element of subversion is present in some of these *canciones de cuna*. In a hand-clapping game played with infants and toddlers, the mother figure is perceived as positive while the father figure is represented in a negative, menacing light.

> Tortillitas de manteca
> Pa' mamá que está contenta.
> Tortillitas de cebado
> Pa' papá que está enojado. (personal collection)

> [Little tortillas made of lard
> For mother who is happy.
> Little tortillas made of barley
> For father who is angry.] (my translation)

The construction of the father in a negative light underscores the possibility that many of these songs were composed by women. Nevertheless, women have been socialized into particular "female" occupations, and the songs portray them in these rigid gender roles (taking care of the children, cooking, cleaning, and so forth). Toor confirms this assertion: "Little girls everywhere play at housekeeping and dressing themselves like adults and their dolls like children. Those who have the means have at their disposition the marvelous world of Mexican toys—clay animals, figures, dolls, tiny utensils, musical instruments—in which everything that adults use is reproduced in miniature" (1987 [1947]: 263).

The constructions of the mother figure appearing in older children's songs and games, for the most part, describe a warm mother-daughter relationship. The songs frequently depict the daughter asking for her mother's advice regarding a possible suitor or depict the mother offering her daughter more experienced counsel regarding proper behavior toward a suitor, as in "Ay mamá, mira don José":

> —Ay mamá, mira a don José
> quiere que le cante y yo no sé.
> —Cántale, mi niña, que dirá
> que eres orgullosa y no te querrá. (Mendoza 1951:62)

> ["Oh Mom, look at Mr. José
> He wants me to sing to him and I don't know how."
> "Sing to him my child, what will he think?
> That you are proud and he won't love you."] (my translation)

Although there is a loving relationship between mother and daughter permeating many of the songs, socially and legally the daughter was under the complete control of the father and, to a certain extent, the mother. For example, the choice of a husband rested with the parents. This is made patently clear in such children's games as "Hilitos, hilitos de oro," a popular game found throughout Spain, Mexico, and Latin America, wherein a dramatic scene is enacted in which the king sends his pages searching for a proper wife for him. The mother of several daughters responds to the pages:

> Vuelva, vuelva caballero
> no sea tan descortés
> de las hijas que yo tengo
> escoja la más mujer. (Villafuerte 1957:16–20)

> Come back, come back sir
> Do not be so discourteous
> From all my daughters
> Choose the most womanly. (my translation)

The page chooses and takes one of the young ladies. The daughter does not utter a word, and we infer that she is flattered to be so honored. It is interesting to note the mother's suggestion that the page take the daughter who is most "womanly" (*más mujer*). Encapsulated in the phrase "más mujer" are a series of significations all related to the conceptualization of women in gender-specific roles: beautiful, hard-working, feminine, and talented in doing "women's" work.

We find that the representation of daughters in these games mirrors the dependency factor in which single women found themselves until recent times. It is a historical fact that if daughters refused to obey the wishes of their parents they would be sent to a convent or, if family honor was involved, put to death. Examples portraying the untimely demise of recalcitrant daughters are most frequently found in novelistic *romances* (Spanish ballads) that trickled down from the adult world to become part of the musical repertoire sung by children. An outstanding example of this tragic image is the ballad of "La Delgadina," a song dating from the sixteenth century that depicts the incestuous desires of a king for his daughter, Delgadina. Her refusal to yield to his amorous advances are punished by imprisonment, where she dies of thirst. Her heart-wrenching appeals for water to her mother, sisters, and brother are ignored while they watch her die (see Herrera-Sobek 1986).

Frances Toor includes a game known as "Mata-rili-rili-rón" in her collection. She describes how the game is played:

> Boys form one line and girls another, facing each other; they advance alternately an equal number of steps and sing:
>
> > Amo-a-tó, mata-rili-rili-rón   (repeat)
>
> One line chooses someone from the opposite and all sing:
>
> > ¿Qué oficio le pondremos?   [What trade shall we give him?]
> > Mata-rili-rili-rón. Mata-rili-rili-rón.   (repeat)
>
> The line that has chosen, decides on the trade and sings:
>
> > Le pondremos zapatero, [We shall make you a shoemaker,]
> > Mata-rili-rili-rón. Mata-rili-rili-rón.   (repeat)
>
> When the companions of the one chosen are satisfied that he is to be a shoemaker, they all sing:
>
> > Ese oficio sí le gusta,   [Indeed he likes his trade,]
> > Mata-rili-rili-rón. Mata-rili-rili-rón.   (repeat)
>
> But if they sing no instead of sí, then the trade can be changed as many times as necessary until one is hit upon which they like. Then both sides sing:
>
> > Celebremos todos juntos,   [We celebrate all together,]
> > Comeremos chicharrón.   [We shall eat crackling.] (267–68)

What is interesting in the above game is that Toor offers a different version for girls. She writes: "A version of this game is to give boys a trade and girls the name of a flower. When they do that, they sing 'Qué nombre le pondremos?' [What name shall we give her?] instead of 'Qué oficio. . . ?' [What trade. . . ?]" (1987 [1947]: 268). Needless to say, the game's message is that boys can aspire to have careers and women can aspire to be flowers!

Catholic ideology regarding proper female behavior is exemplified by the saintly image of the madonna and child that took root in the medieval imagination around the thirteenth century. These two figures are frequently found in children's songs and games. The Virgin Mary is the model of the mother par excellence. She is mostly depicted taking care of the Baby Jesus, and the lyrics repeatedly convey the figure of a demure, devoted mother. Other female saints, such as Santa Ana, Mary's mother, Santa Margarita, Santa Rita, and many others, are similarly portrayed and play an important part in children's lore. The popular lullaby "Señora Santa Ana" can serve as an example.

Señora Santa Ana
¿por qué llora el niño?
Por una manzana
que se le ha perdido.

Iremos al huerto
cortaremos dos
una para el niño
y otra para vos. (personal collection)

[Mrs. Santa Ana
Why is the baby crying?
Because of an apple
He has lost.

We'll go to the orchard
We'll cut two
One for the baby
And another for thee.] (my translation)

Again the lyrics present women involved in the caretaking and nurturing of the child.

As might be expected, with the Most Perfect of Mothers, the Virgin Mary, as their example, it must be a heavy psychological and physical burden on married women to live up to the expectations of motherhood. Indeed, many newly married young ladies chaffed under their recently acquired status, as is evident in a whole series of children's songs and *romances* classified under "La mal maridada" and "La mal casada" [the badly married woman] category. An excellent example is "Ven acá, primita hermana."

Ven acá, primita hermana
Ven acá para contarte
los apuros que pasé
despúes que yo me casé.

A la hora de la comida
es un hombre intransigente
la comida ni muy fría
ni muy tibia ni caliente. (personal collection)

[Come, little cousin
Come and I will tell you
The hardships I endured
After I got married.

> At mealtime
> He became an intransigent man
> The food was not to be too cold
> Not too warm and not too hot.] (my translation)

And in an Asturian lullaby a woman plaintively confesses:

> Todos los trabayos
> para las pobres muyeres,
> aguardando por las noches
> que los maridos vinieren.
> Ea, ea . . .
>
> Unos veníen borrachos
> otros veníen alegres,
> otros decíen—Muchachos,
> Vamos a matar las muyeres.
> ea, ea . . . (Celaya 1972:266)

> [All the hardships
> Are endured by us poor women
> Waiting in the night
> For our husbands to come home
> Ea, ea. . . .
>
> Some come home drunk
> Others come home happy
> Others come home saying: boys
> Let's go kill the women.
> Ea, ea. . .] (my translation)

While such songs depict the unhappy wife, a series of others socialize girls into their future housewifely duties:

> Arroz con leche
> Arroz con leche
> me quiero casar
> con una viudita
> de la Capital.
>
> Que sepa coser,
> que sepa bordar,
> que ponga la aguja
> en su lugar. (Villafuerte 1957:12)

[Rice pudding
Rice with milk
I want to get married
With a widow
From the capital.

Who knows how to sew
Who knows how to embroider
Who knows the proper place
Where the needle goes.] (my translation)

Another game, "En el puente de Avellón," instructs children in daily housewife chores:

Sobre el puente de Avellón
todos cantan y yo también.
Hacen así, así las lavanderas
Hacen así, así me gusta a mi.

Sobre el puente de Avellón
sobre el puente de Avellón
todos bailan, todos bailan y
yo también.
Hacen así, así las planchadoras
Hacen así, así me gusta a mi. (Villafuerte 1957:34–35)

[On the Avellón Bridge
Everyone sings and I do too.
This is the way the laundry women wash
This is the way, and that's the way I like it.

On the Avellón Bridge
On the Avellón Bridge
Everyone dances, everyone dances
And I do too.
This is the way the women iron
This is the way, and that's the way I like it.] (my translation)

The song continues enumerating other housewifely chores. The children imitate the chore as they sing it.

A popular representation of women that runs the gamut of children's songs and games is that of the good-looking girl. This image generally encompasses the stereotypical concepts of beauty prevalent during medieval and Renaissance times. These standards required the feminine figures to be blond, have fair skin, ruby lips, and rosy cheeks. The emphasis on physical beauty as opposed to intellectual achievements or other important human character-istics is pervasive throughout Hispanic children's lore.

> La vuidita
> Yo soy la viudita
> del barrio del rey
> me quiero casar
> y no hallo con quien.
>
> Pues siendo tan bella
> no encuentras con quien?
> Elige a tu gusto
> que aquí tienes cien. (Villafuerte 1957:11)
>
> [The little widow
> I am the little widow
> From the king's neighborhood
> I want to get married
> And I cannot find a husband.
>
> Well, being so beautiful
> You cannot find a mate?
> Choose the one you like
> Here are a hundred men.] (my translation)

Juxtaposed to the good-looking woman is "la vieja" (the hag). This con-struct falls within the purview of the theory of a "master" mother discourse, involving an "angel" versus a "witch" figure, as expounded upon by Kaplan (1992). Psychological and anthropological theories have been entertained to explain the male's fear of women. As Vern L. Bullough asserts: "Few human beings can easily face their own compulsions, and inevitably the male has tended to project his fears and antagonisms in terms of derogatory attitudes toward the female by insisting that women are evil, inferior, and valueless. Thus women should be made to obey, be kept in their place, or assigned to some unreal role which neutralizes them and removes them from the sphere of competition. Emerging from such attitudes are traditions and stereotypes which are used to justify male domination of the female" (1974:16).

Some anthropological theories posited to explain man's dread of women are based on biological and physiological functions. Ernest Crawley (1960) and Theodore Besterman (1960 [1934]) postulated physiobiological explanations, such as the belief of our ancient ancestors regarding the transmittal of human qualities through contact. According to Crawley and Besterman, "primitive" psychology assumed that women were inferior, and therefore men took precautions to avoid frequent contact with them, particularly during feminine physiological functions such as menstruation or childbirth. At such periods, women were viewed as particularly dangerous and were prevented from mingling with males (see Besterman 1960 [1934]: 223–32; Bullough 1974:10).

Of course, Freudian psychoanalysis takes a totally different angle, as is evident in Freud's now famous and controversial theory of "penis envy." Freud reasoned that the female must have great feelings of inferiority due to her lack of male genitalia, which in turn resulted in the male's fear of women (women's deprivation and frustration would lead them to want to castrate him). Karen Horney offers an opposite view: "his original dread of women is not castration anxiety at all, but a reaction to the menace to his self-respect" (1967:142).

Melanie Klein proposed the theory of the "good" and "bad" mother emerging from the early infant's experience of breastfeeding. Thus the breast was viewed as "good" when present and "bad" when absent. Kaplan further explains: "It is easy to see how these two unconscious mothers later become the alternate 'ideal' nurturing and evil 'phallic,' denying mothers" (1992:108). With respect to fear of the mother, Klein states: "I think that the reason why the boy has in the deepest layers of his mind such a tremendous fear of his mother as the castrator, and why he harbours the idea so closely associated with that fear, of the 'woman with a penis,' is that he is afraid of her as a person whose body contains his father's penis; so that ultimately what he is afraid of is his father's penis incorporated in his mother. The displacement of feelings of hatred and anxiety from the father's penis to the mother's body which harbours it is very important" (1975:131).

A Marxist point of view argues that the low status of the elderly in a capitalistic society is due to the uselessness of the aged within the context of a nuclear family. Women, having fulfilled their function as a love object and as producers of children, find themselves without an adequate role in society. This may be one reason why women appear in a degrading, disparaging role in children's songs and games.

The figure of "la vieja" appears in a negative light in children's songs and games. Some songs ridicule her, while others portray her in a fearful manner. I cite a few examples: "Tan, tan / ¿Quién es? / La vieja Inés" (personal collection; Knock, knock / Who's there? / Old Agnes). It is interesting and pertinent to note, however, that in lullabies it is the "bogey man" or "viejo" who is feared:

> Duérmase mi niño
> Duérmase me ya
> porque viene el viejo
> y se lo comerá. (personal collection)

> [Sleep my child
> Go to sleep now
> Because the old man will come
> And will eat you up.] (my translation)

This would certainly accord with my thesis that many lullabies were probably authored by women. As children grow older and invent their own games, they incorporate the true status of women. The "viejo" then turns into a "vieja."

Karen Horney has stated that "At any given time, the most powerful side will create an ideology suitable to help maintain its position and to make this position acceptable to the weaker one. In this ideology the differences of the weaker one will be interpreted as inferiority, and it will be proven that these differences are unchangeable, basic, or God's will. It is the function of such an ideology to deny or conceal the existence of a struggle" (1967:116).

In the various categories of children's songs and games examined here, we are confronted with the fact that the representations of women within them are restricted to a stereotypical few. In these lyrics we recognize the mother, the beauty, the daughter, the wife, and the old hag, but conspicuously absent are professional role models to which a female child can aspire, such as doctors, lawyers, judges, and so forth. Equally important, since these games are played by male and female children, the male child is led to perceive females in limited roles.

These songs and games are extremely charming and are passed from generation to generation. Many of the songs retain the lyrics found in the sixteenth century. It behooves us, therefore, to examine and recognize the pervasive stereotyping of female roles even in such innocent activities as children's songs and games.

WORKS CITED

Anderson, Benedict. 1983. *Imagined Communities: Reflections on the Origins and Spread of Nationalism.* London: Verso.

Besterman, Theodore. 1960 [1934]. *Men against Women: A Study of Sexual Relations*. London: Methuen.

Bullough, Vern L. 1974. *The Subordinate Sex: A History of Attitudes toward Women*. New York: Penguin.

Celaya, Gabriel. 1972. *La voz de los niños*. Barcelona: Editorial Laia.

Crawley, Ernest. 1960. *The Mystic Rose*. Rev. and enlarged by Theodore Besterman. New York: Meridian Books.

Fernández de Lizardi, José Joaquín. 1966 [1816]. *El periquillo sarniento*. México, D.F.: Editorial Porrua.

Garrido de Boggs, Edna. 1955. *Folklore infantil de Santo Domingo*. Madrid: Ediciones Cultura Hispánica.

Herrera-Sobek, María. 1986. "'La Delgadina': Incest and Patriarchal Structure in a Spanish/Chicano Romance-Corrido." *Studies in Latin American Popular Culture* 5: 90–107.

Horney, Karen. 1967. *Feminine Psychology*. New York: Norton.

Hunter College Women's Studies Collective. 1983. *Women's Realities, Women's Choices: An Introduction to Women's Studies*. New York: Oxford University Press.

Kaplan, E. Ann. 1992. *Motherhood and Representation: The Mother in Popular Culture and Melodrama*. New York: Routledge.

Klein, Melanie. 1975. *The Psycho-Analysis of Children*. London: Delacorte Press.

McCosker, Sandra. 1976. "San Blas Cuna Indian Lullabies: A Means of Informal Learning." In *Enculturation in Latin America: An Anthology*. Ed. Hohannes Wilbert. 29–66. Los Angeles: UCLA Latin American Studies Publications.

McDowell, John H. 1979. *Children's Riddling*. Bloomington: Indiana University Press.

Mendoza, Vicente T. 1951. *Lírica infantil*. México, D.F.: Instituto de Investigaciones Estéticas, Universidad Nacional Autónoma de México.

Orozco, José-Luis. 1994. *"De Colores," and Other Latin-American Folk Songs for Children*. New York: Dutton Children's Books.

Reboredo, Aída. 1983. *Jugar es un acto político*. México, D.F.: Editorial Nueva Imagen.

Rousseau, Jean-Jacques. 1974 [1762]. *Emile*. London: Dent.

Toor, Frances. 1987 [1947]. *A Treasury of Mexican Folkways*. New York: Crown Publishers.

Villafuerte, Carlos. 1957. *Los juegos en el folklore de Catamarca*. Suplemento de la Revista de Educación. La Plata, Argentina: Ministerio de Educación de la Provincia de Buenos Aires.

Yurchenco, Henrietta. 1967. *A Fiesta of Folk Songs from Spain and Latin America*. New York: G. P. Putnam's Sons.

5

CAMINANDO CON LA LLORONA

TRADITIONAL AND CONTEMPORARY NARRATIVES

DOMINO RENEE PÉREZ

Fue una mujer, who married a man *con tres niños chiquillos* [*sic*]. Now the man loved his children very much, *pero esta vieja fue muy celosa.* She was *vien* [*sic*] jealous of those kids because he showered them with love every day. She told him how she felt, but nothing changed. One day, she had had enough and told him, "Oyes, hombre. Un día vas a perder lo que quieres mas en este mundo." Well, one day he was working late or *cual cosa,* but he was late getting home. So she took those kids down to the *río* and drowned them, thinking that with them out of the way, she would be able to get more of his attention. *Después cuando el señor regresó a la casa* and found those kids gone, he knew immediately what had happened. The *loca* had killed them. He was heartbroken. *Pues,* he left her and she died of loneliness. *Y cuando ella murió y fue al cielo,* God told her, "You cannot enter the kingdom until you find the lost souls of the children." Because she didn't know where they were, she wanders the earth to this day looking for them.[1]

The story of La Llorona (the weeping or wailing woman) has been passed down in my family for more than five generations. When the wind would moan softly in the fields of my great-grandparents' farm, my mother tells me that the "little grandma" (her name because she was a tiny woman) would suddenly grow quiet and take a deep breath, holding it long enough to catch the attention of my mother and her siblings. She would then exhale, "Oye. La Llorona." The children would run into the kitchen begging to hear the story about the woman who died of loneliness.

For some people of Greater Mexico,[2] La Llorona is a ghost, a boogeywoman who haunts the shores of rivers or lakes. Her physical features are ambiguous, but those who encounter her often tell of a woman dressed in either white or black who initially appears as beautiful and suddenly changes into a hag. Additionally, she is said to possess the face of death or no face at all. Other storytellers, as the folklorist Soledad Pérez notes, focus on La Llorona's fingernails, which they liken to long, razor-sharp knives (1951:74). For those familiar with the tale, La Llorona is a portent of ominous tidings, a woman who lurks along dark and lonely roads or canals, a tortured symbol of some misdeed for which there is no atonement or salvation. In some accounts, reflecting a nationalist perspective, La Llorona is a sexualized mestiza who loved a wealthy Spaniard (or *criollo*) until her selfish and arrogant lover abandoned her for a woman from his own social class.[3]

To many, La Llorona is a tormented soul, wracked with guilt, searching for what has been lost, forever wandering in a physical and psychic borderland. Her confinement emphasizes her location outside or beyond the parameters of the natural world, for, as Gloria Anzaldúa states: "A borderland is a vague and undetermined place created by the emotional residue of an unnatural boundary. . . . The prohibited and forbidden are its inhabitants" (1987:3). However one chooses to view La Llorona, she is, as the Chicana cultural theorist Tey Diana Rebolledo asserts, an icon of the feminine ideal "tied up in some vague way with sexuality and the death or loss of children: the negative mother image" (1995:63). While negative female types are in no way culturally or historically specific to Chicanos,[4] for many familiar with the tale, La Llorona is a woman who traditionally serves as a cultural allegory, instructing people, primarily women, how to live, act, and function within specific established social mores.[5]

To read La Llorona as allegory allows the listener or reader, and in some cases the storyteller, to deconstruct the levels of meaning embedded in the narrative. As the anthropologist James Clifford states, "Allegory draws a special attention to the *narrative* character of cultural representations, to the stories built into the representational process itself. It also breaks down the seamless quality of cultural description by adding a temporal aspect to the process of reading. One level of meaning in a text will always generate other levels" (1986:100). In other words, La Llorona, when examined from or within specific cultural contexts, can assume a number of other meanings.

Folklore, then, acts as a kind of cultural currency through which ideas are exchanged and reinforced within a specific group. Or, as the folklorist Barre Toelken states: "Folklore functions in part as an informal system for learning the daily logic and worldview of the people around us" (1979:27). Within this informal system, La Llorona's story often acts as a deterrent to behavior that is not culturally sanctioned. To function in this manner, she must be firmly established within the culture as a point of reference for negative behavior. For example, as Elton Miles notes, "There is no need to mention [La Llorona's] checkered career because everybody knows the story already" (1988:40). The seemingly static quality of La Llorona's position as a negative cultural figure or villain derives from an apparent and common understanding of her role within the folklore of the culture.

Folklore does not reflect a monolithic set of values, however, nor does it always result in an agreed-upon theme. For instance, the countless variations of La Llorona stories reflect any number of scenarios emphasizing and critiquing behavior ranging from infidelity to murder.[6] Inconstant variables, such as location, time, setting, and narrator, yield such wide variations of stories that Bess Lomax Hawes suggests the only stable element in the story "may be the name La Llorona, itself" (1968:161). However, there is a discernible coding of consistent elements in the stories. Additionally, the storyteller, often several times removed from the alleged encounter (i.e., "My grandmother told me that her sister once saw La Llorona"; "Well, the way I heard it . . ."), assumes the voice of authority in the narrative. He or she interprets for the interlocutor his or her reading of the story either by offering a moral or emphasizing certain elements. Consider the story by F.M.,[7] a Chicano who told his version to Norma Ivers in Yuma, Arizona, in 1981: "'This story is about a young woman who, while on earth, wanted to have a good time, but she had to take care of her baby. To get rid of it, she threw it in the river. . . . When she got old and died, she went up to heaven, but they wouldn't let her in. She had to go back and look for the baby and bury it in a decent manner. . . . She really isn't looking for the baby because she's sorry about throwing it into the river, but because that's the only way she can get into heaven'" (qtd. in Cunningham 1981:73). In F.M.'s rendering of the tale, the young woman murders her child for self-serving reasons and feels remorse only because she is denied entrance into heaven. Here, selfishness and the refusal of maternal obligations are emphasized as themes. Additionally, the moral on one level states the obvious: murder is a sin. Yet, on a different level, the narrator judges the woman for wanting "to have a good time."

Understanding the mutable values and conditions under which this cultural currency is exchanged allows for culturally informed readings of La Llorona that delimit the boundaries of her narrative to allow for revision and cultural critique. As an example of what I consider a culturally uninformed reading, the feminist and folklorist Rosan A. Jordan reinscribes La

Llorona into a static patriarchal paradigm that builds on racist assumptions about Chicanos and Chicanas when she suggests that the myth reflects patriarchally imposed pressure on Chicanas to bear children for Chicano men who need to prove their potency. She even notes a parallel between the "eternal nature of La Llorona's fate and the seemingly unending years of motherhood a Mexican-American woman undergoes" (1985:38–39). Jordan fails to consider a number of important details in her reading, including the subversive possibilities of the narrative itself. She ignores La Llorona's murdering of her children, for instance, and focuses only on what she believes the folktale says about the assumed macho role of Chicano men and subservience of Chicanas, with little consideration for their economic, social, or political oppression. In doing so, she denies Chicanos and Chicanas a powerful symbol of feminine resistance and reinscribes negative stereotypes. Reading La Llorona folklore from a culturally informed position does not eliminate the restrictive cultural values reflected in the myth, but it does allow for consideration of the oppressive forces at work on both men and women in those same values.

As La Llorona's stories have evolved, she, like La Malinche, has been continually repositioned. However, certain elements are consistent: a woman, a body of water, and a haunting cry.[8] Additionally, the stories frequently concern her wandering in search of her lost children. In some versions the woman commits infanticide to free her children from some impending harm or, Medea-like, she kills her children to gain agency or take revenge in some tragic situation.[9] As a cultural figure of femininity, La Llorona is a monstrous feminine or "reproductive demon,"[10] mother as traitor, woman as embodiment of negativity or threat, a predatory specter preying upon "innocent" men and children. Particular to most stories is the distinctive voice of an anguished woman crying out or howling in the night for her lost children, "Ay, mis hijos!" (Oh, my children!). This image derives from preconquest portents of the Spanish invasion of Mexico that included a female voice crying out in the night, "Mis hijos, estamos perdidos!" (My children, we are lost!).

The sound of a woman crying for her children in the months before the arrival of Cortez signals for some the destruction of Aztecan culture through subjugation of and intermarriage with the indigenous people of Mexico (see León-Portilla 1962:6, 9–10). La Llorona, then, is ultimately a figure who "has lost her children, perhaps through no fault of her own" and who is "condemned to wander endlessly, reminding us constantly of our mortality and obligations" (Rebolledo 1995:78). She is mother, sister, daughter, and seer, yet in all instances she is a woman who is condemned to either foresee or bemoan the fate of her children, biological in the tale but emblematic of the indigenous people politically and culturally displaced by conquest.

From a young age, Chicano children are taught, under specific gender constraints and encoded patriarchal inscription, that La Llorona will "get them" if they misbehave or wander too far from home or from sight. La Llorona, as Rebolledo states, "is known to appear to young men who roam about at night. They believe she is a young girl or beautiful woman, but when they approach her (with sexual intent in mind), she shows herself to be a hag or a terrible image of death personified" (1995:63). Boys, through this allegorical tale, are taught to see women as temptresses, embodiments of a malevolent sexuality that could cause them to lose their souls, or as thieving mothers, who will take them away from the security of their "real" mothers and home. Girls are taught that sexuality, when acted on, can lead to isolation and damnation. Often, social class is also a visible component in the tale, as the folklorist John O. West suggests: "The most frequent use of the story is aimed at romantic teenaged girls, to warn them against falling for a young man who . . . is too far above them to consider marriage" (1988:76). In most filmic renderings, the man most frequently out of a Chicana's reach is the Anglo male. The dynamic endurance of the folklore for centuries reinscribes in generation after generation a negative sexuality for women as well as, in some cases, a classist depiction of poor women.

This stratification of classes is particularly emphasized in nationalistic renderings of the tale, most notably casting the woman as a poor *india* and the male as a wealthy Hispano. The story, in this form, speaks specifically to the colonization of Mexico, emphasizing the subjugation of the indigenous population through the creation of cultural mestizos. In most instances the woman is powerless to act against the man, so she murders their "illegitimate" children to exact her revenge upon him. While the man seemingly escapes retribution for his abandonment of the woman and their children, the woman, like the colonialist legacy itself, haunts the man and the people of the town.

The theme of a powerless underclass is particularly relevant to contemporary Chicanas and Chicanos who struggle under the weight of economic and social oppression. It appears in the following La Llorona story, told to the Jungian psychoanalyst and best-selling author Clarissa Pinkola Estés by a ten-year-old boy named Danny Salazar, in which a poor woman who drinks polluted water from a factory gives birth to horribly disfigured children. When offering his account, Salazar is adamant that La Llorona did not kill her children for the reasons cited in traditional tales; in an act of mercy, she kills the children to spare them a difficult life (1995:302). As evidenced by the tale Estés transcribes, Lloronas within the contemporary landscape do not necessarily become lost because of their grief over a man. In fact, Rebolledo suggests that contemporary Lloronas are not only symbolic of women but of Chicano culture as a whole, "whose children are lost because of their assimilation into the dominant culture or because of violence or prejudice" (1995:77). This reading allows for an analysis of La Llorona's symbolic representation of Chicanos and Chicanas who have become lost as a result of the economic, political, social, and cultural violence of Euro-American culture.

While La Llorona has come to signify physical and communal loss, she also contains the possiblity of articulating resistance. In other words, her story can be used to maintain culturally sanctioned behavior, in particular for women, but an interrogation of the female position within the folklore reveals levels of meaning that are infrequentely acknowledged. The cultural anthropologist José Límon argues that La Llorona can be a potent symbol of resistance for Chicanos and *mexicanos*. After carefully scrutinizing the myth, Limón theorizes that encoded in La Llorona's story are the ideas of female resistance, subversion of negative female sexuality, and reclamation of lost Chicano identity and territory.[11] According to Limón, the infanticide demonstrates La Llorona's resistance to patriarchal norms. She murders her children because "she is living out the most extreme articulation of the everyday social and psychological contradictions created by those norms for Mexican women" (1990:416). Upon closer inspection, furthermore, La Llorona does not prescribe a negative sexuality for women, for it is the male lover who is promiscuous, leaving his family behind for another woman. Limón also poses the possibility that La Llorona can recover her lost children, for the river by which she wanders, a traditional element of the tale, is symbolic of rebirth or reclamation. This complex reading of the folktale reveals the ways in which Limón reconsiders La Llorona within the parameters of the traditional narrative.

Limón here builds on the work of Frantz Fanon, who, when speaking of nationalist literature, states that modifications to traditional stories are increasingly fundamental to a national identity: "There is a tendency to bring conflicts up to date and to modernize the kinds of struggles which the stories invoke" (Fanon 1963:240). Similarly, Irene I. Blea investigates these new conflicts by focusing on the cultural meaning behind the folktale to determine what it reveals about women who are born of two distinct cultures

(1992:21–37). Blea, like Limón, argues that La Llorona is a cultural hero-
ine for Chicano culture, symbolizing not only the dispossession of our native land but also reclamation of that lost territory. The work of these critics suggests that La Llorona is being revisioned in the folklore beyond the
boundaries of her singular tragic fate.

Whether the focus is on culturally dictated male or female behavior, class,
or gender oppression, the majority of La Llorona stories falls along a continuum, ranging from traditional to contemporary. These flexible categories are useful for understanding the progression of this migratory legend
about the weeping woman. For the purposes of this study, I identify traditional tales as those that most frequently, but not exclusively, take place in
a rural setting, near a body of water, and where a haunting is said to occur.
The traditional stories also primarily focus on La Llorona as a threat due
to the "loss" of her own children. Variations on this theme, as collected by
Miles, include the despairing widow in poverty who goes mad after murdering her children to end their starvation, La Llorona as a thief who murders her crying child because she cannot quiet him while escaping the authorities, and La Llorona burned at the stake for drowning her children to
spare them from her husband's vengeful rage (1988:38–40). In each of these
instances, the woman's ghostly apparition haunts the site of the original
disaster, most often a body of water.

Contemporary La Llorona tales, in contrast, are defined by their movement toward urban settings, where traditional elements such as water or the
weeping may not necessarily be included, though they often are in subtle
ways. Generally, the emphasis in these stories is on the condition of being
lost, whether politically, economically, socially, racially, or culturally. La
Llorona's journey toward an urban landscape is often reflected in contemporary oral versions of the folktale that construct her as a hitchhiker who
either suddenly appears in one's rearview mirror or who disappears from
the passenger seat once she climbs into the car (Miles 1988:41). In this case,
La Llorona has moved beyond the boundaries of the river to wander along
roadsides, which is symbolic of her people's geographic relocation. La Llorona's movement away from rural settings distances her from natural bodies of water. In the absence of rivers, for instance, such as in the Texas towns
of Alpine and Marfa, La Llorona allegedly haunts the city dump, searching
for her murdered children (Miles 1988:38). As the narrative of La Llorona
becomes "urbanized," other elements of the traditional folktale are replaced
by objects within the urban landscape. For example, in the absence of the
unfaithful lover, an equally oppressive or disabling force, such as bureau-

cratic institutions, corporations, or poverty, is cited for contributing to her despair. However, the traditional image of La Llorona as a threatening figure remains the most significant and persistent element of the narrative.

In addition to the weeping woman's presence in oral narrative, we see these traditional renderings of La Llorona taking place in written narratives by Chicano and Chicana authors as well. Specifically, she is a figure of mourning who weeps for the losses Chicanos and Chicanas have sustained in contemporary American culture, especially women who suffer gender as well as ethnic oppression. She is, at the same time, a figure of revolt against those same losses. Apropos of this point, Toelken, in his consideration of an author's deliberate use of folklore in narrative construction, states: "We may suspect, because of the considerable cultural power of folklore and the depth with which many people register their recognition of their traditions, that a sensitive writer will not use folklore materials lightly, but will be motivated by the conviction that the use of certain images, phrases, and structures will serve as a powerful emotional link between the responses of the audience and the emotional and moral issues in the literature" (1979:335).

To Toelken's mention of emotional and moral issues I would add that an author's use of folklore in her or his literature also reflects political, social, and economic issues of the characters. I would also add that writers revise folklore within their works as a means of revitalizing or updating it to reflect contemporary concerns. Folklore, then, acts as a narrative technique through which writers may allude to a particular cultural myth to provide a meaningful context, one that is culturally coded and understood by a specific audience, for the action that takes place within their narratives. In terms of La Llorona specifically, I contend that contemporary popular culture provides evidence that Chicana and Chicano writers and audiences are finding her a powerful folkloric figure who articulates profound issues of concern.

I hasten to acknowledge that not all Chicano and Chicana writers use the myth of La Llorona in this way. For example, Helena María Viramontes in *Under the Feet of Jesus* (1995) and Rudolfo A. Anaya in *Bless Me, Ultima* (1972) maintain La Llorona's traditional position as a threat to motivate the actions of their characters. Although La Llorona appears in each novel only briefly, she directly influences the behavior and attitudes of several characters who are aware of her traditional positioning. Significantly, in both works La Llorona functions primarily as a threat to men. For instance, in Viramontes's novel, she haunts Gumecindo as he and his cousin, Alejo, steal peaches in the dark. Gumecindo speaks urgently to Alejo during their escapade about La Llorona and her drowned children, prompting them to com-

plete their business as quickly as possible. In this instance, La Llorona functions as cultural allegory, because the young men know that they should not
be out at night or stealing peaches. Their fear of discovery stems not from
the threat of loss of employment or the foreman's wrath but from the mythical woman they have been taught to fear since childhood. As inscribed in
some versions of the myth, La Llorona will "get" the cousins for being out
by the drainage ditch much too late. Due to the proximity of her cries and
the arrival of cropdusters, readers interpret her wails as a warning to the
young men, but the cousins have indicated they do not have the capacity to
understand her warning in this way. Instead they interpret her cry within a
traditional context: she is a threat rather than an aid. Perhaps because Gumecindo takes this threat seriously, he is spared Alejo's fate, for only Gumecindo's quick reactions save him from death when Alejo is submerged in
a shower of pesticides, from which he contracts a debilitating illness.

La Llorona also appears in *Bless Me, Ultima,* again as a significant threat
to men and additionally as a representation of the "monstrous feminine."[12]
Antonio, the young protagonist, has nightmares about the feminine demon
who wails along the shores of the river and "seeks the blood of boys and
men to drink" (Anaya 1972:23). La Llorona is positioned as a vampire who
desires Antonio's innocent soul. Although this dream marks the only time
in the novel she is mentioned, her outlines appear in the siren/mermaid figure
who lives in the cave of the lake and is cited as the source of a drowning in
the reservoir. Antonio learns to fear La Llorona and never knows her re-
demptive or healing powers.

Like his protagonist Antonio, Anaya as a boy was haunted by the physical threat La Llorona poses. In the introduction to his essay, "La Llorona,
El Kookoóee, and Sexuality" (1995), he tells readers that in *Bless Me, Ultima,* his first novel, he looked at his childhood and considered the wide range
of Chicano cultural materials that shaped him as a boy (1995:417). His
choice of La Llorona, he says, illustrates the potency of the myth and how
it affected him as a young boy while walking home at night: "I felt fear,
dread—real emotions which I had to understand and conquer. I had been
warned: Hurry home or La Llorona will get you" (1995:421). Anaya's boy-
hood fear translates into the novel as Antonio's. Although Anaya does not
attempt to revise La Llorona, painting her only as he remembered her from
his childhood, he does stress that, for Chicanos and Chicanas, she resonates
with profound meaning: "to understand those meanings we have to pass
on the stories, we have to re-create the characters in our time. . . . Nothing
is too insignificant to revive and return to the community if we are to save

our culture. We can rescue ourselves" (1995:428). However, Anaya does not attempt to identify precisely what La Llorona's deeper meaning is. He instead leaves that for a new generation of Chicana and Chicano writers and readers to discover and create for themselves.

The boundary between traditional and contemporary tales, however, is neither rigid nor fixed, and a contemporary tale might include some traditional elements. For example, according to West, thieves in a small town once simulated La Llorona's wail to frighten people into believing that the weeping woman was haunting the town. As the people sought refuge, the thieves robbed the unattended houses (1988:35). While the thieves relied on their audience's belief in the traditional narrative, the resulting loss of property and peace of mind are contemporary revisions of the tale, as are the thieves themselves.

In oral and written narratives, La Llorona emerges as a physical threat and a gender-coded allegory proscribing certain behaviors for women. If, as Toelken posits, "Folklore functions in part as an informal system for learning the daily logic and worldview of the people around us" (1979:27), what, then, are contemporary constructions about La Llorona telling us as Chicanas and Chicanos? La Llorona, as a folkloric figure, continually evolves to reflect a new set of cultural concerns. With the continued influx of workers from Mexico to the United States, for example, the folktale is being revitalized as people carry it with them northward, or, as U.S. factories move their plants to Mexico to exploit cheap labor and lax environmental laws, the story is taken back across the border. The crossing of borders and exploitation of Mexican labor may explain why recent La Llorona stories have surfaced featuring the ghostly woman as a *maquiladora* poisoned by polluted water from a factory. As Estés states, the La Llorona story "builds on the psychic issues of each generation" (1995:300), but the dreadful conditions of Mexican factory workers are the source not only of psychic issues but economic and political issues as well.

In addition, whenever two cultures meet, as the performance theorist Guillermo Gómez-Peña states, there is an opportunity for a border crossing (1993:43–44). La Llorona, in a contemporary urban landscape, is the physical embodiment of that border (racial, sexual, physical, or spiritual).[13] She is a transgressive figure strong enough to penetrate the consciousness of an entire culture. As *mexicanos* and Chicanos continue to be violently vilified in Euro-American culture, La Llorona transcends her legendary status as a wandering specter punished for her feminized transgression and becomes emblematic of an entire generation of people who are becoming lost.

For Chicanas specifically, La Llorona is symbolic of historic and contemporary oppression of women by economic and patriarchal forces. By calling upon female Aztec precursors to La Llorona and reinstating her agency, Chicanas are recasting her outside of the boundaries of tragedy, where her actions become a representation of female resistance within a wholly oppressive environment. With increased access to educational and professional opportunities, Chicanas' positions within Euro-American culture and their own culture are beginning to change. By revisioning La Llorona in the traditional narrative or repositioning her in an urban landscape, writers address these new struggles that have followed increased activity outside the home. These authors often indicate that if La Llorona can overcome her tragedy, perhaps contemporary Chicanas can overcome theirs.

A professor of Mexican literature once asked me, "How can you, a college-educated Chicana working on her Ph.D., believe in something like La Llorona? How do you defend your position?"

I'd like to say that I carefully pondered her question, but I immediately replied: "The way I see it, it's better to believe in La Llorona than to have her come knocking on my door some day asking just what it is about her I don't believe."

She smiled and said, "I know. I hear her all the time."

Since then, I have literally been haunted by images of the weeping woman, especially on windy nights. I imagine her wandering on the gently sloping hills of the Nebraska plains where I now live. When the wind moves softly, I see her at a distance. I do not hear her hushed footfalls as the leaves tumble over the ground muffling her trek over the prairie grass. But when the wind funnels through the alleys and corridors of my neighborhood, she pounds against my door, demanding to be let inside, as the house I live in is old and poorly insulated, allowing the wind to seep through the uneven spaces in the door frames. Countless nights I have sat up in bed, startled by the sound of a squealing trumpet bellowing out terrifying notes. On these occasions, I imagine she has come for me, not to take me away but to ask something of me, proof that I have been working, doing something with my life. I also believe that she shows herself to me in these ways for specific reasons: La Llorona opens a path before me that stretches back into my childhood, allowing me to bridge the past and present. I find my connection with La Llorona and my own personal history more than ironic. And while I may have gone for years without thinking about La Llorona, she has been with me, a physical representation of the richness of the storytelling that took place at *quinceañeras,* weddings, graduations, birthdays, and holidays.

NOTES

1. María Pérez, interview with the author, Houston, Tex., March 10, 1998.

2. Like José E. Límon, I borrow this term from Américo Paredes. My intention is to underscore the cultural connections between people of Mexican descent in the United States and Mexico.

3. For a discussion of the "Hispanicized" version of the tale, in which La Llorona murders the children she had out of wedlock when her lover marries another woman of his own higher position in society, see Janvier 1910:134–38, 162–65.

4. Susan V. Smith, who murdered her two children in South Carolina in 1994, might qualify as an Anglo representation of a vilified mother. There are corresponding La Llorona figures in many cultures: Toad or Weeping Woman (Haida, American Indian), Lamia (Greek), Lilith (Jewish), the Woman in White (Filipino), and El Llorón (particular to Durango, Mexico). Maxine Hong Kingston, in "No Name Woman," describes her Chinese aunt who had an adulterous affair and later murdered herself and the child she bore. Spirits like the aunt's weeping ghost lay in wait outside of wells, seeking to pull down people to take their places (see Kingston 1976:16).

5. Scholars, anthropologists, and laypeople have put forth various readings of La Llorona's function. See Barakat 1965; Cunningham 1981; Jones 1988; Kearney 1969; Kirtley 1960; and Leddy 1948.

6. In addition to the variants of the story yielding numerous scenarios and themes, the same story can assume different meanings, especially when told within different contexts (for example, the age, physical condition, and gender of the storyteller and the audience, the location where the story is being told, and the circumstances surrounding the exchange of narratives, such as a family gathering or classroom).

7. In the interview, the Chicano is identified only by his initials. The reasons behind this are not clarified in the collection or the essay. However, one can surmise that the interviewee did not wish to have his identity revealed.

8. Walraven contends that as Mexicans have moved farther north into urban areas, trash dumps have replaced traditional bodies of water as sites for La Llorona's hauntings (1991:208).

9. While this theme is an oft heard primary feature of the narrative, some stories do exclude the revenge theme.

10. I borrow the term "reproductive demon" from Sarah Iles Johnston (1997).

11. Alarcón comments directly on the limitations of Limón's feminist positioning of La Llorona, stating that "La Llorona fails to meet some of the modern and secularizing factors that Chicanas have felt they have needed in order to speak for themselves" (see 1994:110–33).

12. The term "monstrous-feminine" is used by Creed (1990), who argues that the term is a view of the feminine as negative or as a threat. Her argument relies heavily on psychoanalysis, but I am using her term in a different context.

13. According to Rebolledo, La Llorona throughout her history has "brought

together Indian and Spanish folklore and legends." The two traditions since have become interwoven to create a distinct cultural *mestizaje* (1995:63).

WORKS CITED

Alarcón, Norma. 1994. "Traddutora, Traditora: A Paradigmatic Figure of Chicana Feminism." In *Scattered Hegemonies: Postmodernity and Transnational Feminist Practices.* Ed. Inderpal Grewal and Karen Kaplan. 110–33. Minneapolis: University of Minnesota Press.

Anaya, Rudolfo A. 1972. *Bless Me, Ultima.* Berkeley, Calif.: Tonatiuh–Quinto Sol Publications.

———. 1995. "La Llorona, El Kookoóee, and Sexuality." In *The Anaya Reader.* 415–28. New York: Warner Books.

Anzaldúa, Gloria. 1987. *Borderlands/La Frontera: The New Mestiza.* San Francisco: Aunt Lute.

Barakat, Robert A. 1965. "Aztec Motifs in 'La Llorona.'" *Southern Folklore Quarterly* 29 (4): 288–96.

Blea, Irene I. 1992. *La Chicana and the Intersection of Race, Class, and Gender.* New York: Praeger Publishers.

Clifford, James. 1986. *Writing Culture: The Poetics and Politics of Ethnography.* Berkeley: University of California Press.

Creed, Barbara. 1990. "*Alien* and the Monstrous-Feminine." In *Alien Zone: Cultural Theory and Contemporary Science Fiction Cinema.* Ed. Annette Kuhn. 128–44. London: Verso.

Cunningham, Keith. 1981. "La Llorona in Yuma." *Southwest Folklore* 5 (1): 70–77.

Estés, Clarissa Pinkola. 1995. *Women Who Run with the Wolves.* New York: Ballantine Books.

Fanon, Frantz. 1963. *The Wretched of the Earth.* New York: Grove Press.

Gómez-Peña, Guillermo. 1993. *Warrior for Gringostroika: Essays, Performance Texts, and Poetry.* St. Paul, Minn.: Graywolf Press.

Hawes, Bess Lomax. 1968. "La Llorona in Juvenile Hall." *Western Folklore* 27 (4): 153–70.

Janvier, Thomas A. 1910. *Legends of the City of Mexico.* New York: Harper and Brothers.

Johnston, Sarah Iles. 1997. "Corinthian Medea and the Cult of Hera Arkaia." In *Medea: Essays on Medea in Myth, Literature, Philosophy, and Art.* Ed. James J. Clauss and Sarah Iles Johnston. 44–70. Princeton, N.J.: Princeton University Press.

Jones, Pamela. 1988. "'There Was a Woman': La Llorona in Oregon." *Western Folklore* 47 (3): 195–211.

Jordan, Rosan A. 1985. "The Vaginal Serpent and Other Themes from Mexican-

American Women's Folklore." In *Women's Folklore and Culture*. Ed. Rosan A. Jordan and Susan J. Kalcik. 38–39. Philadelphia: University of Pennsylvania Press.

Kearney, Michael. 1969. "La Llorona as a Social Symbol." *Western Folklore* 28 (3): 199–206.

Kingston, Maxine Hong. 1976. *Woman Warrior: Memoirs of a Girlhood among Ghosts*. New York: Vintage.

Kirtley, Bacil. 1960. "'La Llorona' and Related Themes." *Western Folklore* 19 (3): 155–68.

Leddy, Betty. 1948. "La Llorona in Southern Arizona." *Western Folklore* 7 (3): 272–77.

León-Portilla, Miguel, ed. 1962. *The Broken Spears: The Aztec Account of the Conquest of Mexico*. Boston: Beacon Press.

Limón, Jose. 1990. "La Llorona, the Third Legend of Greater Mexico: Cultural Symbols, Women, and the Political Unconscious." In *Between Borders: Essays on Mexicana/Chicana History*. Ed. Adelaida R. Del Castillo. 399–432. Encino, Calif.: Floricanto Press.

Miles, Elton. 1988. *More Tales of the Big Bend*. College Station, Tex.: Texas A&M University Press.

Pérez, Soledad. 1951. "Mexican Folklore from Austin, Texas." *Healer of Los Olmos and Other Mexican Lore*. Publications of the Texas Folklore Society 24: 74.

Rebolledo, Tey Diana. 1995. *Women Singing in the Snow: A Cultural Analysis of Chicana Literature*. Tucson: University of Arizona Press.

Toelken, Barre. 1979. *The Dynamics of Folklore*. Boston: Houghton Mifflin.

Viramontes, Helena María. 1995. *Under the Feet of Jesus*. New York: Dutton.

Walraven, Ed. 1991. "Evidence for Developing a Variant of La Llorona." *Western Folklore* 50 (2): 208.

West, John O. 1988. *Mexican-American Folklore: Legends, Songs, Festivals, Proverbs, Crafts, Tales of Saints, of Revolutionaries and More*. Little Rock, Ark.: August House.

PART 2

PRACTICING TRADITIONS

6.

INDIANIZING CATHOLICISM

CHICANA/INDIA/MEXICANA INDIGENOUS
SPIRITUAL PRACTICES IN OUR IMAGE

YOLANDA BROYLES-GONZÁLEZ

ENTRADA/INTROIT: Among the areas least explored within Chicana/o studies is the realm of spiritual practices.[1] The immense and diverse body of Chicana religious practices defies quantification by social scientists and has largely escaped the purview of academia's theoretical articulations, which have been honed primarily from printed texts. Faced with the ravages and genocide of colonial power struggles for hundreds of years—and particularly in the last century—*mexicana* collective spiritual practices and faith have formed part of the bedrock of day-to-day survival for marginalized communities. Many of those most socially and economically marginalized—indigenous women—have steadfastly served as the unacknowledged high priests and healers of our working communities under siege. *Mujeres* (women) are the chief transmitters of spiritual practices in the home, and to the seven generations, while also often serving as the chief mediators between the home and external religious institutions and sites, be they the Catholic church, religious pilgrimages, spiritual pageants such as Posadas, or at wakes as *rezadoras* (ones who pray), whose prayers help move the deceased to a place of rest.

The primary authorities in this essay are not academics but women who taught me about spirituality, chief among them my Abuelita (grandmother). This piece portrays her at the colonial intersection of race relations, cultural relations, class relations, and gender relations as well as regional specificities. From this personal testimony I seek to show some ways in which indigenous *mexicana* religious practices have transformed and inverted the imperatives of an imposed colonial Catholicism into a means of self-empowerment, indigenous cultural survival, and profound humanistic expression under the harshest conditions. Through the agency and subjectivity of our women elders, indigenous Mexican American communities have forged and transmitted the tools and strategies of a faithful resistance to a systemic and widespread colonial and "post"-colonial dehumanization. In the give and take of struggle, *mexicanas* and Chicanas have learned to fashion faith and religion in our own image: the image of our gender, our "race"/ethnicity, our class affiliations, and the particulars of the local habitat and regional history.

VIVAN LAS SANTAS ANIMAS/REQUIEM: Three years ago, my Abuelita went into spirit. Her name was Polita Gastelum Rodríguez.[2] She was born a working-class Yaqui (Yoeme) in the tribal borderlands, and her powerful and lasting life and legacy remain a matter of bureaucratic invisibility: like legions of others, she never became part of the nation's human inventory through the civil registry. She had no birth certificate, and her place of birth became a fact forgotten amid the turmoil of genocidal wars waged against the Yaqui and all other tribal peoples by the Mexican and U.S. nations. Throngs of mourners at this "nonexistent" woman's three-day funeral blocked traffic in the entire *colónia* where she had uttered innumerable prayers and blessings, including her last prayers and blessings whispered in the course of her extended *agonía*—that process of transition to the spirit-world. Her return to the mother earth was delayed an extra day because of the incessant arrival of additional and still-expected travelers from afar.

In her last weeks, hundreds of people, including me, made the pilgrimage to see her one last time. Among those who visited her in her last weeks and days were the *ánimas benditas* (blessed spirits) of some already gone. Abuelita easily moved between the two sides of existence; her attention shifted seamlessly between the spirits and the visitors sitting in a circle around her bed. In mid-conversation with us, her eyes would suddenly gaze upon this or that deceased relative. As she acknowledged each one's presence by name, she also acknowledged their importance as guides into the spirit world. Virtually immobilized in her last weeks, my Abuela Polita tended almost exclusively to the spiritual preparation for a good death. "En esta vida no hay nada mas difícil que una buena muerte" (nothing is harder in this life than a good death). Yet she did not neglect the flesh, insisting on the appropriate preparation of her simple foods and drink. "Este café está mas frío que mis nalgas" (this coffee is colder than my behind). As for the extended family and kinship network, we already knew our responsibility was to *entregársela a Dios* (to deliver her to God): to let go and assist her passage into the spirit world. Even on my way from the airport to see my Abuelita, I detoured the taxi to La Lomita, the church of our mother Guadalupe. I didn't even have to see my Abuelita to know that it was my turn to give her up to spirit. It was she who had taught me to sense these things from afar.

As part of her preparation for crossing to the other side, she summoned a handful of us and requested some spiritual assistance. She asked Tía Jovita to maintain the home altar adorned with fresh roses from the garden. The home altar is a personal and familial sacred space, an ancient practice rivaling the impersonal and towering domination of church altars. In addition to securing the future of her home altar, my Abuelita asked others of us to settle some outstanding spiritual debts: *mandas* or *promesas*. As we know, it is spiritually harmful to leave this life with unpaid *promesas*. At her request, I visited the shrine of the working-class indigenous outlaw healer-saint Jesús Malverde. Now a popular saint, Malverde devoted his life to feeding the poor by taking from the rich—until government troops caught up with him and lynched him. Thereafter, his powers to assist the poor vastly increased, and he became one of the most renowned healing spirits of the U.S.-Mexican borderlands. Thus he healed my Abuelita's chronic foot sores, which had tortured her for over a decade. Neither modern Mexican medicine nor the American Medical Association doctors in Tucson, Arizona, had found a cure for the tumors. The risk of smuggling my Abuelita in the trunk of the car from one part of our ancestral homelands to the other had been in vain. As a final resort (never petition a miracle worker until you have exhausted all possible earthly remedies), my Abuelita petitioned the spirit of Jesús Malverde: a prominent individual within Sonoran/Sinaloan/Yaqui/Chicana poor people's "Catholicism." *Las llagas desaparecieron* (the sores vanished).

Accompanied by my Tía Nely, I visited the shrine of Malverde that same day. During the dictatorship of Porfirio Díaz leading up to the Mexican Revolution of 1910, Malverde worked to alleviate the ever-growing impoverishment and persecution of the masses. In Sonora and Sinaloa abuses included the capture and sale of Yaquis and Mayo tribal peoples into slavery. The Mexican government shipped them to the *henequen* plantations of Yucatán for fifty pesos a head. Malverde took and redistributed cattle, chickens, jewelry, and money from the Porfirian super-wealthy *hacendado* slave owners.

At the site where Malverde was captured, lynched, and buried by Mexican government troops I delivered the appropriate silver *milagrito* foot in thanksgiving. As a further expression of thanks for my Abuelita's miracle cure, I commissioned a musical *serenata* for Malverde from one of the many groups who wait daily at the shrine and know the proper repertoire. Upon returning to my Abuelita's house, visitors surrounding her bed were engaged in a lively discussion of Malverde. The *plática* became heated when one woman commented "Algunos dicen que no es santo" (some claim he is not a saint). At that moment my grandmother made her only contribution to this discussion. Without even opening her eyes she gently stated "Malverde *sí* es santo" (Malverde *is* a saint). For all those present Malverde was instantly recanonized, devil's advocate notwithstanding. The indigenous American tradition of grassroots popular miraculous narrative (to be distinguished from that of the church) constitutes a significant *contra-decir* (contra-diction, counter-discourse, and counter-memory) in the life of the oppressed. The miraculous utopian space is a form of collective self-affirming protest that extracts some freedom from—and preserves the memory of freedom within—the hardships of everyday life. One theoretician has wisely understood that the miraculous serves to "subvert the fatality of the established order" (Certeau 1984:16–17)—which includes the dogma of official Catholicism.

My Abuelita's spiritual practices were marked by the particulars of her native region, economic class, gender, and race. In her life—as in the lives of many—those practices were at the heart of *lo imprescindible,* the indispensable acknowledgment of the sacred life-cycle and our place within it. As a child at the turn of the twentieth century she witnessed the renewed arrival of the *yoris* (white men/outsiders/colonizers). Earlier waves of colonization had been mild by comparison. Neither the intermittent intrusions by Spaniards (in the early sixteenth century) nor the handful of Jesuits (arriving in 1617 and expelled in 1767) compared with the genocidal power of the emergent nations on both sides of the now-divided ancestral lands.[3] My Abuelita's life began with the Porfirio Díaz dictatorship of the 1880s and ended in the 1990s, shortly before the onset of NAFTA and the Zapatista (EZLN) uprising. Cycles of conquest and resistance: twentieth-century Mexico is ending much like nineteenth-century Mexico. As then, multiple regional popular indigenous uprisings respond to the state's policies and structures of social inequality. Indigenous demands in Sonora and Sinaloa of the 1890s parallel those in Chiapas of the 1990s.[4]

To be publicly identified as Yaqui (or any other tribal affiliation) in the late nineteenth- or early twentieth-century Americas was an almost instant death warrant. Native forms of worship and celebration were forced to the underground of *disimulo* (camouflage). Even the United States did not pass a Freedom of Religion Act until 1978. Until then, Native American spirituality (hence culture) was outlawed. It is not different in Mexico. On both sides of the border, to be indigenous is to be displaced, hunted, sold, relocated, fleeing, or hiding behind "Mexicanness" or, nowadays, "Hispanic." The knowledge passed down through the families reminds us that incessant raids by Mexican or U.S. soldiers reconfigured indigenous family lines and ties on a daily basis. Your changing family unit consisted of those who survived the last genocidal raid with you. Your children were whatever children you managed to grab and run with. My beloved great-grandmother (known publicly as La Tía Celsa) was not a blood relative but the person who protected my grandmother Polita. The rest of Polita's immediate and extended family remain forever blurred and a matter of speculation.

The Yaqui, like all tribal peoples, adopted the survival and protection skills of chameleons. Polita quickly learned the underdog survivalist art of *disimulo:* shielding and camouflaging the indigenous ways within the hide-and-seek of the new nation's *mexicanidad.* Nation formation has always meant forced incorporation. Tía Celsa warned Polita in childhood about the mortal dangers of speaking the Yaqui language while seeing to it that my Abuelita learned Spanish in the twenties. Polita always recalled her first instruction in a European language and its artifacts: "La cuchara, el tenedor" (the spoon, the fork).

With the onslaught of the European language, each tribe also adopted the obligatory Catholic camouflage. It was do or die, but each tribe in the Americas did Catholicism and the Spanish language in its own native register. The Spanish language became Indianized—region by region it became the Uto-Aztecan Spanish of today. Survival also mandated adoption of the Christian pantheon, be it the Christian denominations of the Mexican or U.S. nations. Yet within the Yaqui nation and rituals—as currently within the Chicana/o nation—figures such as Jesus, Mary, and Joseph experienced a radical transformation, marginalization, and inversion/subversion incompatible with Roman Catholic orthodoxy. Far from Rome, native peoples appropriated elements of Catholicism into the Mesoamerican cultural matrixes. Thus each Mexican region has birthed and worships in its own way its own popular saints, most of them de-colonial warrior healers or healing warriors: Jesús Malverde; the Yaqui/Mayo Santa Teresa de Cabora; the Mayo people's Santa Agustina, Santa Camila, Santa Isabel; el Niño Fidencio in northeastern Mexico; Don Pedrito Jaramillo in Texas. These are but a few of the popular regional *santas* and *santos* collectively canonized by native Mexican peoples and disavowed by Rome.

The Yaqui Waehma (a springtime celebration during the Lenten season) incorporates Jesus and Mary for good measure. Some Catholic nomenclature, concepts, and symbols are woven into the Yaqui ceremony in ways that nonetheless preserve the Yaqui foundation of beliefs and meanings. Mother Mary, for example, is enlisted to help symbolize the sacredness of the Yaqui land. Jesus dies on the benevolent human cross formed by the Mother Earth's (Mary's) arms. Yaqui "Catholicism" provides a socially protective veneer as well as ritual protection for the utterly un-Catholic Deer Dancers and Pascola. Yet this humanistic reconciliation of Catholicism with native practices is unacceptable to the Roman Catholic church. Orthodox concepts of sin, confession, and hell are virtually nonexistent. Since the enforcers of orthodoxy are far off in Rome, multiple forms of regional Indianized Catholicism or Catholicized native religion exist in Mexico and the U.S. Southwest. Many critics of borderland culture lose themselves in abstract concepts of "mestizaje," "hybridity," or "syncretism" because they see only the publicly visible "hybridity" without regard to the contexts of cultural genocide, resistance, and self-affirmation that produce it—without regard for the covert, unseen, and unspoken cycles of colonialism that propel the appropriation of selected colonial features. I would agree with Guillermo Bonfil Batalla, who regards syncretism not as a casual or mechanical blending but as a tactic of native resistance. The adoption of this or that Catholic feature (ironically) provides protection and fortifies the overall Native American cultural matrix (Bonfil Batalla 1996:136). What Greg Sarris says about the Pomo tribal people applies to my Abuelita, the Yaqui, and all tribal peoples of today: "To what degree Pomo people were conscious of the historical process and intentionally applied a specific strategy of resistance—disguising the tactical, political nature of the 'blending' in a conspiratorial way—is unclear and perhaps not a relevant concern." Sarris quotes the anthropologist Tim Buckley concerning such practices: "'I think that such tactics and processes are very rarely so conscious or intentional or conspiratorial; I think something more intuitive, unconscious, cultural (and therefore somehow even grander) goes on in these specific kinds of cases'" (Sarris 1993:67n.5). What is certain is the widespread popular awareness of tensions between popular spiritual practices and those prescribed by Catholicism. *Raza's* low attendance at mass is but one symptom of that tension.

My Abuela Polita was not only a Yaqui regionalist but also a member of the international and pan-Mexican Guadalupana Society, consisting of persons who cultivate a special devotion to the deity Guadalupe. She received formal initiation into the Guadalupana Society, sworn to uphold a different order of things. In fact, the widespread veneration of Guadalupe set the cornerstone for the Indianization of Roman Catholicism after 1531: the ultimate act of *disimulo* or camouflage that brought and brings Catholic dogma in line with ancient indigenous forms of worship. Within the indigenous oral tradition we know of Guadalupe's (Coatlashaupe's) various manifestations as the earth mother, often represented through the serpentine earth symbol: Coatlicue, Tonantzin, Quilaxtli, and many more manifestations of earth (feminine) energy.

Polita's *alabanzas* irrevocably document Guadalupe's identification with the forces of nature (terrestrial and celestial), women's power, and the life struggles of indigenous peoples against the (unnamed) colonial powers:

> Fuente perenne
> y pozo de aguas
> santas, que saben
> del mar de gracia.[5]

> [Perennial fountain
> and well of sacred
> waters that know
> of the sea of grace.] (author's translation)

Or, again referencing Guadalupe:

> Es patrona del indio, su manto
> al Anáhuac proteje y da gloria,
> elevad, mexicanos, el canto
> de alabanzas y eterna victoria.

> [She's the patron of Indians,
> her mantel protects and gives glory
> to the Americas,
> raise your voices, Mexicans, the singing
> of chants and eternal victory.] (author's translation)

Or

> ¡Oh Divina Madre
> Mira a tus hijuelos
> Que finos te invocan
> En este destierro!

[Oh Divine Mother
Look at your little children
Who lovingly invoke you
In this exile!] (author's translation)

If you can't beat them, join them: the Spanish transphoneticized "Coatlas-haupe" into "Guadalupe," and the Catholic church finally appropriated the Indian earth mother as "Santa María de Guadalupe"—but not before waging an all-out war against her. Spanish church leaders correctly saw in her a subversive reaffirmation of indigenous spirituality, the consummate Indianization of Catholicism, the colonization of the colonizer. Fray Bernardino de Sahagún complained bitterly of the thousands who flocked to Tepeyac and denounced the cult of Coatlashaupe as "disimulación idolátrica" (idolatrous deceit) and an "invención satánica" (satanic invention) (Sahagún 1950–82:90).

The national and international secular and sacred triumph of Guadalupe also represents the symbolic and (to some extent) real marginalization of Spanish domination, which fervently sought to impose Nuestra Señora de los Remedios in Mexico. The hard-won cult of Guadalupe affirmed native practices in the face of extreme colonial persecution and genocide. What is more, the church's failed effort to eradicate the female principle of Guadalupe marked the failure of the colonial will to subjugate the native in general and (symbolically) native women in particular.

My Abuelita felt closest to Guadalupe while tending to the marvelous plants of her garden. These were as sacred as everything else that inhabits *la madre tierra* (mother earth). She spoke to them while tending them; she also asked their permission and gave them thanks before removing a twig, leaf, flower, or fruit. She taught me prayers I never heard in Catholic school, like the prayer to La Santa Sábila, a plant known in English as aloe vera. The powerfully healing *sábila* plant is thought of as a substitute for Jesus, as the teacher of the "Apóstoles" (apostles).

> Sábila Virtuosa, Sábila Bendita, Sábila Santa, Sábila Sagrada; por la virtud que tú le diste a tus Apóstoles te pido que me alcances esa virtud porque te venero y te quiero para que me libres de Maleficios, Enfermedades, Mala Suerte, que me vaya bien en mis Empresas, en Negocios, y ahuyentes de mi casa el mal y me libres de enemigos en donde quiera que ande; que me des trabajo. . . . en Dios creo y en tí confío.

> Virtuous Sábila, Blessed Sábila, Holy Sábila, Sacred Sábila; by that virtue you bestowed upon your Apostles I ask you to endow me with that virtue, because

I venerate you and I want you to free me from negativity, illness, bad luck, and make my undertakings and doings go well, and keep everything bad from my home, and free me from enemies wherever I may go; give me work. . . . I trust in God and in you. (author's translation)

For Polita, caring for her assortment of medicinal herbs and flowers was as vital as caring for her nine children, her grandchildren, great-grandchildren, and neighbors. Widowed at approximately age twenty-five, she somehow managed to survive and became the spiritual center of a huge family of largely impoverished migrant workers. (Only three of us found our way to any sustained institutional schooling or college education.) Every day, my Abuelita would stand in her garden—a powerful sacred space—and send a *bendición* (blessing) to each of her children, her children's children, and all her relations. A *bendición* also accompanied any of us upon leaving the house or embarking on a journey. She also taught us to bless the sleep of all children in the household.

My Abuelita's spiritual kinship system also embraced all *comadres* and *compadres,* the Guadalupanas (including their families), and the innumerable people she healed in her practice of *curanderismo.* Her eyesight was consumed by cataracts in her old age. Unable to practice healing, she continued working as a teacher, giving verbal instruction to others on how to prepare and administer cures. Of course, the cure could only be commenced by petitioning the *santas ánimas* (guardian spirits). She was a powerful *maestra* (teacher) within the unaccredited popular university of the oral tradition. In colonial Euro-American terms she was "illiterate."

Polita could pray Hail Marys and Our Fathers with the best of them. Many Euro-Catholic concepts were easily assimilable into preexisting indigenous terms and ideas: the sacred cross symbol predates colonization; indigenous peoples thus appropriated the cross of Christ and reinterpreted it by merging it with what has for thousands of years been called the World Tree (El Arbol de la Vida or Yax che'il Kab), the pivot of the universe and the power of the four directions. What some might superficially read as Christian piety is also a declaration of indigenous culture. Similarly, the concept of immaculate conception or virgin birth was widespread in the native Americas (e.g., the birthing of Hunahpú and Ixbalamqué through the maiden Ixquic; the birthing of Quetzalcoatl through Chimalma; or of Huitzilopochtli through Coatlicue).[6] The popular indigenous concept of the god-child called Pilitzintli was easily appropriated as the "niño Dios" (reference to Jesus as "child god"). The Yaqui rebirth Waehma ceremonies coincide with the Easter celebration, because the Catholic church set the date for the resurrection in accordance with the lunar calendar and non-Christian spring rituals. My Abuelita necessarily considered herself a "Catholic," but the Pope might not have. Catholicism in rural Mexico (where most of the population has its roots) usually developed as a fringe benefit attached to and/or paralleling indigenous rites. Historically, today's profession of "Catholicism" by Mesoamerican peoples is an appropriation process born from resistance to colonial violence. Its modalities change with changing circumstances of colonial incursion.

Throughout the centuries, priests have either not been present or involved on a continuous basis among indigenous peoples; they only rarely visited the rural areas of Mexico. Thus Mesoamerican spiritual practices thrived and continued. Through her *historias* (not to mention *padrecito/indio* jokes), Polita *indiréctamente* (indirectly) manifested her distance from the Catholic institution and its clergy. We listeners learned to understand the unsaid, to intuit meanings, to absorb the real significance behind the story told. She often recounted the story of a difficult baptism. It involved walking endless miles from Mojolo, her *ranchito* (hamlet), to the church in Culiacán. She was invited to serve as godmother in the baptism of a baby. Before admitting the group to the baptismal urn, the priest exacted cash payment. The baptismal party was three centavos short. Instead of going ahead with the baptism, the priest insisted on full payment. Polita embarked upon the long walk back to the *rancho*. On her way, she miraculously encountered someone riding to the *rancho* on horseback. She described how the baby was finally baptized only because that horseman shortened her walk considerably and because she was able to locate three more centavos among the poor Mojoleños. In narrating that story, my Abuelita taught us one lesson about priests without passing judgment or uttering conclusions. Narrators of *historias* or *cuentos* know that their listeners can draw their own conclusions. After telling that story, she would usually reiterate that you don't really need priests to perform a baptism or other sacred rites. Thus in 1984 we asked my Abuelita to officiate at my marriage ceremony in the Arizona desert. Before the ceremony she spoke a series of *consejos* to me, words of counsel to guide me in marriage. Through the collective wisdom of *dichos* (proverbs) from the oral tradition she also taught us ethics comparable to those of the Ten Commandments but with more pronounced demands for social equality: "Haz el bien sin mirar a quien" or "Es mejor dar que recibir" (do good deeds without taking into account who benefits; it is better to give than to receive).

Official Roman Catholicism has not endowed me with saints or person-
ages in the image of my gender, race, class, sexuality, or habitat. In fact, Rome
does not recognize those sainted by the people in my ancestral environment.
Understandably so; these saints were often insubordinate revolutionaries
committed to establishing a different social order.

I consider myself fortunate to have been raised with a knowledge of the
Yaqui/Mayo revolutionary Santa Teresa de Cabora (Teresa Urrea). She was
born at the intersection of Mayo and Yaqui territories, and she rose to prominence at a time when a new wave of armed Mexican soldiers, along with
hacendado land-grabbers and sexual exploiters, occupied the Yaqui/Mayo
homeland (today's Mexican Northwest). The dynamics of nation formation
in all regions of the emergent Mexico and United States justified the large-
scale sexual abuse of women by landowners, carpetbaggers, and missionaries. Rape—not marriage—was the bedrock of Chicana *mestizaje* or hybridity.[7] Teresa Urrea was no exception: she was born of the rape of a young
Mayo woman by a landholding *patrón*. Teresa's spiritual/spiritist visions and
sermons of salvation (in the Mayo language) as a young woman served as
catalyst for widespread defection by enslaved and impoverished Mayos.
Various other visionary Mayo preacher-saints emerged in the region. Most
were arrested and sold into slavery. In 1892 an unsuccessful armed uprising was fought in Teresa Urrea's name and with her blessing. This led to her
deportation (*destierro*) to Arizona, where she continued her work as a miraculous healer, as an organizer against Porfirio Díaz, and as a Chicana role
model. Additional northern Mexican uprisings into the twentieth century
were linked to her name and spirit—"Viva la Santa de Cabora" (long live
the Saint of Cabora).

In 1896 Santa Teresa published "Mis ideas sobre las revoluciones" (my
ideas concerning the revolutions), in which she cites comparable indigenous
rebellions throughout the emergent Mexican nation. With self-effacing
humility, she declines credit for the northern Mexican uprisings, citing "un
profundo descontento público contra el despotismo del gobierno" (a profound public discontent against the government's despotism) as the sole
motivating force (Urrea 1896:8).[8]

Teresa Urrea has a place among the best of history's decolonial canonized
visionaries and warriors. As a Chicana/o ancestor, she embodies the grassroots practical wisdom that affirms the necessary union of spiritual and social
transformation. This is the legacy of other grassroots leaders, such as Gan-
dhi, César Chávez, Dolores Huerta, Martin Luther King Jr., Malcolm X, or
the Mothers of East Los Angeles.[9]

Yaqui mythology provides an equally powerful race-gender-class-regional affirmation through the story of the impressive girl Yomumuli. The spiritual practice of symbolic narrative (*cuentos*, or stories from the oral tradition) transmits a powerful knowledge of native women's agency (obscured by the mythology of imperialism). Like all stories told to me by my grandmother (or anyone else), this one served as an important site of theoretical reflection. Although too lengthy to tell here, the story of the young girl Yomumuli situates a woman as the creator of all Yaqui tribal life ("Todos los indios fueron creados por ella"; [all Indians were created by her]). Yomumuli furthermore serves as a magical tribal mediator between mortals and the guardian spirits (or Surem); she is the creator, translator, and voice of prophecy.[10] Only Yomumuli is able to understand the prophetic messages of the speaking stick. By transmitting those messages she is able to warn the Yaqui of the advent of colonization and Christianization. Displeased with the message, she migrates to the northern skies yet continues to serve as guardian spirit. This sacred story implicitly deifies Yomumuli as an authority predating Christ and colonizers. As a child I could fully identify with the figure, because I imagined my grandmother was telling me her own story in code; by extension it was me. This sacred figure allowed for such self-affirming acts of womanist spiritual imagination to counter the colonial imaginary in general and the marginalization of women in particular.

Because my Abuelita taught me a Yaqui/Chicana spirituality in what is now the Arizona/Sonora borderlands, I am always ambivalent and somewhat reluctant to answer that recurrent question: "Are you Catholic?" It is never clear to me what is meant. I have always known that there is the straight Catholicism of priests and the catholicized native religions and rituals. At a young age I realized I was Catholic and not Catholic. I attended Catholic school while at the same time learning from my Abuelita's "Catholicism," in which she implicitly disavowed priests—for reasons related to and different from the stories of priestly sexual abuse I heard from my victimized classmates. She embraced root concepts (which resonate in all the world's religions) and marginalized the church institution. From her I came to realize that among the colonized, "Catholic" becomes a code term signifying acceptability, a protective veneer that shields against further inquisition and genocide. My Abuelita taught me reverence for those "Catholic" powers that most deeply converged with native teachings, such as El Sagrado Corazón (compatible with the indigenous *nahuatl* Yolteotl concept of the "sacred heart"); our Lady of Guadalupe, mother of the universe; and *el niño Dios*, who also predates colonialism. She taught me an expanded and thus different pantheon of saints; a different *sentimiento;* and a different and decolonial way of the cross: "Mi'ja persígnate así: Por la Señal de la Santa Cruz, De Nuestros Enemigos Líbranos Creador. Santo Dios, Santo Fuerte, Santo Inmortal, Líbranos de Todo Mal," an untranslatable sign of the cross devoid of any mention of the patriarchal Jesus, of the Father or the Son. (She knew that one too.) Her catholicized native spirituality in her own image was an ancient and contemporary liberation theology. Thus she taught me how to liberate the spirit even in the most adverse circumstances. She modeled for me how not to be judgmental with the admonition, "Allá está Dios" (God is there). During our times alone together she made sure I knew all the prayers of blessing, petition, thanksgiving, and all times in the life-and-death cycle. In our *pláticas,* she also was an articulate social observer who was quick to point out the contradictions and foibles of what she called "los civilizados" (the civilized ones), the people who felt "modern" and superior to the "lowly" Indian masses. In her later years she initiated me into the vast medicinal knowledge and powers of *curanderismo.* Through her example, she showed me the long process of becoming human, of being human, and of *buena educación,* which has nothing to do with institutionalized schooling, in *ixtli,* in *yóllotl—rostro sábio y corazón fuerte—*wisdom (countenance) in action, holistic word and deed, the word made flesh. The importance of the indigenous concept of "formar rostro" (making face and heart) is reflected in the contemporary lexicon. One common way to warn someone against undertaking a negative action foregrounds the human "rostro": "¿Con qué cara vas a hacer eso?" (With what face will you do that?). Those are the kinds of words that continue to counsel me. Although my Abuelita is gone into spirit, and I mourn her absence in the flesh, I also know of her continued spiritual presence in me and other members of her huge family. I call upon her particularly in difficult times, mindful of the words spoken to me by Chumash elder, Pilula Khus: "Sometimes they can help us more from the other side."

Polita Gastelum Rodríguez's life and spiritual practices reveal a blueprint of twentieth-century social processes that created "Mexicans" and "Chicanas/os" as well as "Catholics" from multiple regional Indian tribal cultures (Silko 1991). Her life stands for the lives of millions of our women elders, no matter what they call themselves. The historical changes in ethnic labels or names (with new national, regional, tribal, and personal names imposed) for many did not erase the Mesoamerican consciousness and presence of indigenous womanist values and identity. Many names have changed, but the underlying practices and spirit remain the same. The native spirit of the Americas,—woman, Indian, and poor—will continue to Indianize and humanize the imposed patriarchal Catholicism. This synthesis, whereby native peoples appropriate compatible Catholic ideas into Native American spirituality, constitutes one of the extraordinary humanistic achievements of the Americas. Native peoples have harmonized oppositions and hierarchies of gender and sexuality, race, and culture—oppositions rooted in colonial devastations and greed.

The institutions within which we labor—be they church, university, school, hospital, beauty salon, or home—are all linked to the political economic order of the society that devalues native women. However, as native women, Chicanas are not lacking in a rich legacy of sociospiritual practices and affirmations in our image. These sustaining practices, and the class-, gender-, race-, and region-based social visions they embody, continually prefigure and inspirit a different order of things, domains of freedom, equality, dignity, and self-affirmation.

I want to close with the *mujerista sentimiento* of the divine that was published anonymously in a book on Latina liberation theology:

> I have never thought of describing God because for me it is not a person, it is like a sentimiento [deep feeling], a force that makes me move, which pushes me in difficult moments. It is a force, something I cannot explain. But if they would ask me to draw God, I would draw my grandmother smiling. Because she is the only person that I believe has filled me so much that I can compare her to God. I would draw a picture of my grandmother with her hands open, smiling, as if to say, "Come with me because I am waiting for you." God is strength for the lucha [struggle], strength to keep going ahead, to encourage. . . . For me it is always a force that moves me. And even if everybody would say that I am bad, that I cannot do it, that force says that I can do it, that I am special, that I am capable of moving mountains. But it is something outside of me that comes to me in the darkest and most difficult moments.[11]

ASI SEA

NOTES

This essay will be included in my book-in-progress entitled *Essays in Chicana Herstory,* a compilation of analytical essays written at the intersection of human *testimonio,* academic research, and the linguistic styles of the heart and spirit. These essays will form part of the New Chicana Writing. I want to acknowledge the students in my Barrio Popular Culture class at the University of California at Santa Barbara, summer 1999, for their enthusiasm, their engaged presence, and their comments.

1. As I write this essay (1996), research and writing on Chicana spiritualities is in its infancy. The few books published include Isasi-Díaz and Tarango 1989, Rodriguez 1994, and Turner 1990.

2. Her name reflects the reality of most naming in the Americas, where indigenous names became European ones. I recall the words of the local Chumash elder Tony Romero: "Many people ask, 'If you are Chumash, how come you have a Spanish name?' They don't understand" (personal communication with the author, April 28, 1987). Native peoples, like African slaves brought to the Americas, were given the Hispanic names of their owners on the plantations (haciendas), missions, or mines. Most of today's *raza* families carry these these slave names. As such, my grandmother's family names also reflect this history of slavery.

3. Writings on Yaqui culture and social history include Savala 1980, Hu-DeHart 1981 and 1984, Spicer 1980, 1984 [1940], and 1988, Molina, and Painter 1986.

4. For more information on the devastating effects of GATT (General Assembly on Tariffs and Trades) and NAFTA (North American Free Trade Agreement) from the perspective of indigenous women, consult *Indigenous Woman* 2 (1) 1995, especially Castillo 1995. The journal is available through IWN, P.O. Box 174, Lake Elmo, MN 55042, (612) 777–3629.

5. All prayers and *alabanzas* stem from the native oral tradition, as transmitted to the author by her grandmother, Polita Gastelum Rodríguez.

6. The significance and symbolism of virgin birth in indigenous culture is examined by Girard 1979.

7. Foundational for an understanding of the sexual violence within Chicana/o history is Antonia Castañeda's "Sexual Violence in the Politics and Policies of Conquest: Amerindian Women and the Spanish Conquest of Alta California" (1993).

8. For a cogent description of Teresa Urrea's life, see Mirandé and Enríquez 1979. Also interesting is the documentary novel by Domecq 1990.

9. For an excellent analysis of the Mothers of East Los Angeles, see Pardo 1990.

10. For a thorough moral history of the Americas from an indigenous perspective, see Silko 1991.

11. This is the testimony of a Puerto Rican woman named Inéz. It is collected and published bilingually, along with other beautiful *testimonios,* in Isasi-Díaz and Tarango 1989:17.

WORKS CITED

Bonfil Batalla, Guillermo. 1996. *México Profundo: Reclaiming a Civilization.* Austin: University of Texas Press.

Castañeda, Antonia. 1993. "Sexual Violence in the Politics and Policies of Conquest: Amerindian Women and the Spanish Conquest of Alta California." In *Building with Our Hands: New Directions in Chicana Studies.* Ed. Adela de la Torre and Beatriz M. Pesquera. 15–33. Los Angeles: University of California Press.

Certeau, Michel de. 1984. *The Practice of Everyday Life.* Trans. Steven Randall. Berkeley: University of California Press.

Domecq, Brianda. 1990. *La insólita historia de la Santa de Cabora.* México, D.F.: Editorial Planeta.

Girard, Raphael. 1979. *Esotericism of the Popol Vuh.* Trans. Blair A. Moffett. Pasadena, Calif.: Theosophical University Press.

Hernández Castillo, Rosalva Aida. 1995. "Reinventing Tradition: The Women's Law, Chiapas." *Indigenous Woman* 2 (1): 4–7.

Hu-DeHart, Evelyn. 1981. *Missionaries, Miners, and Indians: Spanish Contact with the Yaqui Nation of Northwestern New Spain, 1533–1820.* Tucson: University of Arizona Press.

———. 1984. *Yaqui Resistance and Survival: The Struggle for Land and Autonomy, 1821–1910.* Madison: University of Wisconsin Press.

Isasi-Díaz, Ada María, and Yolanda Tarango. 1989. *Hispanic Women, Prophetic Voice in the Church: Towards a Hispanic Women's Liberation Theology.* San Francisco: Harper and Row.

Mirandé, Alfredo, and Evangelina Enríquez. 1979. *La Chicana: The Mexican-American Woman.* Chicago: University of Chicago Press.

Painter, Muriel Thayer. 1986. *With Good Heart: Yaqui Beliefs and Ceremonies in a Pascua Village.* Tucson: University of Arizona Press.

Pardo, Mary. 1990. "Mexican American Women Grassroots Community Activists: Mothers of East L.A." *Frontiers: A Journal of Women's Studies* 11 (1): 1–7.

Rodriguez, Jeanette. 1994. *Our Lady of Guadalupe: Faith and Empowerment among Mexican-American Women.* Austin: University of Texas Press.

Sahagún, Bernardino de. 1950–82. *General History of the Things of New Spain: Florentine Codex.* Trans. Arthur J. O. Anderson and Charles E. Dibble. Santa Fe, N.Mex.: School of American Research; Salt Lake City: University of Utah.

Sarris, Greg. 1993. *Keeping Slug Woman Alive: A Holistic Approach to American Indian Texts.* Berkeley: University of California Press.

Savala, Refugio. 1980. *The Autobiography of a Yaqui Poet.* Ed. with background and interpretations by Kathleen M. Sands. Tucson: University of Arizona Press.

Silko, Leslie Marmon. 1991. *Almanac of the Dead.* New York: Simon and Schuster.

Spicer, Edward. 1980. *The Yaquis: A Cultural History.* Tucson: University of Arizona Press.

———. 1984 [1940]. *Pascua: A Yaqui Village in Arizona.* Tucson: University of Arizona Press.

———. 1988. *People of Pascua.* Tucson: University of Arizona Press.

Turner, Kay Frances. 1990. "Mexican-American Women's Home Altars: The Art of Relationship." Ph.D. dissertation, University of Texas at Austin.

Urrea, Teresa (Santa Teresa de Cabora). 1896. "Mis ideas sobre las revoluciones." *El Independiente* (El Paso), 12 August 1896. PHS 8 (Patronato de la Historia de Sonora. Archivo de la Revolución Mexicana. Mexico, D.F.).

LAS QUE MENOS QUERÍA EL NIÑO

WOMEN OF THE FIDENCISTA MOVEMENT

CYNTHIA L. VIDAURRI

"Somos las que menos quería el Niño" (we're the ones Niño liked the least). This is the classic response from many women when asked about their involvement in the Fidencista movement, a folk medical and religious following based on the practices, beliefs, and teachings of a Mexican *curandero* named José Fidencio de Jesús Constantino Síntora, more commonly referred to as El Niño Fidencio. Niño Fidencio died in 1938, but his influence continues today in a movement that blends folk Catholicism and traditional medicine. Fidencistas are loosely organized into *misiones* (missions) under the direction of *materias*.[1] In a trance, *materias* take on Fidencio's spirit to perform healing rituals. Fidencistas are concentrated throughout northern Mexico and the southwestern United States but are also found wherever Mexicans or Mexican Americans have migrated, such as Illinois and Wisconsin.

Walking through the streets of Espinazo, Nuevo León, in northern Mexico, during one of Niño Fidencio's feast days (October 17 and 19 and March 17) is enough to suggest that he did indeed want women to carry on his work.[2] Unlike the experience of women in formal religious and health institutions, Fidencista women occupy all levels of the movement's structure and perform the same range of healing rituals as their male counterparts. Women participate in all aspects of the celebration. Before the actual trip, they construct vestments for the *materia* and the *misioneros,* negotiate for musicians and *matachines* to perform at the feast, and plan the logistics of the pilgrimage. Trips sometimes involve complicated international border crossings. In Espinazo, women lead the faithful in musical veneration, organize processions to the various holy sites, cook for the entire mission, and function as Niño's assistant when the *materia* is in a trance with his spirit. The presence of many children at the feast day celebrations suggests that women's most long-standing contribution is their ongoing socialization of children into the Fidencista tradition.

Most of the existing research on the Fidencistas concentrates on Fidencio himself or on the broader documentation of the movement. But the overwhelming presence of women, the extent of their involvement, and their contributions compel us to look beyond these approaches. Barbara June Macklin and Dore Gardner's work reflects the experiences of Fidencista women more specifically (see Macklin 1980; Gardner 1992), and my own research has led me to view the Fidencistas not only as a folk medical and religious movement but also as a *movimiento femenil*—a movement based on female perspectives, approaches, and skills. This essay offers an explanation as to why the existing Fidencista movement is also a women's movement. I have chosen as an example the experience of one Fidencista *materia*, Nieves Reyes Aguiñada, who has devoted her adult life to the service of Niño Fidencio. She was born on August 5, 1925, during the height of Niño Fidencio's fame. Even though she never met him in person, her life was to become inextricably intertwined with his. While each woman's path to Niño Fidencio is marked by very personal experiences, her story is characteristic of Fidencista women.

FIDENCISTA MOVEMENT ORIGINS

The Fidencista movement originates from the life and work of José Fidencio de Jesús Constantino Síntora, who was born in 1898 in Guanajuato, Mexico. Orphaned at a young age, he eventually came to live in Espinazo, Nuevo León, where he worked for the family of Enrique López de la Fuente. The specific details of his life are imprecise, but a number of stories exist about his path to Espinazo and toward becoming a *curandero*. In Espinazo, Fidencio met Teodoro von Wernich, a German-born spiritist whom Fidencio cured of a previously incurable ulcer. In gratitude for this healing, Wernich promised to make Fidencio famous.[3] Under the direction of López de la Fuente and von Wernich, Fidencio's healing power gained great acclaim, and he became known simply as El Niño Fidencio.[4] Tens of thousands of pilgrims, in search of medical and spiritual care, converged in Espinazo. Niño Fidencio worked continuously, treating every type of ailment with his repertoire of herbal medicine and spiritual rituals. The Niño phenomenon was closely followed by reporters, whose newspaper accounts fueled Niño's fame. All this public fervor drew the attention of the medical community, which feared that the public health was in jeopardy when the growing crowds stressed Espinazo's limited infrastructure. The highlight of Niño Fidencio's healing career came in 1928, when the Mexican president Plutarco Elías Calles came to Espinazo to be healed.[5] The relationship between church and state under the Calles administration had been tense, especially after the anticlerical provisions of the constitution were implemented. In turn, the church went on strike in July 1926, and for the next three years all formal rites were suspended (Meyer and Sherman 1987:587). Fidencistas believe that Calles's Espinazo trip was a step toward a reconciliation between church and state, in which Fidencio was a principal party.

Personal accounts of cures, newspaper stories, and countless photographs propelled Niño Fidencio's notoriety to regions far beyond Espinazo, and by 1935 it had developed into a cult (Zavaleta 1999:9). This cult developed at a time when Fidencio's health was failing, and on October 19, 1938, Niño Fidencio died. The stories surrounding the circumstances of his death are as mysterious as the stories about his life. The life and passion of Niño Fidencio would elevate him to folk sainthood, and his legacy would be the foundation for the next generation of Fidencistas.

BUSCANDO CORAZONES—BECOMING NIÑO FIDENCIO'S MATERIA

The contemporary Fidencista movement is fueled by its most vibrant and crucial component—the *materias*. Unlike most charismatic movements that die with the charismatic leader, Niño Fidencio lives on through *materias* that become Niño's body on earth. Through them, he continues to dispense medical cures and emotional advice.

The recruitment and retention of *materias* is crucial for the long-term viability of the movement. It is believed that while under von Wernich's tutelage, Niño Fidencio learned how to "transport his spirit," and in preparation for his eventual death he had trained some of his followers to take on his spirit. In his teachings, Niño Fidencio predicted the coming of many *materias*. He stated, "Yo me tengo que morir, después de mi muerte vendrán muchos Niños Fidencios, pero recuerden que sólo hubo uno y ése soy yo" (I must die, after my death there will come many Niños Fidencios, but remember there was only one and that is me). Fidencistas interpret this to mean Fidencio would manifest himself through many *materias*. He would need many *materias* because no single individual could contain his spirit in its entirety. After death, Niño comes *buscando corazones* (looking for hearts), hearts that are large enough to contain his. By becoming Niño's *materias,* women believe they are fulfilling a holy calling. Even though there is a general perception among Fidencistas that women were not Niño's first choice for *materias,* they believe women's hearts are more disposed to accepting Niño Fidencio. In October 1988, Fidencistas commemorated the fiftieth anniversary of Niño's death in Espinazo. This was probably the largest single gathering of *materias* in the movement's history. At this event, approximately four hundred, or 85 percent, of the *materias* were women. Although most of the older *materias* are registered with one of the two major Fidencista groups in Espinazo, there is no formal mechanism to obligate someone to be registered.[6]

The call to serve Fidencio is much like the process of becoming a *curandero,* in which an individual receives a calling to service and is bestowed a *don* (gift) to heal. This *don* comes directly from God; not meeting this obligation is a direct reproach of God. Similarly, *materias* receive a calling to serve Niño Fidencio, and not meeting this call violates a sacred obligation.

Materias believe they are the "chosen ones"—preselected to do Niño's work. Niño does not need permission to use their body, but he will not take them by force; *materias* must give themselves freely and willingly. The realization of being a "chosen one" usually comes through a life-threatening or life-altering situation such as a critical illness. This may occur to the *materia* herself or to a loved one. Doña Nieves's route to becoming a *materia* was determined for her at an early age in one of these critical moments.

Born in Upland, California, she was far from her relatives in Mexico and the center of Fidencista activity. About 1933, her mother took her and her siblings to meet their relatives in Coahuila, Mexico. On this trip, her younger brother, Santiago Reyes, became very ill and would not respond to any medical treatment. Doña Nieves's godmother, Chavalita, told her mother to take Santiago to Lolita Salazar, a *materia* for Niño Fidencio. In exchange for healing Santiago, Doña Nieves was promised to Niño Fidencio's service by her mother. Santiago fully recovered, but Doña Nieves was not told about the commitment made in her name.

She grew up, married, and had children, unaware of her obligation to Niño Fidencio. She and her family moved close to Corpus Christi, Texas, and around 1960 she began to suffer from an undefined ailment; this general malaise lasted for a year and a half and was characterized by exhaustion, headaches, fever, and chills. Her doctor prescribed numerous medications that left her chronically lethargic. This period put stress on her family and caused her to feel guilty for not taking care of them. It was during this time that she felt compelled to find Niño Fidencio. A friend showed her a button with Niño's picture on it, and she remembers not wanting to return the button. That same day she prayed to God at her altar asking about Niño Fidencio. She felt he could cure her malaise but was afraid of dabbling in something evil or getting caught up with charlatans. Her doubts were soon resolved. After praying, she napped and woke up contented and full of energy. Her husband returned from work to find her cleaning the house, with dinner ready. She saw her improvement as proof that she was on the right path. Her husband was frightened at first but was impressed with the overwhelming changes to her well-being. She sought out Niño Fidencio and saw him manifested for the first time in a *materia* named Cuquita González. It was Cuquita who revealed to Doña Nieves that she had the *luz* (light, gift) to be Niño's *materia*.

There is no orthodox process by which one becomes a *materia* like Doña Nieves, but there are similarities in the paths taken. After receiving a calling, *materias* are guided by an experienced *materia* through a period of *preparación* (preparation or training). This training period requires the novice and her family to make personal sacrifices. This is a time of introspection that involves prayer, meditation, and physical penance. After this formative period, the senior *materia* determines when the novice is ready to take on Niño's spirit.

There was a period in the movement when novice *materias* traveled to Espinazo to be tested by Victor Zapata, the *revisador general* (inspector general), or Victoriano Hernández, the *segundo revisador* (second inspector). In a trance state, *materias* were quizzed about Niño Fidencio's life, philosophy, and healing knowledge. Upon successfully passing the inspection, *materias* were acknowledged by the Fidencista leadership. After the *revisadores* passed away, no one took on the formal function of inspector general. Because they had proved themselves to the Fidencista leadership, *materias* who went through this rigid inspection are perceived as higher in status than those who did not. It is important to note that this process pertains to becoming Niño's *materia* and not becoming a *curandero*, although some *materias* are *curanderos* in their own right. To be a *curandero* implies having a gift to heal independent of Niño Fidencio. Doña Nieves insists adamantly that she is not a *curandera* but rather a servant of Niño Fidencio.

Materias carry out Niño's work in their own communities, where they develop a following through word of mouth when a devotee comments on the cures received through that *materia*. The work usually takes place in a room, with an altar to Niño Fidencio, set aside exclusively for this activity, and some of the busier *materias* have constructed separate spaces that serve as shrines where the *misioneros* gather.

Doña Nieves, still searching for a permanent cure to her malaise, made her first trip to Espinazo in 1960 with Cuquita. There she experienced her first *curación* (healing) at the *charquito* (little puddle) where Niño Fidencio himself once conducted healing rituals. When they returned from Espinazo, Doña Nieves was prevented from proceeding to her home by Materia Anita, so she could go through her *preparación* (training). For the next six months, she and her eldest son Emilio stayed in Piedras Negras, Coahuila, while she prepared to become a *materia*. Her husband quit his job to be with her and support her through this process, and her son was withdrawn from school. Not having a place to live, they slept in their car during that six-month period. This hardship is perceived to be part of her spiritual development. In March 1961, Niño Fidencio's spirit manifested itself for the first time in Doña Nieves. She traveled to Espinazo to successfully present herself before the *revisador general*, Compadre Victor Zapata.

In January 1962, Doña Nieves and her family moved to Robstown, Texas, where they purchased a home adjacent to the railroad tracks, where trains once stopped to refuel. Proof that this was where Doña Nieves was to serve El Niño came when the real estate agent who sold them the property donated his commission to Niño Fidencio.

There were great demands for Niño's services. For the next seven years, Doña Nieves worked day and night, stopping only for brief naps and light meals. The limited time she had for herself was spent in meditation. During this period, a temple was constructed using the wall-sized concrete braces that once supported the train fuel tanks. On September 7, 1965, the "Mixta Help of Charity and Mercy, Fidencio Sintora Constantino" temple was issued a certificate of incorporation by the State of Texas. Here, Doña Nieves dedicated herself to El Niño's work. At its height, the mission counted on a hundred active Fidencistas and their children. Today, a log with the names of people who came seeking Niño Fidencio serves as testimony to the vibrant activity at the mission.

MATERIAS AND SOCIAL INSTITUTIONS

As Macklin points out, Mexican American folk healers enjoy greater personal independence and acquire power and authority through their work, but these often come at great expense for a Fidencista woman (1980:130). The decision to carry on this work can be a source of conflict with the social institutions that are most important to her—family, church, and sometimes legal and medical institutions. Following El Niño can be in direct conflict with her family's belief system. Even when they hold similar beliefs, the family must alter their relationship with the *materia,* who has many new demands on her time and attention. Husbands and children are most directly impacted by this change in the household structure, but *materias* often state that they are willing to lose their husbands if necessary to carry on Niño's work.

Some *materias* report conflict with the Catholic church, often being told by parish priests that they are involved in charlatanism or worse, the devil's work. Some priests in the Espinazo area have worked out a relationship with Fidencistas, even though the bishop's office has issued public admonishments. Doña Nieves's son, Emilio, was most impacted by her work. His religious training in Catholic schools did not acknowledge Niño Fidencio, and priests told him that what his mother did was wrong. His loyalty was divided between his mother and the church.

In extreme cases, the *materias* experience conflicts with medical and legal institutions. Like Niño Fidencio, some have been accused of practicing medicine without a license or of various forms of abuse when outsiders do not understand a dramatic healing ritual. Having a member of a medical profession, such as a nurse or doctor, in a Fidencista mission is a source of pride because it indicates acceptance by a representative of an institution that historically has denounced traditional medicine.

EVALUATING WOMEN'S PARTICIPATION

The extensive participation of women in the Fidencista movement is not surprising when it is evaluated from a broader historical, social, and cultural perspective. Three specific circumstances account for the continued participation of women: Niño Fidencio's connection to women; the context in which the movement originated; and the precedents set by women who took early leadership roles.

Niño Fidencio is said to have had a deep respect for women, especially his mother. As a sign of respect for his mother, Fidencio changed his surname to her family name. In Spanish-speaking countries, it is customary to use both the father's and mother's surnames with the paternal surname placed immediately after the given name. Niño Fidencio's birth records record his name as José Fidencio Constantino (father's surname) Síntora (mother's surname). It is uncertain when the name change occurred, but the engraving on his tomb, where he was buried with a rosary given to him by his mother, reflects this change—Fidencio de Jesus S. Constantino (Garza Quiroz 1991:1). Some stories claim that Niño's first healing act was to fix his mother's broken arm.

Niño Fidencio is closely connected with the Virgin of Guadalupe, the most powerful of Mexican Catholic and nationalistic images. He became known as El Niño Guadalupano (child of Guadalupe), and images of Niño Fidencio with Virgin of Guadalupe iconography continue to reinforce this connection. According to some stories, when an autopsy was conducted after his death the doctors found an image of Guadalupe stamped on his heart.

Niño himself transcended gender roles. When he worked for the López de la Fuente family, the children came to call him "mamá." One of his sobriquets was "mamá de los huérfanos" (the orphans' mother). He was said to be fond of housework and was an expert tortilla maker (Riley 1999:2). As a healer, *partera* (midwife) work was said to be his favorite. The non-gender-specific tunics now worn by *materias* in a trance are like those Niño wore.

Niño Fidencio's work and the movement it inspired originated in an isolated area where, as in all frontier experiences, gender lines become nebulous and men and women do whatever is necessary to survive. Women have always taken on the responsibility of providing health care, and in places where institutional medical treatment is not readily available it is logical for this role to be expanded and to be highly valued. Likewise, in the absence of a formal church or priest women have taken on the maintenance of religious practices and the spiritual training of children.

While it may be a common belief that Fidencio wanted men to carry on his work, it would have been an impractical expectation. At the time of his death, many men in the Espinazo region were migrating to work in other parts of the country or the United States. It was a practical response for women to fill the roles normally ascribed to men.

This absence of men from the region may explain why some of the significant members of the fledgling movement were women. The first *materias* might have well been women. There still exists a story that Niño Fidencio, shortly before his death, sequestered three women to teach them to take on his spirit; they in turn would teach others. Early on, leadership roles were taken by women. The first temple to El Niño was started in Coahuila by Damiana Martínez and Cipriana Zapata; and Garza Quiroz identifies Señora María Longoria viuda de Garza as a Fidencista who called herself *decana de los cajitas* (the *cajitas'* deacon) (1991:82). In the contemporary Fidencista movement, Comadre Cipriana, the daughter of Victor Zapata, is the presiding spiritual leader.

CONCLUSION

As a university student in the 1970s I was influenced by feminist literature, but I could never completely reconcile it with my observations of women's behavior in my own community and experiences. Both of my grandmothers were very "traditional" Mexican American women by their era's standards, and yet their daily lives were filled with activities not commonly perceived to be traditional. Between them their experiences included working outside the home, running a family business, doing heavy physical labor, and managing their own money, to name a few. Yet my grandmothers, like Fidencista women, would never consider themselves feminists by the definitions I learned at the university.

When considering the frontier circumstances in which the Fidencista movement began, Fidencio's connection with women, and the precedents for female leadership roles set early on, it seems inevitable that women would be at the forefront of today's movement. When viewing the Fidencistas as a *movimiento femenil* and evaluating their feminine power in its organic context, it is easy to understand how these women see their participation as an extension of their familial and social roles. Doña Nieves and other Fidencista *materias* are *femeniles* in a way that is culturally appropriate for them. There are countless examples of women doing what is necessary to survive in their own terms that would appear to the outside observer as being feminist. By couching Fidencista women's participation as "feminist," we are applying a concept of attitude and behavior that is born out of U.S. Anglo experience. I would argue that Latinas have a brand of feminism that is crafted from our own experiences and is culturally appropriate to us. When asked if she thought that by being a *materia* she was being a feminist, Doña Nieves responded, "Es un sacrificio muy grande por un capricho" (it's a great sacrifice for a whim). To think that Fidencista women would choose this work simply to challenge male authority and to increase their own social status diminishes their sacrifices and greater contributions to the communities they serve.

NOTES

1. *Caja, cajón, cajita, vaso, vaso preferido,* and *materia* are terms for people that take on spirits. I found that *materia* was most commonly used by both men and women Fidencistas. I hesitate to use the closest English equivalent, "medium," because of its New Age connotations.

2. Observations summarized in this essay include field research in Espinazo starting in 1996.

3. Macklin 1973 claims that Fidencio was actually working for von Wernich and not López de la Fuente when he healed von Wernich.

4. His followers claim that the term *niño* was used because of his innocent, child-like nature; others claim it refers to the belief that Fidencio never developed adult male genitalia and always spoke in a prepubescent boy's voice.

5. Some accounts have Calles coming to Espinazo looking for a cure for his daughter, and more sinister accounts have Calles and the army coming to kill Niño Fidencio because he was perceived to be a disruptive influence on church-state matters. Another claims that Calles took the army to kill Niño Fidencio because the medical community accused him of practicing medicine without a license and being a menace to the public health.

6. These estimates come from field research conducted by myself and Joe S. Graham in Espinazo.

WORKS CITED

Gardner, Dore. 1992. *Niño Fidencio: A Heart Thrown Open.* Santa Fe: Museum of New Mexico Press.

Garza Quiros, Fernando. 1991. *El Niño Fidencio y el Fidencismo.* Monterrey: Editorial Font, S.A.

Macklin, Barbara June. 1973. "Three North Mexican Folk Saint Movements." *Comparative Studies in Society and History* 15 (1): 89–105.

———. 1980. "'All the Good and Bad in This World': Women, Traditional Medicine, and Mexican American Culture." In *Twice a Minority: Mexican American Women.* Ed. Margarita B. Melville. 127–48. St. Louis: Mosby.

Meyer, Michael C., and William L. Sherman. 1987. *The Course of Mexican History.* New York: Oxford University Press.

Riley, Luisa. 1999. "Fidencio, el niño Fidencio." October. <http://www.cnart.mx/cnca/cimagen/luna9b.html>.

Zavaleta, Antonio N. 1999. "El Niño Fidencio and the Fidencistas." August 26. <http://unix.utb.edu/~vpea/article.html>.

8

TRANSGRESSING THE TABOO

A CHICANA'S VOICE IN THE MARIACHI WORLD

LEONOR XÓCHITL PÉREZ

> So long as music reaffirms what everyone expects, it can manage to seem apolitical, to serve as a mere frill. But as soon as it transgresses some deep-seated taboo, it can bring boiling to the surface certain antagonisms or alliances that otherwise might not have been so passionately articulated.
> —Susan McClary, *Feminine Endings: Music, Gender, and Sexuality*

Of the ten male and female players in the Mariachi Juvenil (youth mariachi), we four girls stood out. Rachel, my sister, played *guitarrón* (a portable acoustic bass, indigenous to Mexico); Irene played *vihuela* (a small acoustic rhythm guitar); and Dora and I played *violín*. Since we didn't have uniforms and we weren't told what we should wear to our first performance, we decided to coordinate our apparel. We agreed on blue jeans and purple blouses. When Don Chuy, our mariachi teacher, first saw us at our junior high school auditorium, his jaw dropped. He held his head in disbelief and yelled out, "¡Ay Díos mío! ¡Todas en pantalones de mezclilla!" (Oh my God! All of you in jeans!). Don Chuy was so upset that he threatened not to let us perform. We were told that in the future we must wear dresses. A school administrator calmed him down as we quickly took our positions on stage. As the curtain opened, our mariachi group started its first song. The audience was stunned. There was dead silence and then came a loud roar of laughter from approximately two hundred junior high school adolescents. Immediately I felt a knot in my stomach, and then my knees started shaking. The blood rushed to my face, and my eyes began to water. I wanted nothing more than to run off that stage. We managed to finish our performance, and at the end Don Chuy shook his head and said, "¡Nos chiflaron!" (they whistled at us!). In Mexico a certain type of whistling is an expression of disapproval.

In 1974 my junior high school was one of the first in the Los Angeles area to institutionalize mariachi music as an alternative to the classical music traditionally taught in the public school system. At that time, however, mariachi groups in the low-income community of East Los Angeles most often were found in the *cantina*. These groups were mainly composed of immigrants who wove in and out of bars at night and charged clients for performances *al talón* (by the song). Because of limited financial resources, most people in my community only hired mariachis to perform at a few cultural and religious celebrations and at some serenades. It's no wonder my peers laughed at the sight of us. We were kids, male and female, who were imitating adult male mariachis in what seemed an inappropriate cultural context. Although my junior high school did have a *folklórico* group (Mexican dance troupe), it was mostly composed of Mexican immigrants whom we called "T.J.s" after Tijuana, the Mexican border town through which most of them crossed to get to Los Angeles. Therefore, the sight of the more assimilated Chicanos playing mariachi music in blue jeans added humor to the moment.

What would persuade a school district to establish such a program? Various forces promoted the inclusion of mariachi as a legitimate cultural form of expression in the music curriculum of some U.S. schools. One force was the "Chicano cultural renaissance," a product of the Chicano movement of the 1960s and 1970s that promoted the pursuit of self-definition and pride in Chicano cultural roots as a form of protest against domination by mainstream society (Meier and Ribera 1993). The Chicano cultural renaissance was mainly promoted in colleges and universities through newly emerging Chicano studies and ethnomusicology departments. The Institute of Ethnomusicology at the University of California at Los Angeles, established in 1961, housed the nation's first university-based group, Mariachi Uclatlán (Loza 1993). It became a model for other institutions and encouraged Latinos and non-Latinos to learn this musical genre. A second force in the mid-1960s was Mariachi Los Camperos de Nati Cano, a professional mariachi group based in Los Angeles that established the first nightclub where mariachis performed on stage as a dinner show. Through their performances at the restaurant, Mariachi Los Camperos started to reach a new audience of highly assimilated middle-class urban immigrants and their children (Fogelquist 1996). Other forces, such as the advent of bilingual/bicultural education and the genesis of mariachi festivals, also contributed to establishing mariachi as a legitimate cultural form. The music educator Belle San Miguel Ortiz is credited with setting the stage for the first mariachi conference in San Antonio, Texas, in 1979, which evolved from the mariachi program for schools that she began in 1966 (Fogelquist 1996). Together these forces promoted the inclusion of mariachi in the music curriculum at the primary, secondary, and university levels in the West and Southwest.

The inclusion of women in this traditionally male-dominated genre was an unexpected outcome of the mariachi curriculum in the school system. However, social and cultural factors quickly formed a glass ceiling that, to this day, has kept women from participating fully in most groups and certainly not beyond the school or semiprofessional level. Therefore, I propose that the transgression of the taboo against female players by traditionalists "brings boiling to the surface certain antagonisms or alliances that otherwise might not" be so fervently voiced (McClary 1991:27). Despite these antagonisms, alliances, and restrictions on full participation, women nevertheless benefit. As mariachis, they escape from traditional gender roles, gain power, and acquire a voice. The developments in mariachi music, however, not only empower women but also highlight the transitional and often confusing gender roles assigned to female mariachi musicians.

Little is known about the experiences of women in mariachi. The academic literature is scant (Clark 1996; Hart 1997; Jáquez 1995; Pérez et al. 1998; Rojas 1998), and not one dissertation has been written exclusively on this topic. Most of the publications on women in mariachi exist in the media and focus mainly on the three most recognized professional mariachis in the United States: the pioneers Rebecca Gonzáles, Laura Garciacano Sobrino, and Mónica Treviño (De la Cruz 1995; Hanly 1990; Quintanilla 1995; Treviño and Bentancourt 1996). Thus I offer my story, as a woman in mariachi performance for fifteen years, as a means of further exploring the female voice in this musical tradition.

I performed in mixed-gender mariachi groups for eleven years before I took a ten-year break. In November 1995 I picked up my violin and started playing once again. My return to the mariachi world, this time as an educated Latina in the process of obtaining a doctoral degree in higher education research at UCLA, has offered me an opportunity to articulate and analyze my experiences as a female in mariachi through a feminist theoretical framework. Specifically, I am guided by standpoint theory, which exposes perspectives on society that are not always visible; however well-intentioned one may be, the multiple relations of humans with each other and the natural world may not be apparent when perceived through one's personal views. A standpoint, however, is not only an interested or biased position but a position from which to launch the process of change (Hartsock 1987).

I develop my standpoint by writing my story. According to the feminist Chandra Talpade Mohanty (1991), for women of color, writing one's story does not serve to describe only an individual's struggle, as is often the case with the Euro-American autobiography. Instead, one speaks from within a collective as a participant in a larger struggle. This process is also known as validity-as-reflexive-accounting, and it allows for interaction between the writer, the topic, and the sense-making process (Altheide and Johnson 1994). Furthermore, writing one's story facilitates an understanding of a woman's perspective from the "micropolitics" of her everyday life and, therefore, beyond the feminist politics of organized movements. This process also leads one to the formation of a politicized consciousness of self-identity.

Writing my story in order to find my voice as a woman in mariachi (my standpoint) brought to the surface certain contradictions in my life. One conflict originated in the tension between my involvement in mariachi performance and my family's participation in the East Los Angeles Pentecostal church. Although our pastor advocated separation from anything that was "worldly" or not Protestant, I knew much about Catholicism, spiritualism, and *curanderas* (Mexican folk healers). My mother was born in the United States but was raised in Mexico. She was Catholic prior to marrying my father and often missed the rituals of the Catholic church. She therefore retained certain Catholic practices, such as not eating meat on Fridays and making *capirotada* (bread pudding) during Lent. When we were ill, she took us to my Tía María, who was a spiritualist, for healing. I'd watch my aunt slip into a trance as she summoned our family's spirit guide, Hermana Clarita (Sister Clara). And when we reached the height of our rebelliousness as teens, she took us to a *curandera* named Olga for *límpias* (cleansing). My father, the pastor, and our church congregation never knew about these experiences, of course, because my mother swore my three sisters and me to secrecy.

My entire family was involved in music. A healer prescribed violin lessons as a cure for my mother, to remedy her love-sickness as a teen, but she discontinued private instruction after only a few years. My father, who also was born in the United States but was raised in Mexico, was the son of a seasonal farm worker and did not have the privilege of taking private music lessons. He did, however, play a few songs that he learned by ear on the piano and the guitar. Each of my three sisters played instruments, and most of the music they performed was classical or church-related.

We never listened to mariachi music as I was growing up because it was secular and had an association with the bar scene, thereby making it "worldly" or "del mundo" and unsuitable for entertainment in our Christian home. Upon hearing of my decision to join a mariachi group at my junior high school, my father told my mother that I was being groomed to become a *callejera* (a woman of the street; also one who drifts away from home). Despite my mother's choice to contradict Pentecostal church expectations by practicing certain "worldly" and/or Mexican traditions herself, she too had difficulty supporting my interest in mariachi music.

These contradictions and the tensions they created made my identity formation as an adolescent a painful experience. Given the socially constructed dichotomy of acceptable or unacceptable behavior in my community at that time, I always seemed to be participating in some form of inappropriate behavior. Only recently, as a Latina graduate student, have I begun to resolve the contradictions in my life. I am learning to accept this tension as part of embracing, instead of compartmentalizing or denying, my multiple identities. In *Borderlands/La Frontera: The New Mestiza* (1987), Gloria Anzaldúa writes: "The new *mestiza* copes by developing a tolerance for contradictions, a tolerance for ambiguity. She learns to be an Indian in Mexican culture, to be Mexican from an Anglo point of view. She learns to juggle cultures. She has a plural personality, she operates in a pluralistic mode—nothing is thrust out, the good the bad and the ugly, nothing rejected, nothing abandoned. Not only does she sustain contradictions, she turns the ambivalence into something else" (1987:79). Anzaldúa maintains that to work out a synthesis for the contradictions in accepting multiplicity, the self adds a third element that is greater than the sum of its severed parts. That third element is a new consciousness—a mestiza consciousness. It was with this mestiza consciousness that I started to reflect and to write, thereby developing my standpoint and finding my voice as a female in the mariachi world. I accomplish this task through writing in the style of "U.S. Latina autobiography" (Torres 1991), which through content, form, and language reflects the fluidity of my multiple identities that include an emerging scholar, Chicana, and mariachi.

THE TRANSFORMATIVE POWER OF MARIACHI

Anzaldúa describes well the options for Chicanas in communities like East Los Angeles: "For women of our culture there used to be only three directions she could turn: to the Church [*sic*] as a nun, to the streets as a prostitute, or to the home as a mother. Today some of us have a fourth choice: entering the world by way of education and career and becoming self-autonomous persons" (1987:17). Although I publicly agreed that college, the new fourth option, was the route to freedom from the three common life options for Chicanas in my community, in private I was very aware of my academic failings in junior high and high school and therefore doubted my ability to succeed in higher education. Garfield High School, my alma mater, is now nationally recognized because of the work of the math teacher Jaime Escalante. However, when I attended Garfield between 1976 and 1979, no one seemed to be "standing and delivering."[1] I managed to graduate in the top third of my class with a only a C average. Even if I had been academically prepared, I viewed college as too far away in the future to satisfy my burning desire, since a young age, to express myself and be autonomous. And so in my world as an adolescent there was a fifth option: to be a mariachi.

The experience of being a mariachi was transformative. It provided an alternative to the traditional Chicana gender roles and the expectation that I form an identity based solely on my sexuality as childbearer, nurturer, and sexual partner. Simply by wearing the traditionally male *charro,* the suit worn by mariachis, my gender identity was altered. Dress is a coded system of nonverbal communication that aids human interaction in space and time. The codes of dress include visual as well as other sensory modifications to the body that set off cognitive and/or affective processes in the viewer (Eicher 1995). The meaning placed on clothing is based on socialization within a particular cultural context as well as on an individual's improvisations when applying learned meanings of dress within specific social situations (Roach-Higgins and Eicher 1992). Among the visual codes of the *charro* suit is the *botonadura,* the silver buttons that line the outer side of the pants. The *charro* suit was originally worn by Mexican ranchers and did not at first include the *botonadura.* Not until the eighteenth century did the ranchers of rich families begin to use colors, adornments, and other accessories. The emperor Maximiliano de Habsburgo adopted the attire of the Mexican rancher, using the color black for the first time, thus attaching another code to the *charro* suit. Eventually, the black color and silver *botonadura* of the traditional *charro* suit became codes for wealth and power. It has changed little over time and currently is the same in Mexico and the United States. Today, the codes of the *charro* suit in the United States elicit ethnic pride and emotions tied to the many important life events at which mariachis perform.

In contrast to the *charro* suit, the codes of traditional dress for Chicanas in many ways promote the gender roles of sexual partner, childbearer, and nurturer. Anzaldúa (1987) points out that *la gorra, el rebozo, y la mantilla* (the hat, shawl, and veil) convey the message that women must be protected. She further explains that culture and religion seek to protect us from the supernatural, both the divine and undivine, and adds that Christianity and most other religions see women as carnal, animal, and closer to the undivine and conclude therefore that they must be protected.

The white color of the *vestido de quinceañera* (a dress worn at a Mexican girl's fifteenth birthday celebration as a rite of passage into womanhood) also promotes the gender roles of Chicanas. The dress is a public announcement that a young woman is pure and ready for marriage. She is a *mujer buena* (a good woman) because she is on the good side of the *virgen/puta* (virgin/whore) dichotomy under which many Chicanas in my community are classified. When it came time for me to celebrate my fifteenth birthday, I had already been wearing the black *charro* suit for two years and wanted nothing to do with wearing a white *quinceañera* dress. I was a *virgen* but didn't feel I had to prove it by wearing the dress. In addition, I wasn't eager to get married. I begged my mother not to force me to have a *quinceañera*, but she insisted. And so the long and laborious process began. I picked twenty-eight of my closest teenage friends and relatives, fourteen male and fourteen female, to be my court of honor, and for three months we had meetings to discuss every conceivable aspect of the *quinceañera*.

Although I didn't resist much at the beginning, various occurrences prior to the *quinceañera* added to the tension of unwillingly going through a cultural ritual. Two days before the celebration, we had a live goat locked up in our backyard to be slaughtered for the *birria* (marinated goat meat). It escaped and chased my sister Paulina and me around the front yard. We climbed onto my mother's Toyota and waited for a neighbor to rescue us. On the day before the celebration, no one warned me that the goat had been slaughtered. I opened the refrigerator door, and the sight of the goat's head on a plate near two bowls of its blood sent me screaming and trembling to the front of the house. On the day of the *quinceañera*, we were late to the church by an hour and a half because my mother was putting the finishing touches on the dresses—frilly, satin, peach-colored gowns—that she had sewn for all the young women. Jannie, one of the girls in the *quinceañera*, became so dehydrated waiting in the sun that when the ceremony started she fainted at the altar. By the time we were finished with the ceremony, I was enraged. The only way I knew to mentally and emotionally escape what had been imposed on me was to resist participation in the rest of the celebration by becoming intoxicated. I drank as much beer and champagne as Philip, one of the boys in the *quinceañera*, could sneak out from the bar for me. For the rest of the evening, various sisters, cousins, and friends kept me from the public eye and thus from humiliating my parents. The next morning, I experienced my first hangover. My head throbbed, I was extremely thirsty, and no matter how many times I brushed my teeth I could still smell alcohol on my breath. Even so, I started the ritual of putting on my *charro* suit in preparation for a mariachi performance. I put on my leather boots, white blouse, black skirt lined with the silver *botonadura*, black coat, and red tie. I was happy to be out of the *quinceañera* dress and in my *charro* suit again. Nothing else that hung in my closet could make me feel as good as my *charro* suit did.

In performing mariachi music, I was able to behave in ways not normally considered appropriate. For many Chicanas there is what Anzaldúa (1987) calls a tradition of silence. A young woman who is raised well is not an *hocicona, lengua larga, repelona,* or *chismosa* (big mouth, complainer, longtongued, or gossiper). She also never questions. I was called many of these labels and frequently annoyed my mother with my questioning. She would often complain by saying, "¿Dónde? ¿Quién? ¿Cuándo? ¡Chihuahua! ¿Porqué tienes que saber todo? ¡Preguntona!" (Where? Who? When? Geez! Why do you have to ask and know about everything!). I recently asked my mother when I started talking, and she jokingly said, "¡Ay, desde que naciste! Y la abrías tan grande cómo la tenías" (Ay, since you were born! And you'd open it as wide as it was). Although she now speaks fondly of my gift of gab as a child, I remember how much my mouth would get me into trouble. In performing mariachi music, I satisfied my need for verbal expression. I was encouraged to use my mouth and with it to project the *gritos* (yells) and *coros* (choruses) that characterize the music. When I sang and sustained notes, people listened and I was never silenced. In *boleros* (romantic mariachi music), I sang the words of love and seduction without compromising my status as *virgen;* my violin embraced the singer's voice as the *adornos* (musical accompaniments) wrapped themselves around the beginning, middle, and end of vocal phrases.

The mariachi pioneer Laura Garciacano Sobrino, who was the second woman in the United States to perform professionally in male-dominated mariachi groups, recounted to me an occasion when mariachi performance provided a space in which to dramatically and loudly unleash her feelings. After experiencing a major conflict with an influential person in the mariachi world, she reached a moment of catharsis at a performance with a mixed-gender group. She said: "Little by little, about twenty minutes into the show, all of a sudden from way down deep in my belly I felt this *grito* coming up, from way down there. I just felt it. It was like 'Oh my God! What is going on?' I felt it travel through my body and all of a sudden, I gave the most wonderful *grito*. A mariachi *grito*. These guys turned around and looked at me and I just let it out."[2]

Many Chicanas are confined by the expectation that they be submissive and stay close to home. Being a *callejera* is not respectable. My experiences in being a *callejera* by playing mariachi, however, provided access to places, people, and events that broadened my horizons. My involvement in mariachi performance exposed me to the mariachi scene at various colleges and universities in the Los Angeles area. My mariachi mentor, Don Chuy, who was a traditional mariachi from Zacoalco de Torres, Jalisco, was influential in the movement to teach mariachi in the higher education system (Flores 1982). In 1961, he directed the first university-based mariachi, later known as Mariachi Uclatlán, at the UCLA Institute of Ethnomusicology (Loza 1993). He also directed Mariachi Nuevo Calistatlán in the 1970s at the California State University in Los Angeles. It was during this time that the Mariachi Juvenil to which I belonged disbanded because of a lack of funds. Don Chuy couldn't conceive of disrupting my mariachi training and insisted that I join Mariachi Nuevo Calistatlán while still in junior high school. That mariachi training was extensive and valuable. However, the most positive outcome of playing with Mariachi Nuevo Calistatlán was the exposure to the college environment and students.

Despite the growing participation and positive experiences of women in mariachi performance, traditionalists often contested the new female presence. Laura Garciacano Sobrino describes a typical encounter. At her first performance with an all-male mariachi, the oldest member said to the musical director, "'¡No! Nunca he tocado con una vieja; no voy a comenzar ahora'" (qtd. in Hanly 1990:48; No! I've never played with a woman; I'm not going to start now [my translation]).

My parents were the first to contest my participation in mariachi. When I played with Mariachi Nuevo Calistatlán, they realized that my passion for mariachi was deep and that it had become part of my identity. I recently asked my mother why she objected to my playing with the mariachi, and she said, "Tenía miedo que te vayas a ir con un hombre" (I was afraid that you'd go with a man). A few of my cousins became pregnant out of wedlock when we were adolescents, and my mother was concerned that my involvement with this group, my turning into a *callejera,* would lead me to compromise my status as a "good Christian girl."

I remember clearly the day that Elsa, one of the students from California State University, Los Angeles, dropped me off after a mariachi rehearsal; my parents asked her to come into our home. I hid in the kitchen as I heard them tell her in the living room that I would not continue to rehearse or perform with the group. The shock and the anger was overwhelming. Mariachi was the only constant and good thing in my life. It was the only place where I felt I excelled. If I chose to continue playing mariachi, that meant that I was actively turning away from my parents; I couldn't bear the thought of being rejected by them. Therefore I surrendered to their demands, and for more than a year I didn't touch my violin.

My parents' restriction on playing mariachi was the beginning of a difficult and rebellious period in my adolescent life. However, my imposed leave of absence neither stopped my love for mariachi nor helped improve my academic record. Plaza de La Raza, a community cultural arts and education center, more than the school system was instrumental in nurturing my growing intellect. It was for me, as it has been for many Latinos since the early 1970s, a cultural oasis where arts and education were respected and promoted. Through their Media Arts Education Program, I wrote articles for the youth newspaper, *La Paloma,* as well as articles for special editions of local community newspapers. Self-Help Graphics was another center that nurtured my talent and intellect. In 1978 I was one of seven youths hired, through a National Endowment for the Humanities grant, to promote the Mexican Day of the Dead celebration, which Chicanos in my community had almost forgotten. When I graduated from high school I attended Los Angeles Community College, but in my first semester I failed academically and dropped out.

Exhausted by tensions at home and my failure to succeed in college, I decided to apply for an internship I heard about through Plaza de La Raza to work as a student reporter for the Robert F. Kennedy Memorial Foundation in Washington, D.C. Much to my surprise, I was accepted, and it wasn't long before I decided to take the offer. Various problems, however, jeopardized my actually leaving home. It was not proper for a woman to leave her home single and unprotected, much less to go to the other side of the country by herself. My mother was not in favor of my leaving, but I pleaded with my oldest sister, Doraluz, to exercise her influence. My mother was concerned about how I was going to survive on the stipend of four hundred dollars a month. My father, who was the main provider for the family, had died of cancer seven months prior, and she had no way to support me. What my mother didn't know was that Don Chuy had put me in contact with Dan Sheehy, the director of the only mariachi in the Washington, D.C., area at that time. Mariachi de las Américas (now Mariachi Los Amigos) would become my financial savior and pseudofamily. And so, at the age of eighteen, I packed my bags and went on my way. My mother's parting words to me were, "If something goes wrong, then I'm going to be the first one to tell you, 'I told you so.'"

A NEW MARIACHI WORLD: EMPOWERMENT AND CONFUSION

My association with Mariachi de las Américas was my first move out of school-based mariachis and into playing professionally. In Washington our audiences were predominantly white. The mariachi was out of its cultural context, and I therefore escaped the cultural pressures connected to being a female mariachi. I was far away from my mother and mariachi traditionalists; thus I never worried about being criticized for crossing gender boundaries or being pressured to participate in gender-based cultural practices. In Mariachi de las Américas I wasn't a "female mariachi" but simply a mariachi. I was empowered to define myself as I pleased and to live my life as I saw fit.

I was not only empowered by the anchoring of my mariachi identity but also by the informal education I received from the many interesting places at which I performed. A September 1980 performance schedule reads: Department of Agriculture, Cannon Caucus Room–House of Representatives, FBI courtyard, Fort Richie, Department of Justice, Hyatt Regency–Presidential Dinner, Commerce Building, Immigration, Vint Hill Farms Army Base, St. Timothy's School, and Mt. Vernon College. I also traveled with Mariachi de las Américas to various states on the East Coast as well as in the South. I especially remember a performance at the Mexican embassy. After the reception, I sat on the steps for a long while, fondly gazing at the mural by Roberto Cueva del Rio that lines the wall of the grand staircase.

At the end of my one-year internship, it was officially time for me to go home. In my mother's mind, I was on "temporary leave." However, I called her and told her I wasn't ready to come home because I hadn't had enough. I stayed in Washington, D.C., and played with the Mariachi de las Américas for five years.

When I returned to Los Angeles in 1985, I once again encountered the complexity of mariachi performance when situated in its own cultural milieu. On the one hand, the transformative power of playing mariachi in Los Angeles was more striking because I crossed gender boundaries; on the other hand, the effort to reshape and define my participation in terms of cultural expectations was more heightened, more compelling, and more urgent. The mariachi world, which I had left behind five years earlier, looked much different. The class system based on variations of the traditional mariachi had further developed.

I didn't know what position women held in this new climate. It appeared, however, that people in East Los Angeles were no longer shocked and amused by Chicanos connecting to their roots through mariachi music or by the idea of a "female mariachi." It had been at least eleven years since mariachi was institutionalized in the school system in Los Angeles. Students who played mariachi throughout their secondary education now graduated from high school not only as individuals but also as cohorts of mariachis who stayed together and went on to play semiprofessionally. I imagined that the families of the Chicanas in these semiprofessional groups accepted them more easily, as mariachi performers, than my family had accepted me. I also felt that I couldn't penetrate the tight bond that they, both males and females, had developed in their formative years as mariachis in the school system. Eventually, the demand for a mariachi music curriculum became so great that the music educator Adolfo Martínez and the former principal Victoria Castro formed the Latino Music Magnet at Belvedere Junior High School. To this day, the school buses in youth from all parts of Los Angeles to learn mariachi as well as other forms of Latino music. Even in my Pentecostal church, leaders decided to put one foot in that which is "worldly" and create the "Christian mariachi." I never considered playing with these mariachis nor with Boyle mariachis, immigrants who stand on Boyle Street waiting to be hired, because these two groups were most likely to contain the greatest number of traditionalists. By this time, various colleges and universities had established mariachi programs, but I was no longer affiliated with anyone in area colleges. It was at this moment that I realized how important my mariachi mentor, Don Chuy, had been to my persistence in the Los Angeles mariachi world. Unfortunately, he died in August 1982, while I was in Washington, and was not present to help me find my place in this new mariachi world.

My self-ascribed fifth option in life, to be a mariachi, simply disappeared. Ten years went by before I found my place in the mariachi world. During those years, it was extremely painful for me to watch mariachis perform. I wanted so badly to be among them on stage. My family eventually developed a more positive attitude about mariachi music and started to attend the annual Mariachi U.S.A. festival created by Rodri Rodríguez in Los Angeles in 1990, but I never joined them; it was just too painful.

After becoming frustrated by not being able to succeed in the workforce without a formal education, I took the new fourth option in life for Chicanas (Anzaldúa 1987) and in 1991 enrolled in higher education. It was there in 1995 that I reclaimed my passion. As I walked through Schoenberg Hall at UCLA, I heard the sounds of mariachi. My entire body reacted. My heart raced as I looked into one of the rooms and saw Nati Cano of Mariachi Los Camperos directing a room full of youths. It triggered memories of my beginning in the mariachi genre. I told Nati Cano my story, and he informed me that UCLA had a group, which I immediately contacted. When I informed my mother that I had joined a mariachi, she exhaled and said "¡Ay gracias a Dios! A ver si ahora vas a estar en paz" (Oh, thank God! Hopefully you will now be at peace). She paid for the *botonadura* of my new *charro* suit to show that she now supported my passion for mariachi performance.

Reentry into the mariachi world was not what I had expected. I believed that by 1995 the conflicts and tensions related to women playing mariachi had been resolved. I was wrong. Although women played in mariachi in greater numbers, and their participation was not as strongly contested, their influence on the music and its performance was greatly limited.

THE EMERGING IDENTITY OF THE FEMALE MARIACHI

The media's focus on predominantly male high-profile mariachi groups promotes the idea that there are only a handful of women in the mariachi world. I call this idea "the mariachi myth." The accessibility of mariachi training in the school system and the transformative qualities of mariachi performance have attracted hundreds of women of all ages, from all places, and of all ethnicities to this musical tradition in the United States. Most women, however, play in school-based and semiprofessional groups. Professional groups who receive most of the public and media attention, such as Sol de México and Mariachi Los Camperos, have responded to the growing number of female mariachis and the public's demand to see more of them. However, it appears that they only have "token" positions for not more than one woman at a time. When the musical director from Mariachi Los Camperos, Nati Cano, was asked if more than one woman could perform in his group, he jokingly said, "'Bueno, eso ya es demasiado'" (qtd. in Hanly

1990:50; well, that's a bit much [my translation]). When he allowed the first female, Rebecca Gonzáles, to join his group, Cano admitted, "Hubó gente que se molestó, fue una rupta de la tradición, de la imagen del macho" (qtd. in Hanly 1990:50; there were people who were bothered; it was a rupture from the tradition of the image of the macho [my translation]).

Since gender identity is not necessarily consistent with sex category, it is possible for females through mariachi performance to cross over into the male gender domain and display behaviors not traditionally ascribed to women. However, this gender crossover has diminished. Interestingly, as the numbers of female mariachis have increased in school-based, semiprofessional, or professional groups, the distinction between male and female roles have become accentuated. Even though many Latinas have moved away from traditional gender roles in the last twenty-five years, the contemporary female mariachi usually conforms to the gender expectations characteristic of traditional Mexican culture. This traditional male-female dichotomy is accomplished through the heightening of female sexuality: by identifiable "female" characteristics in dress, such as the feminized versions of the traditional *charro* suit in all female groups; how a female mariachi wears her hair; through the instruments women are encouraged to play; by how a female handles her body on stage; and most importantly by the biologically based criteria, the male voice, used to measure what is legitimately "mariachi." By creating woman as a highly feminized Other, traditional mariachi directors protect the macho image of the mariachi genre.

Women in mariachi always have worn skirted versions of the *charro* suit. However, the black traditional *charro* suit and its powerful meaning are currently being exchanged for brighter pastel *charro* suits by most all-female groups. Pink is the color of choice for the all-female group Reyna de Los Angeles (queen of Los Angeles). The color pink is the classic symbol of femininity and youth. Similarly, the all-female group Mariachi Angeles Del Cielo (the angels from the sky), a semiprofessional group in San Antonio, Texas, wears powder blue and white uniforms. Powder blue and white are the colors of the sky and the clouds. The image of "angels in the sky" evokes an association with goodness and purity. Perhaps these groups wear these colors, which in the United States are symbols of femininity, as a sign of gender pride. However, these new visual codes prevent women from identifying with the traditional connotations of power and wealth of the male *charro* suit and reinforce traditional conceptions of subordinate female roles. Barbara Pérez Díaz, who has been a mariachi for more than twenty years, said, "'I wouldn't be caught dead in a pink suit . . . I'm happy with black'" (qtd. in Treviño and Bentancourt 1996:93).

When I started playing mariachi in 1974, there weren't any strict codes on how a female should wear her hair. Having straight and thick hair, it was easy for me to simply brush it and let it sit neatly on my shoulders. In returning to the mariachi world, however, it wasn't long before I discovered that women in mariachi were now expected to tie their hair back, usually with a big bow that matches the color of the *charro* suit tie. Prior to my first performance in a group, I was called by the director and given specific instructions to tie my hair. For women, pulling one's hair back has a functional purpose if a *sombrero* is worn, but such large and heavy hats are rarely used outside of high-profile performances. Therefore, when I resumed wearing my hair loose, it wasn't long before both male and female mariachis protested. In one case, a male trumpet player told me that he and several other male members felt that my hair would look better if it were tied back. I was appalled, because I could never imagine telling *them* how to wear their hair. On another occasion, I was approached by a female performer who said it wasn't "mariachi" to wear my hair loose. I was speechless. I wondered where she got the notion that female mariachi identity includes such a hairstyle.

In mariachi performance, women's sexuality is also heightened by the instruments they are encouraged to play. It is a common belief that women in mariachi play only certain instruments because of biological limitations. There may be some constraints to playing certain instruments, such as the trumpet because of the strength required to play it or the *guitarrón* because of its size; however, not all mariachi women are incapable of playing these instruments. In a conversation with Rosi, a female trumpet player, she explained that an instructor discouraged her from playing the trumpet because it would be too physically demanding for her. She wondered how he could arrive at this conclusion without giving her an opportunity to try. Claudia, a full-time mariachi guitarist and vocalist, was not allowed to play the *guitarrón*. Her mother didn't like the way she looked playing it. She thought it was "too big." In a recent conversation with one of the members of Mariachi Los Camperos, I was told that it is better for women to play the violin, because when they raise their arms *las mujeres lucen mejor el cuerpo* (women can better display their bodies). Therefore, though supposedly women have physical limitations, I believe that women are usually guided toward playing certain instruments because performing with such instruments is more aesthetically pleasing. It isn't surprising, then, that women would be discouraged from playing the trumpet and the *guitarrón*. Playing the trumpet distorts the face and requires the exposure of saliva, and the size of the *guitarrón* can hide most of the female body.

Movement on stage is perhaps the most obvious way in which sexuality is heightened for the female mariachi. It is more acceptable for female than for male mariachis to dance to *sones, cumbias,* or other rhythmic pieces on stage. Recently, during a performance of a mixed-gender mariachi in a local restaurant, a male mariachi swiveled his hips as the female mariachis danced to the *cumbia*. During the group's break, I overheard the restaurant's owner reprimanding the male mariachi for dancing on stage. In contrast, the performances of the all-female Reyna de Los Angeles often have choreographed dance sequences, although they are short and not done for all songs. Perhaps the most notorious for dancing is Mexico's well-known all-female group Las Perlitas Tapatías (the Tapatía pearls), who whip off their *charro* skirts and dance in tight leggings (Treviño and Bentancourt 1996).

It has been said that women do not continue to perform in the mariachi genre after a certain age because they simply get married and quit (Treviño and Bentancourt 1996:93). I suggest, however, that it is not a lack of dedication that keeps women from persisting in mariachi but rather the fact that women who marry, have children, and/or are beyond childbearing years are commonly either consumed by their new roles, discouraged from continuing, or lose interest in performance because of the focus on their sexuality. As a result, the majority of women in mariachi are usually single and/or young. For example, the members of the all-female group Las Adelitas are between fourteen and twenty-four years of age; members of the all-female group Angeles del Cielo are between fourteen and twenty. The few who have managed or chosen to play beyond these years and who either are married and/or have children handle these life events as would be done in any other profession. In reference to dual roles, childbearing and mariachi playing, Laura Garciacano Sobrino has said, "'Most committed mariachi women take maternity leave and go back to work'" (qtd. in Treviño and Bentancourt 1996:93). However, I know of one woman, Maribel Medina from Mariachi Mexicapán, who performed throughout most of her pregnancy, temporarily trading in her *charro* suit for a skirt and *poncho*. She performed on a Sunday, and the following Tuesday she was in the delivery room. It must be noted that her husband is the musical director of the group. However, other women in his mariachi have also performed during their pregnancy.

The extent to which females have crossed gender boundaries and influenced the mariachi genre has been limited to their participation in the group or to minor changes that do not threaten to change the sound of mariachi. According to the musicologist Susan McClary (1991), most members of a given social group internalize the norms of their chosen music and thus respond appropriately. They can detect even minor stylistic infractions and respond with either delight or indignation, depending on how they identify themselves with respect to the style at hand. After listening to a live performance by the all-female group Reyna de Los Angeles, one man indignantly told me that women are the downfall of mariachi. He objected to the high-pitched voices of this all female group, a deviation from the deep male sound. This type of response, which I have heard from various men in the mariachi world, is the strongest barrier against the mariachi genre becoming legitimately both male and female.

CONCLUSION

It is a common belief that the women in the few all-female groups in the United States, such as Reyna de Los Angeles, Las Adelitas, and Angeles del Cielo, are breaking new ground by shaping the female identity in mariachi performance. However, this assertion is questionable, given that every one of these groups is directed by men (José Hernández, José Salinas, and René Benevítez, respectively) and that these men are shaping the female identity in mariachi performance. Hernández works behind the scenes, choosing repertoire and writing the musical arrangements for his group (Quintanilla 1995:E2); thus he determines what is interpreted as the female sound in his mariachi group. Currently, repertoire for female groups tends to focus on *rancheras* and *boleros;* Reyna de Los Angeles commonly plays love songs by pop singers such as Gloria Estefan and Selena. Perhaps if women were choosing repertoire and writing arrangements for themselves, their performances might differ.

Culture has been described as a creative process through which performers and performances, whether they be verbal, dramatic, or artifactual, not only follow but revise and revitalize accepted rules, thereby acting out and challenging aesthetic conventions and social values (Babcock 1993). Therefore, I suggest that women become aware of the gender politics of the mariachi world and take leadership roles. Women in mariachi should become new mestizas (Anzaldúa 1987) and transcend the confines of the emerging male-female dichotomy. Embracing diverse influences, they can shape for themselves the female presence and sound in mariachi.

In January 1998, the mariachi pioneer Laura Garciacano Sobrino received

word that nine women had left José Salinas's all-female group Las Adelitas. Shortly thereafter, we both attended one of their meetings. It was inspiring to see the courage that these women have to start their own group.
They named their new group Las Alondras. An *alondra* is a bird, and like
birds they are lifting themselves to greater heights. Topics discussed at the
meeting included: interest in highlighting their education at stage performances; redesigning the female version of the *charro* suit; the possibility of
wearing their hair loose for performances; instituting a collaborative instead
of a hierarchical leadership style; and hiring various mariachi instructors
instead of having one musical director. Time will only tell if this new experiment in the performance of mariachi by these women will begin to perma-
nently transgress the taboo.

Chandra Talpade Mohanty (1991) is right. The process of writing my story
did result in a politicized consciousness of self-identity. As I wrote this essay, my tacit knowledge of the gender issues in mariachi performance was
unveiled. For many of us, mariachi has provided a space in which to experience opportunities not normally found in other contexts. It has allowed
us to be animated and strong, to be more economically independent, and,
by being *callejeras,* to meet people and visit places we would not normally
have access to. As mariachis we are able to escape from traditional gender
roles, gain power, and acquire a voice. At the same time, our ability to
maximize this experience has been hindered by social and cultural factors
that have formed a glass ceiling. It keeps many of us in school-based, semiprofessional, and/or all-female groups and thus from full participation in
this male-dominated tradition.

Ironically, as I finished writing this essay, the members of the mariachi
group in which I performed chose to rename the group and disassociate
completely from our university. They decided to go "professional." Unfortunately, my life as a graduate student, as well as other responsibilities, kept
me from joining them in this venture.

My newly formed consciousness of the position of women in the mariachi genre left me in a precarious position. What would I do now? I chose to
challenge the barriers revealed in my essay by tapping into my mestiza consciousness (Anzaldúa 1987). From this source, I realized that as a Chicana,
mariachi, and emerging scholar, I am armed with additional tools with which
to transgress the taboo and carve out a space for myself, and other women
like me, in the mariachi world.

I started the process of transgressing the taboo by conducting research on
and writing about women in mariachi. At the urging of the ethnomusicolo-

gist Terry Liu, I submitted and had accepted a proposal to hold a session on the position of women in mariachi for the Southern California Chapter meeting of the Society for Ethnomusicology. I then contacted Laura Garciacano Sobrino and invited her to be on the panel. In a long overdue reunion, she shared with me that she too wants to find a forum to discuss and influence the status of women in the mariachi world. Inspired by our talk, she reached over, grabbed my hand, and said, "Come with me to Tucson!" Having been invited to hold a workshop at the Tucson International Mariachi Conference, Laura spontaneously decided to lead the first-ever workshop for women in mariachi. Together in Tucson, Laura and I raised the consciousness of other women so that they too can transgress the taboo by shaping for themselves the female voice and identity in the mariachi world.

Since our meeting, Laura and I have developed a web page on the Internet (Pérez and Garciacano Sobrino 1998). On this web page, we are documenting the history of women in the mariachi genre. We are also developing a section in which women will be able to register themselves and be acknowledged as part of the mariachi tradition.

Through writing my story, I divulged the meaning of mariachi in my life. It is a passion that is anchored in the core of myself. Ignited in me as an adolescent, this passion has sustained me emotionally throughout my life. The insights I've gained through this process of writing have released me from the emotional residue of inhibiting memories. In telling my story, I revealed my standpoint, found my voice, and reclaimed my love for mariachi music. I recently started practicing my violin again and developing a list of songs; I know now that I cannot live without playing this music. Therefore, I am preparing to start the search for a group to join. I will once again reenter the mariachi world.

NOTES

1. *Stand and Deliver* is a 1988 film about Escalante's work teaching math at Garfield High School, starring Edward James Olmos and Lou Diamond Phillips.

2. Laura Garciacano Sobrino, personal communication with the author, Montebello, Calif., April 23, 1998.

WORKS CITED

Altheide, David L., and John M. Johnson. 1994. "Criteria for Assessing Interpretive Validity in Qualitative Research." In *Handbook of Qualitative Research*. Ed.

Norman K. Denzin and Yvonna S. Lincoln. 485–99. Thousand Oaks, Calif.: Sage Publications.

Anzaldúa, Gloria. 1987. *Borderlands/La Frontera: The New Mestiza.* San Francisco: Aunt Lute.

Babcock, Barbara A. 1993. "'At Home No Women Are Storytellers': Potteries, Stories, and Politics in Cochiti Pueblo." In *Feminist Messages: Coding in Women's Folk Culture.* Ed. Joanne N. Radner. 221–48. Urbana: University of Illinois Press.

Clark, Jonathan. 1996. "Mariachis Femeniles." Radio Bilingüe, San Jose, Calif.

De la Cruz, Elena. 1995. "Una Verdadera Reina del Mariachi." *La Opinión,* July 22, sec. D.

Eicher, Joanne B. 1995. "Introduction: Dress as Expression of Ethnic Identity." In *Dress and Ethnicity: Change across Space and Time.* Ed. Joanne N. Radner. 1–5. Washington, D.C.: Oxford University Press.

Flores, Elsa. 1982. "Don Chuy, el último de los grandes mariachis." *La Comunidad,* Suplemento Dominical de *La Opinión,* April 11.

Fogelquist, Mark. 1996. "Mariachi Conferences and Festivals in the United States." In *The Changing Faces of Tradition: A Report on the Folk and Traditional Arts in the United States.* Ed. Betsy Peterson. 18–23. Washington, D.C: Research Division Report 38, National Endowment for the Arts.

Hanly, Elizabeth. 1990. "Las Mujeres en el Mariachi: ¿Y Ahora . . . Quién es el Rey?" *La Familia de hoy* 1 (4): 48–50.

Hart, Karen. 1997. "Banning Together: The Implications of the Female Presence in Mariachi Music and Performance." Ms.

Hartsock, Nancy C. M. 1987. "The Feminist Standpoint: Developing a Ground for a Specifically Feminist Historical Materialism." In *Feminism and Methodology.* Ed. Sandra Harding. 157–80. Bloomington: Indiana University Press.

Jáquez, Cándida F. 1995. "Women's Participation in Mariachi: Ideology and Consciousness." Committee on Institutional Cooperation Fellows Conference, November. University Park, Pa.

Loza, Steven. 1993. *Barrio Rhythm: Mexican-American Music in Los Angeles.* Urbana: University of Illinois Press.

McClary, Susan. 1991. *Feminine Endings: Music, Gender, and Sexuality.* Minneapolis: University of Minnesota Press.

Meier, Matt S., and Feliciano Ribera. 1993. *Mexican Americans/American Mexicans: From Conquistador to Chicanos.* New York: Hill and Wang

Mohanty, Chandra Talpade. 1991. "Cartographies of Struggle: Third World Women and the Politics of Feminism." In *Third World Women and the Politics of Feminism.* Ed. Chandra Talpade Mohanty, Ann Russo, and Lourdes Torres. 1–47. Bloomington: Indiana University Press.

Pérez, Leonor Xóchitl, and Laura Garciacano Sobrino. 1998. *A History of Women in Mariachi Music.* <http://www.mariachi-publishing.com/womenmariachi/index.htm>.

Pérez, Leonor Xóchitl, Sarah L. Truher, Laura G. Sobrino, and Marie-Claire Salla-berry. 1998. "Women in Mariachi: Breaking the Rules, Reclaiming and Reinter-preting Tradition." Society for Ethnomusicology Southern California Chapter Meeting, February 28. University of California at Los Angeles.

Quintanilla, Michael. 1995. "Mariachi Queen Laura Sobrino and Her Band Are Breaking Barriers." *Los Angeles Times*, September 17, E1–E2.

Roach-Higgins, Mary E., and Joanne B. Eicher. 1992. "Dress and Identity." *Cloth-ing and Textiles Research Journal* 10 (4): 1–8.

Rojas, Raymundo E. 1998. "Mariachis Femeniles." Ms.

Torres, Lourdes. 1991. "The Construction of the Self in U.S. Latina Autobiogra-phies." In *Third World Women and the Politics of Feminism*. Ed. Chandra Tal-pade Mohanty, Ann Russo, and Lourdes Torres. 271–81. Bloomington: Indiana University Press.

Treviño, Laramie, and Alejandro Bentancourt. 1996. "Mariachi muchachas: (Pink trajes and all!)." *Latina Magazine Bilingüe*, December, 92–93.

PART 3

TRANSFORMING TRADITIONS

MEETING LA CANTANTE THROUGH VERSE, SONG, AND PERFORMANCE

CÁNDIDA F. JÁQUEZ

As a symbol of Mexican national identity, mariachi performance currently enjoys an international presence that extends beyond the borders of Mexico and the United States into parts of Europe and Asia as well as Latin America. Within this broader performance complex, U.S. mariachi groups form a distinct cultural and social community. Daily practice reveals intersecting issues of traditionalism, nationalism, ethnicity, race, and gender that collectively constitute the production of mariachi's social meaning. Drawing upon Judith Butler's conception of performing gender (1990), this essay explores how multilayered meanings embedded in mariachi performance aesthetics and ideologies form a dialectical relationship between coherency and fragmented dualities, inconsistencies, and internal contradictions located in historicity, lyrical content, and women's entry into the professional mariachi ranks.

The relationship between historicity, lyrical content, and women's entry into the professional mariachi ranks delineates a social performance practice site that is particularly rich in exposing how coherency operates within a web of dualities, inconsistencies, and internal contradictions on a performative plane. Viewing mariachi as a social practice allows for a nuanced discussion of mariachi performance as enmeshed in community daily life. Variegated conceptions of traditionalism, nationalism, ethnicity, race, and gender provide the basic materials from which musicians and audiences create their performative experiences. The historical background to the emergence of urban mariachi sets the tone for how contemporary historical meanings produce a sense of place and time for U.S. mariachi as a social practice. The linkages to a historical past in Mexico draw out notions of regional and ethnic identity and nationalism woven in songs' lyrical structures and content. The words themselves become the invitation to the musicians' skills and motivation in a performative statement that draws upon audience participation.

Women's entry into the ranks of professional mariachi highlights how traditionalism, nationalism, ethnicity, race, and gender are worked out in performance contexts as part of a social practice. Because women's presence in mariachi challenges some of the basic conceptions of who should perform this music and how it should be done, the tensions revealed expose key conceptualizations of traditionalism, nationalism, ethnicity, race, and gender in their active, performative usage. The mariachi performance community considered in this essay is located in the area around Austin, Texas.

HISTORICITY

The contemporary urban mariachi tradition emerged as a symbol of Mexican identity during the postrevolutionary period of the 1920s. In the wake of Mexico's emergent nationalistic agenda, governmental policies evinced rapid, wide-scale reform for a country recovering from over a decade of instability. As part of this agenda, many writers and prominent thinkers argued for the ideological rejection of European forms as cultural models, of which the fine arts played a substantial role. It was a bold rejection of earlier attitudes that had valorized European culture as the scale against which cultural value and progress had been measured. In the arts in general, the look inward focused on those cultural forms construed as uniquely Mexican in their origins. This turn inward was marked by a primitivist aesthetic oriented toward discovering the true roots of *mexicano* culture (Blanquel 1985; Villegas 1985).

In terms of music, the sources were seemingly unlimited in regards to rural mestizo musical forms. The tri-ethnic heritage of these musical expressions (European, in particular Spanish, indigenous, and African) engendered regional musics differentiated primarily by instrumentation, repertoire, and rhythmic organization. Music practice existed as part of a broader context of regionally identified cultural expressions that included such things as dress, food, and subsistence practices. In this sense, the Jalisco region is cited by scholars as the origin of mariachi. The mariachi ensemble began as a Jaliscan string group typified by one or two violins, harp, and a regional guitar. By the 1930s it had developed into the urbanized form we currently recognize—trumpet, violin, *guitarrón* and *vihuela* (regional guitar-like instruments), Spanish guitar, and, occasionally, the Jaliscan harp (Fogelquist 1975; Pearlman 1988; Sheehy 1979). The Mexican postrevolutionary period was marked by intense, though sometimes sporadic, urbanization under nationalistic political agendas. Among other things, rural inhabitants pursued developing economic opportunities and resources in emergent city centers (Katz 1974:32–33). Mestizo musicians participated in these developments.

A mariachi musician in his mid-nineties told me how he had come to the square as a young man around the late 1910s. His original plan had been to come to the city to look for work to support himself and send funds back to his family.

> I had a difficult time. I was young and really didn't have many skills. In those days, you had to compete with many other young men who were looking for work. You sometimes could get a job or two for [a] short time if you were lucky. I played a little guitar and knew maybe two or three songs, so I went around here [Plaza Garibaldi] and played for people as they were eating and drinking. I would play the same songs over and over again—earning whatever people would give me. There were some groups here also playing. I had a pretty good voice and this one group took me under their wing . . . and that's how I became a mariachi!

Scholars have documented the earliest known recordings of mariachi ensembles that had traveled to Mexico City as early as the Porfirio Díaz presidency, just after the turn of the century; however, it was not until after the 1920s that the mariachi tradition commanded an international presence (Sonnichsen 1986a, 1986b) in Mexico's romantic nationalist search for its cultural roots (Blanquel 1985).

The advent of technological developments in radio and later in recording became important factors in the development and dissemination of mariachi as a popular, urbanized expression. What had begun as a regional ensemble quickly developed into a national symbol of pride and ethnic identity. A group's success was in no small part due to its ability to musically reflect, in an expanding repertoire, not only Jaliscan musics but other regionally identified mestizo musics from throughout Mexico. In one sense, musicians responded to the diversity of their urban audiences. In another sense, it was part of an ongoing exchange developed among rural musicians in their itinerant movements in internal migratory patterns within Mexico (Mendoza 1961). It is difficult to trace the emergence of urban mariachi as a distinct performance tradition within the United States. The ethnomusicologist Steven Loza has documented mariachi business ventures in southern California performance venues as early as the 1930s (1993). Some musicians recount an urban mariachi family history that includes a professional presence in the United States as early as the late nineteenth century, again as part of larger migratory patterns, but this time between Mexico and the United States.

As writers such as Gloria Anzaldúa have noted (1987), the politics of identity for Mexican-descent communities this side of the border engender a complexity that is not reducible to the either/or proposition (Mexican or American) that may be invoked, particularly when it comes to issues of cultural identity. The betwixt-and-between conundrum points to a relationship that is mitigated by its own set of contradictions as the process of cultural synthesis demands an ongoing process of retrenchment. Cultural forms necessarily engage these issues.

It is precisely on this point that the ideological basis of mariachi fundamentally differs between the United States and Mexico. Within the United States, Mexican-descent communities exist in a marginalized position from which issues of ethnic identity involve cultural expressions shaped by purposes relevant to contextual circumstances. As Américo Paredes (1963) argues in a discussion of the origins of the *corrido*, expressive forms in the United States by people of Mexican descent arise out of a particular set of historical circumstances. As such, this expressive culture should not be subsumed under a framework that uncritically theorizes it as an extension of Mexico (Paredes 1963) or an imported, bastardized version devoid of originality or distinct meanings. Themes of nationalism, historicity, and ethnic identity that are engendered in mariachi and invoked in the Mexican context take on particular meanings within U.S. Mexican-descent communities as mariachi evolves as a social practice meant to fill the needs and expectations of this particular community. This is perhaps nowhere better illustrated than in the lyrical content of the songs themselves and the performative practice.

LYRICAL CONTENT

Throughout the Southwest and urban centers with significant Mexican-descent communities, professional mariachi performance has emerged as a powerful cultural symbol of ethnic identity. Issues of representation concerning authenticity, traditionalism, and intra-ethnic diversity form the fabric within which musicians and participants consciously engage musical aesthetics as they locate themselves within broader societal structures. Mariachi has historically been a male-dominated tradition that evolved into a male-dominated profession.

A survey of lyrics reveals a male-centered voice that traverses the dominant themes of lost love, love's injustice, women's beauty, and regional or national pride. The traditional *traje* (outfit) is a symbol of male frontierism and landed wealth, as it evokes the figure of the well-dressed *charro*—a figure romanticized by the Mexican film industry during the 1940s and 1950s with such singing film stars as Miguel Aceves Mejía, Pedro Infante, and, more recently, Vicente Fernández. The singers were inevitably accompanied by the sounds of a mariachi, who sometimes were clothed in modest *zarapes* that romanticized the group's rural origins. The frequent appeal to *lo ranchero,* an interpretation of country life as a masculinized sphere of influence, only cemented these images, as the singer would sing from atop his horse or at a country dance or social event—usually in the process of pursuing a reluctant female. As Manuel Peña notes, the evocation of *lo ranchero* has deep roots as a conception of Mexican nationalism within Chicano culture.

> Romantic nationalism in Mexico has exerted a unifying influence by appealing to the glory of the nation's "unique" heritage. As components of this nationalism, the concept of *lo ranchero* and the symbols that cluster around it—of which *música ranchera* is one—have contributed to the ideology by ennobling the existence of hacienda and rural life in general, portraying this existence as idyllic. Since the 1930s the principal vehicles for this portrayal have been film and music, often used in combination. (1985:10–11)

The mariachi repertoire is primarily comprised of *sones, polcas, valses, huapangos, boleros,* and *rancheras.* Though instrumental pieces exist, songs with words dominate. The various song forms or types can be distinguished primarily by meter, tempo, and rhythmic organization. Although *ranchera* music is often defined according to the themes it addresses (in its appeal to *lo ranchero*), it also has a specific musical meaning.

In a *ranchera,* the rhythmic organizing principle as forwarded by the rhythm section (guitar, *vihuela,* and *guitarrón*) often falls along a quadruple or triple meter with the stresses on the first and third or first beats, respectively. Many instrumentalists and singers who are new to the tradition (although sometimes already competent musicians in other musical genres) find the harmonic form and structure deceptively easy to learn; however, they find the *ranchera* stylistic and expressive qualities some of the most difficult to produce. The explanation behind this musical conundrum lies in the chief difficulty of reproducing the affective sentiments and qualities so strongly associated with *ranchera* music. Aspiring Spanish-language popular singers in *mexicano* traditional musics are expected to have command over the vocal inflections, vibrato, and extreme timbre shifts associated with a good *ranchera* singing style. Indeed, in some circles the measure of a good singer of *mexicano* traditional musics is how well a singer can sing a *ranchera*. It becomes the litmus test against which all other abilities are measured.

As an example of this process, the *mexicano* popular music singer Lola Beltrán is skilled in a number of Latino popular music genres; however, it is in *ranchera* music that she is thought to excel, and her name has become synonymous with the genre. This has contributed to her popularity and international presence in Spanish-language venues. In addition to these aspects, a poetic Spanish-language competence is demanded to fully understand the multiple levels of the language being used. Not only does the declamatory style need to be sensitive to syllabic stresses and articulations, double entendre or abstract meanings must be made concrete in their delivery. Even with this technical expertise under control, the expectation is that the technical efforts coalesce into a specific kind of general *ranchera* expressive quality that must be invoked for a singer to successfully perform the piece. It is the *sentimiento,* or active evocation,[1] of a particular kind of historical past that gives life and meaning to the performance.

It is this complexity that is to be commanded and expressed in a good *ranchera* performance. Although the lexical meaning of the words of some *rancheras* deal explicitly with these themes (e.g., "México lindo" [beautiful Mexico], "El rancho grande" [The big ranch], "La ley del monte" [Law of the countryside]), others appear more subtle in their references. "¡Ay Jalisco!" is an example of a *ranchera polca*. It also brings to the fore a series of gender issues that Peña refers to in a general way when speaking of "manliness" as a quality that the *ranchera* invokes (1985:11).

In the world of the idealized rural life and its nationalization as a symbolic core of Mexican culture, love relationships adopt a tenor that is equally provocative in its abstract appeal to idealized circumstances. This is not to say that these idealized circumstances mean that love relationships meet with unmitigated success; on the contrary, many *rancheras* focus on romantic difficulties such as betrayal, misunderstanding, a competing relationship, or unfulfilled desire.

What remains constant and idealized are at least two characteristics that define this stance. The first is that the song texts remain male-centered in their genesis (dominant composers associated with this genre include José Alfredo Jiménez, José Angel Espinoza "Ferrusquilla," Manuel Ezquivel,

Felipe Valdés Leal, and Tomás Mendez) and execution—a male-centered voice dominates the narrative. The second is that the gender relationships are idealized and "normalized" into a dynamic wherein the male figure becomes the pursuer and the female figure assumes a passive role as the object of desire.

"¡Ay Jalisco!" (see the lyrics at the end of this essay) is often performed as the epitome of regional identity predicated upon a sense of nationalism. Its rapid tempo as a *polca* provides an exuberant introduction to what becomes a narrative in which love for a country's region is inscribed upon the body of a young woman, ripe for pursuit. The city of Jalisco takes as its lover the state of Guadalajara in which it is located. The state or homeland is thus feminized, casting woman as the object of desire as an allegory of man's allegiance to his country or land. Issues of courtship and pursuit—"por una morena echar mucha bala / Y bajo la luna cantar en Chapala" (for a brown-skinned woman, fire a lot of bullets / and sing under the moon in Chapala [stanza five])—cement women's availability "lo mismo en los Altos / Que allá en la Cañada" (the same Los Altos as in / Over there in La Cañada [stanza four]).

In actual performance, the focus can easily fall upon issues of regional identity in the performative style and audience participation. A family whose ancestral roots are specifically located in Guadalajara turns in their seats to let out *gritos*[2] of approval as they recognize the instrumental introduction. The mother and her sister shout out "¡eso!" (that's it!) as encouragement to the musicians. The mariachis turn to this table and address their performative statement toward the two women. The two women laugh at the description of Jaliscan women as beautiful and without equal, but only join in singing on the places where Jalisco and a sense of nationalism predominate. Their selective interpretation is neither unusual nor passive.

In another performance context, issues of ethnicity come into focus. A young man and his white girlfriend are sitting at a table with his parents and his siblings. An older brother sings out the lines in stanza four to mock his younger brother's sense of cultural identity because his girlfriend is not Mexican. The mother laughs and scolds the older brother, but by the time the fifth stanza is sung she has her hand on her hip to support her place as a valued Mexican woman. The father joins in the gesturing by shaking a finger and laughingly stating "Ya ves" (you see)[3] to his young son.

Regardless of how strongly these exchanges engage nationalism and ethnicity in the personification of women as an object of desire (synonymous to land to be kept, conquered, and fought for), these are not themes likely to be as overtly raised in other social situations, such as dinner or living-room conversations.

The context of musical performance provides the departure point for creative expression that deals with these potentially explosive issues in a comparatively nonthreatening environment. Though discussion of these issues is framed under the humor and celebratory nature of the performance situation, they carry no less potential danger as pivotal issues for many people of Mexican descent in the United States. It is often a precarious balance between how far things can be taken and when the boundaries have been crossed. A chair is slammed down, and a group in the corner of the church social hall is broken apart by the bride's father with help from his brothers. A young man and his girlfriend are invited to leave, as his cousin holds up his hands saying he didn't "mean nothing by it." The performative frame has been ruptured, and the song lyrics (being performed by a mariachi) that the cousin jokingly referred to in talking about the young man's sister have exceeded the boundaries, as the mariachi and its social practice figuratively (and literally) edge toward the door.

In looking at these issues from the perspective of social control, this is not a world created by equally empowered men and women. The ideological construction of women's bodies and the social control of those feminized bodies as objects of sexual desire in sum take the most efficient route in invoking a cultural metacommentary that validates pursuit and ownership of women. In this sense, the lyrics invite multiple meanings that, under social strictures, must engage this cultural metacommentary—whether or not cultural production unpacks its basis (by selective, interpretive listening practices) or perpetuates it (critical commentary on interracial relations). Within mariachi as a social practice, these processes invoke a context wherein women have not been totally excluded as musical performers or participants. They have a presence; however, it seems that the only mildly acceptable role for women in mariachi performance, and indeed Latino popular musics in general, is that of La Cantante (the female singer)—a role that is even contemporarily reprised in certain mariachi circles as the only truly proper role for women's participation.

WOMEN'S ENTRY INTO THE PROFESSIONAL MARIACHI RANKS

Current trends in the United States reflect an emergent position for women, as they are becoming increasingly represented not only as instrumentalists but as composers and directors as well. During the summer of 1994, I had the opportunity to work with musicians at Plaza Garibaldi in Mexico City. In particular, I was able to work closely with the permanent singer and only female member of the Mariachi de Marina. In general, these musicians maintained that one of the primary differences between U.S. and Mexican mariachi was that the U.S. groups frequently included women instrumentalists on a permanent basis.

It is difficult to speak of exact figures, but it seems that these perceptions of professional U.S. mariachi have some basis, though with some important qualifications. From past work with southwestern mariachi school programs, conferences, and workshops, I have found women and young girls well represented among these amateur or semiprofessional musicians; however, among the largest, most financially successful groups, sometimes referred to as "show mariachis," male musicians dominate the ranks to the almost total exclusion of women, the main exception being an all-women's group based in southern California, Mariachi Las Reynas (the queens), founded within the last five years and, despite excellent musicianship, still regarded as a kind of novelty group. In addition, the number of female participants decreases the further one travels up the rankings of the semi-professional and professional groups.

It is on the basis of these observations and views expressed to me by musicians (both male and female) that I have begun to understand how women's presence in mariachi is created, defined, maintained, and changed on the grounds of conflicting ideologies. It requires little effort to uncover the patriarchal strictures that these apparent gender ideologies imbue. But what exactly can be said beyond noting women's oppression as a kind of binary opposition (Solie 1993:1–20)? Our discussion so far has presented materials that might be interpreted as validating a binary oppositional relationship between men and women as socially constructed beings. The duality does indeed exist on the level of lyrical content, but we have already seen how lyrical content can provide the departure point for a mariachi performance practice that is exceedingly context-sensitive in that people are relating to one another in their performative contexts as they produce mariachi's social meaning in actual lived practice.

In this sense, the polarities and dualities are never clear. The binaries do not function as mutually exclusive relationships but rather as two points along a continuum that can perhaps be partially "magnetized" to pull social expression and practice to one side or another in a given moment. This conception also centralizes how expressions can simultaneously engender elements of seemingly contradictory polarities. This is particularly true in figuring out how women's presence as musicians in mariachi is socially constructed. Even among male musicians who are willing to accept women as instrumentalists, the language portrays the nuances of these highly gendered spaces: "Well, of course a good violinist or singer is good—no matter woman or man"; "we have had some good women musicians on the violin"; "she sings mostly, though sometimes she'll play guitar when we're short a player." While the statements are clearly meant to validate women's presence in mariachi, they also illustrate the unequal acceptance of women in all spheres of musicianship.

Women are not accorded roles, for example, as guitarists or trumpet players as automatically or unconsciously as they are the more socially acceptable roles of violinists or singers. In perhaps the most extreme example, I know of only two female professional *guitarrón* players. It is as if this bass instrument is simply too large and ungainly to be dealt with by a female physique ideologically constructed as too weak and ineffectual.[4] Not incidentally, the *guitarrón* provides the undergirding bass line over which the entire ensemble rests, so it is also as if such musical power should not be located in female hands.

Within the Austin, Texas, mariachi community there have recently been many changes. During the course of my field research, it was not unusual to learn that from week to week certain groups had re-formed or that particular musicians had left one group for another. In addition, Austin mariachi groups frequently borrow musicians from other groups to meet their personnel needs. This general time of change was marked by younger musicians who wanted to improve the state of mariachi performance, both as a practice and a perceived art form.

A mariachi newsletter for the Southwest was founded, and the first Austin Mariachi Espectacular concert sold out the venerable downtown Paramount Theater. The point was aptly and loudly made by organizers that mariachi "had arrived" by occupying a space that was usually reserved for well-established or world-renowned performers such as Ray Charles or the Tibetan Monks. Early critics had doubted that an all-mariachi concert would attract enough patrons to break even. The successful evening ended with a call for expanding the concert and making it an annual event.

Within the Austin mariachi community, El Mariachi Continental is one of six professional groups. With one exception, groups pursue mariachi as an evening and/or weekend profession in addition to a day job. Each mariachi has one main manager or leader and may keep as many as ten players on call. One group, deemed by the others as the best and certainly the longest in existence, is resistant to accepting women on a permanent basis. The leader clearly states that "it's traditional that only men play." The other three groups have women instrumentalists, and one ensemble has a female music director and composer. Mariachi Continental is unique in that it is the only group under a woman's management.

During interviews and substantial videotaping sessions focused on work evenings at an Austin Mexican restaurant, Elida consistently and strongly divulged some of her feelings on what mariachi is and what it should be. At times, as in many other instances with women mariachis, I felt as if she had been waiting for someone to come and hear her story. It was as if I was being taken by the shoulders and would not be let go until I "got it right" and learned the full extent of her story. Elida had immigrated to the United States as a young woman with no formal musical training. Her daughter Carmen had become interested in music and had begun to learn the violin in school orchestra programs. By the time Carmen had reached high school, she had become interested in learning how to play some kind of Mexican music. One of the important considerations for moving the family from one part of town to another was that Carmen would be able to participate in a local high school mariachi program.

Elida emphasized that she felt she had taught her children that they had a great deal to be proud of as Mexican-descent people. For Elida, Carmen's participation in mariachi symbolized this cultural pride through involvement with a long-standing tradition. The problems began when Carmen sought to continue mariachi performance within the local professional ranks. Elida recounted the evenings when her daughter would return home late at night having finished playing and Carmen would tell her about problems dealing with an all-male mariachi group who had only reluctantly recruited her for a temporary trial. Because she was not openly accepted, she even had difficulties assuming what should have been one of her most accepted roles, that of a singer. This inconsistency was laid bare during the first taping session, during which Carmen exhibited skill and poise as a particularly fine *ranchera* singer.[5] As Elida revealed, it wasn't long before she decided to seize the earliest possible opportunity to begin their own mariachi group. Acceptance for Mariachi Continental within the broader mariachi community has been strained at times. The competitive edge for a finite number of engagements leaves little room for even-handed acceptance even among the male-managed groups.

In assuming mariachi leadership and the main management position, Elida has assured herself control of an opportunity to promote her daughter's abilities as a developing musician in a positive, as opposed to antagonistic, environment. Elida has also begun thinking about her group as a possible alternative for other talented young women who face the same problems as her daughter. Just before I left the area, Elida had added a woman *vihuela* player who had participated in the local high school mariachi program and had graduated only to discover limited playing opportunities.

It will be interesting to follow what new traditions Elida begins in her position as mariachi director. Her direction of the group is already seen in local circles as somewhat unusual. She does not really sing or play an instrument. Consequently, during a performance she can often be found standing in the middle of a mariachi ensemble directing with her body—hand motions to the rhythm and melody sections, a nod to the side, and a continual monitoring of the performance situation in making repertoire selections that seem most appropriate. In a telling analysis of the assumptions connected with women's roles in mariachi, many audience members (as well as people who have viewed video clips of this process) wait expectantly for her to burst into song sometime during the evening.

The position of Mariachi Continental, indeed its very existence, points to the inequitable power relationships that exist for women as they seek to control their own cultural production as musicians. They negotiate tradition-bound strictures that are naturalized in an appeal to a historical past that makes them appear timeless and enduring—"it's traditional that only men play." Through these strictures in mariachi as a male-dominated sphere, women must negotiate access to playing opportunities and performative roles that span much wider than that of La Cantante, an image that does not easily recede into the background. In some sense, all women mariachis (whether they actually sing or not) must negotiate the expectations that define who they are and what they should be doing. The strength of strictures that limit access to the professional ranks for women is amply illustrated in the limited numbers of women who, despite the necessary training (in workshops and the local high school program) do not enjoy the same professional opportunities.

CONCLUSION

We have viewed mariachi as a social practice in its performative expression involving musicians and audience participants. By locating the discussion in historicity, lyric content, and women's entry into the professional mariachi ranks, intersecting issues of nationalism, traditionalism, race, ethnicity, and gender have been shown to be mutually constitutive. The dualities, inconsistencies, and internal contradictions explored are not social puzzles in need of solutions; rather, they collectively define a performative plane that forms a coherency in the act of a performative statement (despite the dualities) in daily practice.

As one final comment, in case we have become too comfortable with the notion of a mariachi performative plane, while the experiences of women who inhabit this plane within the Austin mariachi community may be similar, their responses are unique. The question is not whether women experience these strictures, but rather how they respond to them and become active agents while negotiating them. María Castro, herself a product of the Austin high school mariachi program (her father teaches the classes), has chosen to circumvent some of the difficulties of a female mariachi performer by inventing a different performative context. She regularly performs as a solo singer while accompanying herself on guitar at a local Mexican restaurant. As such, she is able to perform within the mariachi tradition with a greater degree of control over her own musical expression. In addition to the traditional *boleros, huapangos,* and *sones,* she regularly includes her own compositions as well as drawing on other musical sources.

She is particularly well known for her renditions of songs by Loretta Lynn ("Honky Tonk Girl," "You Ain't Woman Enough to Take My Man") and Patsy Cline. She states that she enjoys performing those songs and identifies with these women solo singers as strong performance figures. In another sense, she admits that she enjoys the "poke" toward mariachi traditionalism in drawing these seemingly divergent/contradictory musical traditions together. I cannot help but think that musical theoretical analysis has a bit of catching up to do with the María Castros of the world—her dress evokes the appearance of La Cantante in its bright colors, Spanish flair, and bits of lace. A flower draws up her hair and her bouncing steps click the pointy ends of two-inch heels into the floor as she sings it will be "over [her] dead body" that another woman will take her man.

> ¡Ay Jalisco no te rajes!
> (M. Esperón and E. Cortázar)

Ay Jalisco, Jalisco, Jalisco
Tú tienes tu novia que es Guadalajara
Muchacha bonita la perla más rara
De todo Jalisco es mi Guadalajara

Me gusta escuchar los mariachis
Cantar con el alma sus lindas canciones
Oír como suenan esos guitarrones
Y echarme un tequila con los valentones.

Ay-ay-ay-ay
Jalisco no te rajes
Me sale del alma
Gritar con calor, abrir todo el pecho
Pa' echar este grito
Que lindo es Jalisco, palabra de honor.

Pa' mujeres, Jalisco primero
Lo mismo en Los Altos
Que allá en La Cañada
Mujeres muy lindas rechulas de cara
Asi son las hembras de Guadalajara.

En Jalisco se quiere a la buena
Porque es peligroso querer a la mala
Por una morena echar mucha bala
Y bajo la luna cantar en Chapala.

Ay-ay-ay-ay
Jalisco no te rajes
Me sale del alma
Gritar con calor, abrir todo el pecho
Pa' echar este grito
Que lindo es Jalisco, palabra de honor.

Abrir todo el pecho
Pa' echar este grito
Que lindo es Jalisco, palabra de honor.

[Oh Jalisco, Jalisco, Jalisco
You have your girlfriend, it's Guadalajara.
Young, beautiful woman, the most rare pearl
Of all Jalisco is my Guadalajara.

I like to listen to the mariachis,
To sing with soul their beautiful songs.
To hear the sound of those guitars,
Let me go ahead and drink a tequila with the braggarts.

Ay-ay-ay-ay
Jalisco don't give up!
It comes from my soul
To shout with great joy
How beautiful is Jalisco! word of honor.

For women, Jalisco is first
The same in Los Altos as in
Over there in La Cañada
Women very beautiful, with very cute faces
That's how the females of Guadalajara are.

In Jalisco one loves in good faith
Because it's dangerous to want the bad one.
For a brown-skinned woman, fire a lot of bullets
And sing under the moon in Chapala.] (author's translation)

NOTES

1. The initial idea of an evocation of a particular historical past came from a con-versation with Manuel Peña, September 1997, in Fresno, California.

2. A high-pitched yell that often uses some falsetto. In the context of a musical performance, it signals enthusiastic approval and encouragement to the performers. It is considered a specifically Mexican expression and may be called upon in other contexts where ethnic identity is particularly salient.

3. A literal translation is "You see what happens." In this context, it carries con-notations of a call for caution and some corrective measure to be taken.

4. The *guitarrón* requires some force in both hands. The left hand must quickly depress octaves and rapid scalar flourishes with strings that are fairly thick. The right hand must literally "pull" the strings away from the instrument body to produce the proper sound.

5. *Ranchera* refers to a song type that invokes a particular musical singing style and aesthetic. The declamation of the text strives for a kind of impassioned musical interpretation that follows the inspiration of a given text.

WORKS CITED

Anzaldúa, Gloria. 1987. *Borderlands/La Frontera: The New Mestiza*. San Francisco: Aunt Lute.

Blanquel, Eduardo. 1985. "The Mexican Revolution." In *A Compact History of Mex-ico*. Ed. Daniel Cosío Villegas et al. 145–61. Mexico City: El Colegio de México.

Fogelquist, Mark. 1975. "Rhythm and Form in the Contemporary Son Jalisciense." M.A. thesis, University of California at Los Angeles.

Katz, Frederich. 1974. "Labor Conditions on Haciendas in Porfirian Mexico: Some Trends and Tendencies." *Hispanic Historical American Review* 54 (1): 1–47.

Loza, Steven. 1993. *Barrio Rhythm: Mexican-American Music in Los Angeles*. Urbana: University of Illinois Press.

Mendoza, Vicente T. 1961. *La canción mexicana: Ensayo de clasificación y antología*. México, D.F.: Fondo de Cultura Económica.

Paredes, Américo. 1963. "The Ancestry of Mexico's *Corridos:* A Matter of Definitions." *Journal of American Folklore* 76:231–35.

Pearlman, Steve Ray. 1988. "Mariachi Music in Los Angeles." Ph.D. dissertation, University of California at Los Angeles.

Peña, Manuel. 1985. *The Texas-Mexican Conjunto: History of a Working-Class Music*. Austin: University of Texas Press.

Sheehy, Daniel. 1979. "The 'Son Jarocho': The History, Style, and Repertory of a Changing Musical Tradition." Ph.D. dissertation, University of California at Los Angeles.

Solie, Ruth. 1993. "Introduction: On 'Difference.'" In *Musicology and Difference: Gender and Sexuality in Music Scholarship*. 1–20. Berkeley: University of California Press.

Sonnichsen, Philip. 1986a. *The Earliest Mariachi Recordings: 1906–1936*. Notes. Arhoolie Records, Folklyric 9051.

———. 1986b. *Mariachi Coculense de Cirilio Marmolejo: 1933–1936*. Notes. Arhoolie Records, Folklyric 9052.

Villegas, Daniel Cosío. 1985. "The Present." In *A Compact History of Mexico*. Ed. Daniel Cosío Villegas et al. 145–61. Mexico City: El Colegio de México.

RANCHERA MUSIC(S) AND THE LEGENDARY LYDIA MENDOZA

PERFORMING SOCIAL LOCATION AND RELATIONS

YOLANDA BROYLES-GONZÁLEZ

> Me gusta cantarle al viento
> porque vuelan mis cantares,
> y digo lo que yo siento
> por toditos los lugares.
>
> Atravesé la montaña
> pa' venir a ver las flores,
> no hay cerro que se me empine
> ni cuaco que se me atore.
> —From "La feria de las flores,"
>   *canción ranchera* by Jesús "Chucho" Monge
>
> I like to sing to the wind
> because my songs fly
> and I say what I feel
> throughout all places.
>
> I crossed the mountain
> to come see the flowers,
> there is no mountain too high
> nor horse that will falter.[1]

La canción ranchera. Música ranchera. "Ranchera" (country or rural) songs and music(s). What is this so-beloved and so-maligned music? And how to understand the ecstatic, tragic, and profound flow between that music and the people who cherish it, the communities who know and sing the songs and pass them on across generations and geographies? How do we grasp this enduring popular *raza* music, whose traditions and underground superstar idols are dismissed (or not even perceived) by academic culture critics?[2] Dismissed along with it is the humanity of the people who carry the weight of the tradition, the low-income *raza*.[3] This dismissal is evident in many of the epithets for *raza* collectives living below the poverty line yet rich in cultural expression and legacy: *peladas/os* (lumpen proletariat), *broncs* (north of the border), *nacas* (south of the border), *borrachos/as* (drunks; with their *música de cantina* [bar music]), *la chusma* (the masses), *gente con el nopal en la frente* (people with a cactus on their forehead), *rancheritos y rancheritas* (hicks), *mojados y mojadas* (wetbacks), *la plebe* (the masses), *la palomilla* (the gang).

La canción ranchera is one of the most powerful musics of our time, with a following deeply rooted in oral traditions of poetic imagery and musical expression. Families and communities transmit the musical refrains, sentiments, melodies, and life stories associated with various songs across multiple generations and across the geographies of long migrations criss-crossing the Americas—"Hey, that's my cousin Hector's song. . . . Do you remember when he . . . "; "Play me my Abuelita's favorite: 'La ley del monte' [Law of the countryside]. Remember how she always . . . ." How to understand the seemingly simple yet profound poetry of the people, the power, and resonance of *ranchera* songs?

Like the songs, the artists who perform them become idolized, iconized, and legendary. Closely identified with the beloved songs, the singers who interpret them rank near the top of the pantheon of popular heroes, beloved for their ability to articulate the sensibilities and experiences of the people: Lydia Mendoza, Lucha Reyes, Jorge Negrete, Pedro Infante, Lola Beltrán, Las Jilguerillas, Las Hermanitas Huerta, Vicente Fernández, David Zaízar, José Alfredo Jiménez, Esteban Jordán, Valerio Longoria, Andres Huesca, Juan Gabriel, Joan Sebastian, Chalino Sánchez, and many more etched in the collective memory.[4]

Among the earliest and most revered of these popular transnational idols was the legendary Lydia Mendoza. Born in 1916 in Houston, Texas, she was performing music by the age of seven and recording before the age of twelve. Although she is unknown among academics, her phenomenal performance career spans two-thirds of the twentieth century. At age seven she began to learn guitar from her mother; shortly thereafter she began performing within the newly established family performance collective. In 1928 she became one of the first *raza* recording artists when she and her family recorded a handful of beloved songs from the oral tradition, including "Cuatro milpas," one of the most powerful and enduring anthems from the Mexican Revolution of 1910:

Cuatro milpas tan sólo han quedado
del ranchito que era mío
ay, ay, ay, ay
de aquella casita tan blanca y bonita
lo triste que está.

[. . .]

Y por eso estoy triste morena,
por eso me pongo a llorar
recordando las horas felices
que juntos pasamos en mi dulce hogar.[5]

[Only four corn fields remain
of my little ranch
Ay, ay, ay, ay
of that small house, so white and beautiful
how sad it stands.

And that is why, my sad dark one,
that is why I weep
remembering the happy hours
we spent together in my sweet home.]

Mendoza's rise to popularity was launched in 1934 with the enormous and almost instant success of her recording of "Mal hombre," which is not a *ranchera* song but is sung in *ranchera* style.[6] With that recording she initiated a career that always included womanist perspectives (in addition to other *ranchera* thematics). The already popular song "Mal hombre" became even more popular through her voice, which convincingly delivered a stinging social commentary denouncing the unfair treatment of women:

Luego hiciste conmigo lo que todos
los que son como tú con las mujeres,
por lo tanto no extrañes que yo ahora
en tu cara te diga lo que eres:

Mal hombre,
tan ruin es tu alma que no tiene nombre.
Eres un canalla, eres un malvado,
eres un mal hombre.[7]

[Then you did with me what all men
who are like you do with women,
so therefore don't be surprised if
I tell you to your face what you are:

Evil man
your soul is so despicable that it has no name.
You are a scoundrel, you are a wicked man,
you are an evil man.]

From her earliest solo recordings to her last (a span of over sixty years),
Mendoza's repertoire provides us with a rich discursive site for investigat-
ing the sexual and gender politics of *raza* working-class communities as well
as the feminisms and womanisms of the oral tradition that have been the
unacknowledged precursors to (and which continue to parallel) more recent
academic feminisms. At a time when it was largely a taboo subject within
academic discourse, Lydia Mendoza openly sang about sexuality, as in one
of her favorite songs, "Mujer paseada" (experienced woman). This song
departs from widely held academic (and popularized) stereotypes and discourses concerning "traditional" working-class notions of women's virginity and chastity. In this song, the lover proclaims that it simply does not
matter that the loved one has had abundant sexual experience. Thus, it
openly enacts a particular sexuality and sexual agency by valuing as a life
partner a *mujer paseada,* a sexually experienced woman:

Así te quiero mujer,
no le hace que seas paseada.
Te quiero porque te quiero
de las entrañas del alma.[8]

[That is how I love you, woman,
it matters not that you are experienced.
I love you because I love you
from the depths of my soul.]

These and other collective songs performed by Mendoza and other women
rehearsed narratives of identity and cemented a strong platform for the
continued circulation and negotiation of womanist (*mujerista,* feminist)
values and movements since time immemorial. This is an untapped discursive realm for anyone interested in tracing feminist/*mujerista* origins and
voices as well as masculinist narratives.

Lydia Mendoza forged one of the longest performance and recording careers in the history of American music. Her struggles to establish herself as one of the first public and professional entertainers and recording artists paved the way for thousands of others to follow. Mendoza's extraordinary transnational resonance was made possible in part by the advent of the new sound recording industries in the 1920s. Radio and phonograph technologies facilitated her widespread resonance, which at some levels is the very resonance of the people whose collective songs were channeled through her body and voice. She was a musician trained in the ancient oral tradition of *música de talón:* wandering street musicians who commingle among their principal constituents and sing the collectively cherished songs the people request. Mendoza was obliged to know by heart the repertoire of the oral tradition, weaving and mending the cloth of working-class *raza* culture, those shifting strands of collective consciousness enacted in the circle of songs. She continued the practice of singing traditional songs by popular demand until the late 1980s, when a debilitating stroke ended her musical career.

Mendoza's musical repertoire encompasses a diverse array of borderlands Mexican musical forms from the oral tradition—the *canción ranchera, corridos* (narrative ballads), *huapangos, boleros*—as well as musical styles and genres that migrated to the borderlands and beyond (such as tangos, *milongas, pasodobles*). I focus here on Lydia Mendoza and the *canción ranchera,* perhaps the most popular and enduring of Mexican love song genres. Mendoza and the *canción ranchera* are vastly underresearched domains, in contrast to the *corrido,* for example. Neither Mendoza nor the *canción ranchera* have enjoyed any sustained critical attention.[9] Mendoza nonetheless is a living legend and a towering figure in U.S., Mexican, and Latin American cultural history. Her audiences have fondly given her a number of nicknames—"La Alondra de la Frontera" (lark of the Borderlands), "La Cancionera de Los Pobres" (singer of the poor), "La Gloria de Tejas" (the glory of Texas)—each highlighting and marking important attributes of class origin and affiliation; of geographic place; of the immense pride people projected onto her; and of her musical artistry, her voice as pleasing and migratory as that of a songbird capable of transcending unnatural boundaries and national borders.

Besides performing *ranchera* songs on a regular basis, Mendoza self-consciously embodied the gendered rural/ethnic "ranchera" (country) or "norteña" (northerner's) persona in her performances. She designed, sewed, and hand-decorated all her characteristic bold-configured and highly stylized Mexican *regional* (rural) sequined and brightly flowered dresses. She manifests the *ranchera* aesthetic in her dress, her song stylistics, and her musical repertoire. Her image grew and was established first and foremost in remote rural migrant agricultural communities throughout Texas, northward to Michigan, and later to the West. Mendoza traveled the agricultural migratory labor routes and established herself in that down-to-earth image by playing for pennies among the people, living and suffering with them. She was one of them and sang the songs in that unmistakable and unembellished strong yet natural voice. In many ways she cultivated and helped define a rural-based aesthetic that later found its way into the imaginary of the cities.

My purpose here is to examine how Mendoza's crucial network of popular *ranchera* songs constructs social meaning, including a common ground across differences, of working-class identity formation and thus social empowerment. Her agency in that process is prime. For a more sustained and encompassing treatment of Mendoza and Mexican popular musics, I refer readers to my bilingual book, *Lydia Mendoza's Life in Music/La historia de Lydia Mendoza—Norteño Tejano Legacies.*[10]

IMAGINED COMMUNITIES: THE COUNTRY AND THE CITY, CENTERS AND PERIPHERIES, EL RANCHO AND THE NATION

There exists a powerful mythical space within *raza* culture, a historical and imagined space that no one—even those who have never been there—can escape, evade, or ignore. It is a space of sociocultural origin that pervades and infuses contemporary *raza* existence, even in its most urbanized and sophisticated self-fashionings. It is that rural place of origin, known as "el rancho," where we lived before we moved to the cities and where the people can trace their deepest roots: the land. When *raza* refers to "mi tierra" (my land), the reference is not to any nation-state but to that physical rural geography of origin. Most of what we know (or don't know) as "rancho" is the domain of the rural landbase, of homeland, of the ancestral lands from which untold millions have been displaced, removed, and dislocated on all sides of all national borders. Today, *rancho* or *ejido* is the domain of difficult subsistence farming in remote places, where a few families or clans cluster together and work for the most part collectively: A few *milpas* (corn patches), and in their midst the *calabazas* (squash) and bean plants growing in symbiotic relationship with the corn stalks; A handful of other plants and some animals; *Las casitas* (the little houses) made of diverse natural materials, often with thatched roofs. A river flows nearby and provides water, a place to bathe and wash clothes, a place where lovers meet, a place to weave stories into legends, and a place to sing the old songs or *canciones*. From those *canciones*, which have come down through the centuries, the *canción ranchera* evolved at the turn of the century. The *ranchera* features a simpler harmonic structure and rhythm and a more elaborate melodic line than the *canción*. "Ranchera" generally refers to the popular rural musics of the various geographical regions, and the *canción ranchera* thus serves as a major repository for *rancho* iconography.

Lydia Mendoza's repertoire is on the evolutionary cusp, embracing both the *canción* and the *canción ranchera*. Her enduring popularity—as well as that of her repertoire—speaks to the extraordinary love for song (particularly the love song) and its centrality among the native peoples of the Americas in what is today Mexico, Latin America, and the the United States. The crucial centrality of song is documented by the Nahuatl-speaking peoples in expressions such as "Only through songs does our pain on earth subside" or "Wherever I walk, wherever I sing, is a blooming of flowers, a swelling of song, and there my heart is alive."[11] How to analytically express the working-class "structures of feeling" that are transmitted, evoked, and negotiated by the *canción ranchera* within the lived and changing realities of the Mexican twentieth-century diaspora of *la gente ranchera* (the rural people)?

Musics are major markers of shifting popular identities within the push and pull of twentieth-century capitalism. The industrialization, urbanization, and migration that has accelerated sharply since the 1930s in Mexico and the United States has created tension between the rural and urban cultural spheres—replete with mutual stereotyping and derision and power struggles articulated in part through musical traditions. Localized social tension is enmeshed in the violent larger process of nation formation, global capitalist development, and the historically attendant regionalist (rural) uprisings seeking to claim local autonomy in the face of a centralizing hegemonic power and globalizing economic interests. The emergence and dissemination of the *canción ranchera* plays a crucial role in that tension between the rural and the urban, between the deeply rooted rural and the uprooted overnight metropolis. In fact, the *canción ranchera* is a part of the contested space between the two overlapping cultural geographies of a migratory people with long roots. Seen historically, the emergence and mass popularization of the *canción ranchera* is inversely related to *raza's* presence on the landbase. In the 1930s most *raza* still lived and worked in rural environs; today over 90 percent live in urban centers. The *canción ranchera*—replete with *rancho* scenarios, symbols, and remembrances—grew in pop-

ularity and predominance in the 1930s and 1940s with the sharply rising
raza exodus to the cities. The move to urban centers urbanized the popu-
lace and countrified the cities. As early as 1936, the *ranchera* star Jorge
Negrete eked out a living singing *rancheras* in New York City on a National Broadcasting Company radio show. Lydia Mendoza played an important
role in this process of countrification, transforming the city into a rural
imaginary. Her voice helped establish and consolidate the imagined communities of U.S. Mexicans and Mexican immigrants during one of the greatest migratory periods. Lydia Mendoza's presence and voice became a space
of reintegration, reflection, and collectivity during periods of extreme dis-
location and relocation. Initially through her travels and tours along the
migrant labor trails and later through the emergent media of radio and the
recording industry, her voice and repertoire physically gathered displaced
workers into listening collectives and auditory communities. Her voice established a focal point and presence among the massive migratory movements (forced and/or voluntary) of the thirties, and it continues to do so in
the present.

Throughout these decades many songs remained constants in her repertoire; one example is "Canción mixteca" (Mixtec song) which gives strong
expression to the *sentimiento,* the pain and melancholy of uprootedness and
migration from the beloved place of origin:

> Qué lejos estoy del suelo donde he nacido,
> inmensa nostalgia invade mis pensamientos
> Y al verme tan solo y triste cual hoja al viento
> quisiera llorar, quisiera morir de sentimiento.
>
> Oh tierra del sol!
> suspiro por verte,
> ahora que lejos
> me encuentro sin luz, sin amor.
> Y al verme tan solo y triste cual hoja al viento
> quisiera llorar, quisiera morir de sentimiento.[12]
>
> [I am so far from the land of my birth,
> an immense nostalgia invades my thoughts
> and seeing myself alone and sad like a leaf in the wind
> I want to cry, I want to die—so deep is the feeling.
> Oh, land of the sun,
> I sigh, wishing to see you
> now that I am far away and

I find myself without light, without love
and seeing myself alone and sad like a leaf in the wind
I want to cry, I want to die—so deep is the feeling.]

Mendoza remained a constant presence throughout the changes and turmoil of the record-breaking immigration northward from rural Mexico after the Mexican Revolution and during the forced deportations southward under the racist scapegoating policies of the U.S. government. Those deportations included forced repatriations (1930s and 1950s) of *raza* peoples, akin to many other Indian removal policies.

However simple the *canción ranchera* may seem on the surface, its meanings and performance are linked to questions of power and politics.[13] Working-class interests, strategies, and mobilizations ("social history") have always been reflected in rural musics. Music forms a discursive space in which migration, urbanization, and nation formation are filtered, processed, assessed, critiqued, denied, danced, and cried. Mexican revolutionary leaders always brought rural musicians with them when they seized Mexico City, symbolically displacing the Eurocentric tastes imposed by the "national" traditions of elites. Upon recognizing the tenacity of the rural, the Mexican postrevolutionary nation and its elites even try to harness (appropriate) rural iconographies within the homogenizing narrative of the nation, a tacit recognition of the one million peasant lives that were lost in battle. The president orders *ranchera* music to be played at festive events, and mariachi bands from the *ranchos* of Jalisco are enlisted as "national" symbols. Yet the *rancho* remains antithesis of the nation-state and of the nation's maneuvers of forced incorporation (usually through land seizures) and homogenization (through the educational system). The *ranchera,* by contrast, works to cement local allegiance; the imagined community is not the nation but the *rancho,* the communally held farmlands. The *canción ranchera* dramatically proclaims a non-national order of things ("¡Ay, mi casita de paja!" [Oh, my little straw house!]) and produces counternarratives of popular rural identity at a historical juncture (from the late nineteenth century to the present) when rural life and culture are being decimated by extensive government/corporate-sponsored land seizures. In Mexico, common *ejido* lands were seized by foreign capital during Porfirio Díaz's dictatorship of thirty years, and in the United States, *raza* lands were seized by the forest service and by the massive Anglo land theft of westward expansion. In the context of continual land struggles—as diverse as those over the Tierra Amarilla in New Mexico, the Yaqui River in Sonora, Arizona's Big Mountain, or that

of the Zapatistas in Chiapas—the *canción ranchera* creates a popular poetics of space that tenaciously remembers and even idealizes rural lifeways
under attack as the nation-states sell out to foreign investors. The *canción
ranchera* typically pays homage to local particulars of geographic region and
physical rural particularities, not to the nation.

Among the *ranchera* songs that Lydia Mendoza recorded in 1928 with her
family, for example, is one extolling the beauty of Monterrey, where they
had family roots. Significantly, the northern Mexican metropolis of Monterrey is described in almost strictly rural terms:

> ¡Ay tierra de mis ensueños,
> quien estuviera en la orilla!
> Y ¡Ay, que chulo es Monterey,
> con su Cerro de la Silla!
>
> Es tierra de bendiciones
> toda buena y toda noble,
> porque allí se apareció
> la Virgencita del Roble.
>
> Que me entierren en el campo
> en una tumba sencilla,
> donde pueda yo mirar
> ese Cerro de la Silla.[14]
>
> [Oh, land of my dreams,
> would that one be at its outskirts!
> And oh how beautiful is Monterrey
> with its Saddleback Mountain!
>
> It is a land of blessings
> all good and all noble,
> because it was there that
> our Lady of the Oak appeared.
>
> Let me be buried in the country
> in a simple tomb
> where I can see
> that Saddleback Mountain.]

Like many *rancheras,* this one conjures not only the land (*el campo*) but also
the domain of popular spirituality that runs so deep (encapsulated here by
reference to the miraculous narrative of the Virgencita del roble). The nar-

rative tenor is the common heartfelt longing for a return to the beloved homeland—the return that immigrant populations often yearn for and rarely achieve. That yearning becomes a constant within the *ranchera* song tradition. Mendoza also sang "Mexico lindo y querido" (dear and beloved Mexico), which became among the most famous "yearning" *rancheras* and the signature song of the *charro cantor* (singing horseman) Jorge Negrete. In that song—and in numerous others like it—the homeland Mexico is constructed as a rural landbase and not as a national territorial geography. The longing for "Mexico" is not a nationalism but a ruralism and regionalism rooted in the land itself:

> Que me entierren en la sierra
> al pie de los magueyales
> y que me cubra esta tierra
> que es cuna de hombres cabales.[15]
>
> [May they bury me in the wild
> at the foot of the maguey fields
> and may the earth
> that is the cradle of honest men
> be my coverlet.]

Even in popular usage, *mi tierra* (my land) refers to regional cultural geographies and not to "country" as nation-state. Similarly, the *ranchera* tenaciously extols the particulars of the *rancho* and *pueblito* (small town), even after being successfully transplanted into the big city. Thus the rural-urban binary is not only oppositional but also complementary. Rural and urban are (to this day) in constant dialogue and interchange; they are spheres of mutual influence. Ironically, the more migration there is to cities the more rural the cities become. (The recent urban *quebradita* dance movement—featuring rural attire and musics—provides ample testimony to this.) The migration to cities has historically been from the country. Thus the city becomes an outpost of the country. And for all the migration to the cities, there is always a contingency of familial relations who stay behind in the *rancho,* adding to the exchange between the two. For all of the rural imagery in Mendoza's songs, she spent most of her life in big cities—just like José Alfredo Jiménez, the most prolific composer of *ranchera* songs at mid-century.

Mendoza's voice has been heard and loved in rural and urban contexts since the 1930s, providing an affirmative social space amid the increasing-

ly restricted geopolitical and economic contexts of the twentieth century—
which currently include the devastating economic aftermath of NAFTA,
severe human rights abuses against *raza* peoples in the borderlands, and the
environmental degradation of the planet (which always includes the mis-
treatment of peoples). Across times and changing contexts, *ranchera* music
helps feed and give expression to the soul of *raza* workers in the state of siege.
Mendoza's voice and guitar transcends physical and temporal boundaries,
serving as a consolidating agent across generations and across regions; she
has become a multivalent counterforce to the displacement, uprooting, exile, migration, and Euro-homogenization and assimilation emanating from
elitist Euro-American policies and practices, institutions, and transnational capital as well as the repressive apparatus of the nation-state. Through
her recordings and itinerant performance career beginning in the 1920s,
Lydia Mendoza contributed immensely to the creation of a far-flung auditory community, thus enacting a transnational (supranational) *raza* sociocultural circuitry and cohesion that in many ways supersedes the "imagined
community" of nation-states. Bonfil Batalla describes the importance of such
resistant grassroots cultural expressions within the contemporary reality of
raza people's "restricted cultural spheres" or the "reduced universe of social life" on the economic margins of society (1996:136). Within those restricted cultural spheres the *canción ranchera* has survived and thrived while
many other song and cultural forms (some with heavy corporate backing)
have retreated and even vanished. The sheer exuberance of the *canción
ranchera* (along with its general proliferation) needs to be understood within
and outside of this context of social restraints bred by expanding capitalism and Third World governments who protect profits and not working
peoples who produce the profits.

PERFORMING SOCIAL RELATIONS THROUGH COLLECTIVE SONG

Notwithstanding its immense popularity, the *canción ranchera* is widely
dismissed by some as insignificant or "merely" love songs and by others as
escapist or apolitical. Others have reduced the *ranchera* to the "treacherous
woman" trope, ignoring the preponderance of other images. What I seek
to analyze here are the ways in which the *canción ranchera* functions as a
living working-class social practice that variously enacts and rehearses social relations, locations, and meanings—a particularly necessary exercise in
these times of harder work for lower wages, expanding prisons, and ram-
pant violence in urban centers and within U.S. foreign policy. George Lip-

sitz has examined how contemporary musical cultural production is an important site of self-creation and re-creation, particularly among peoples marginalized by the oppressive nation-states: "At a time when transnational capital and repressive state apparatuses hold the upper hand everywhere, cultural production plays a vital role in nurturing and sustaining self-activity on the part of aggrieved peoples. Culture enables people to rehearse identities, stances, and social relations not yet permissible in [national] politics. But it also serves as a concrete social site, a place where social relations are constructed and enacted as well as envisioned" (Lipsitz 1994:137). Music has figured among the most prominent of individual and collective self-constitutive practices and domains for *raza* peoples since before colonization. Songs are invaluable resources in which communities rehearse, codify, and transmit what Bakhtin has called "the unofficial truth . . . about the world" (1984:91)—the marginalized knowledges of *raza* in the Americas. Those sung knowledges encompass a broad spectrum, including everyday human values strategically deployed in the face of adversity; diverse knowledges of gender relations and sexual relations; the historical and humanistic knowledges of *corridos;* the verbal play and cultural vocabularies of lullabies; and the spiritual knowledges of hymns or *alabanzas* (song chants). The flow of song in Chicana/o communities functions as a free shared space or forum for the collective to air a host of contending ideas, ideologies, interests, values, love configurations, tragic circumstances, humorous situations, social analyses, theoretical positions, emotions, and collective rural (or ruralized urban) memory in all its registers, harmonies, and contradictions. I can only sketch and summarize here some aspects of the *canción ranchera* as living social practice.

Channeling Human Flow and Desire

For those singing, listening to, or dancing a *canción ranchera,* the music and lyrics work together as a cultural channel of human flow and desire. Among the unique characteristics of the *canción ranchera* is its boldness and directness; admired performers have the ability to hit at the root of a highly charged emotion, to capture a *sentimiento:* "¡Si piensas abandonarme, mejor quitame la vida!" (if you plan to abandon me, you may as well kill me instead!). The *ranchera* emotes without much narrativizing; you fill in the blanks with your own desires. There is a powerful engagement of passion, a release of deep happiness or deep sorrow, love, hatred, or unmitigated enjoyment—often linked through memory to other contexts in which that song was experienced or to the loved ones who cherish the song.

These songs serve as a momentary and autonomous space of rehumaniza-tion, often culminating in the ritualized *grito* or piercing primordial scream, which powerfully releases emotions through the body (or bodies) and soul. *Ranchera* songs and *gritos* often function as a collective sociotherapy ac-knowledging and healing wounds—or tearing them open again. The plea-sure or pain summoned forth by the *canción ranchera* and its attendant *gritos* is simultaneously emotional, mental, and physical, often including dance as a prime component. One of the features that distinguishes the *canción ranchera* from the *corrido,* for example, is the emotional tension and upheaval created and sustained by the *ranchera,* while the *corrido* maintains a detached narrative tone.

How to understand the vibratory field of the rhythmic and harmonic flow of the *ranchera*? And how does it affect the social biofield? The sensory nature of oral tradition is little understood. It requires *all* the senses for its transmission. Beyond words, its beats and melodies evoke deep memory and transfer subtle essences that flow and travel—like wind, water, and fire—from one person to another. That flow moves within the physical and spir-itual universe. The musical beats, harmonies, melodies, and words produce sublime effects: laden vibratory and auditory fields of memory, collectively validated and cherished musical fields that help define social relations and social movement.[16] The deeply emotional and collectively charged quality of *ranchera* music has the ability to tap into deep levels of being. As such, it is able to bridge the gap between the deep unconscious and conscious aware-ness in the here and now. The ineffable powers of musical flow, of musical intervals, defies description; yet they directly touch and reorganize deep levels of being, of desire, and of meaning. Musical vibrational fields can enhance or suppress electromagnetic fields, altering their relationships. Vibration alters all chemical and physical processes.

Among the existential realms touched and transformed by the vibration-al field of music is the untold suffering and indignities experienced at the workplaces of physical wage labor. Music is a physically and spiritually transformative process. Seen in this way, we can only fathom the survival-ist importance of musical rehumanization by examining it in the context of dehumanizing working-class jobs and chronically violent *raza* histories.[17] The social powers of music variously function within Mexican, Latina/o, and Native American culture as a prime humanizing force or as an alterna-tive force or counternarrative in the face of evil or debilitating circumstances.

Remembering the Mesoamerican Cultural Matrix/Homeland

Many love songs—in particular the *ranchera* variety favored by Lydia Mendoza—are much more than songs about love. The love situation is always supported by vocabulary, imagery, values, customs, landscapes, material culture, and symbols from the cultural matrix of Mesoamerica, the deep roots of Mexican culture and its changing and unchanging symbols of identity. Love (and its attendant grief, disappointment, ecstasy, passion, death, and birth) happens amid cornfields, cactus, trees, *rebozos,* birds, beloved rural geographies, and the larger natural environment, such as the open sky, and amid the deep connection to and love for the land and rural places of origin (*el rancho*) and its icons and symbols from the plant and animal kingdom ("¡Ayyyyy, que laureles tan verdes!" [Oh, how green are the laurels!]). Significantly, the markers of *raza* popular spiritual practices and sacred spaces also figure prominently. In short, the *canción ranchera* circulates as a meaning-full storehouse and symbolic repository of the indigenous *raza* cultural matrix. Frequently referenced items, such as horses, geographical landmarks, specific plants (i.e., corn or the maguey plant), the woman's *rebozo,* the saints, and spiritual markers, function as what Charles L. Briggs has called "triplex signs" (1988:2). Each of these loaded signifiers encompasses at least three interrelated spheres of meaning. They evoke an entire way of life and the land-based self-sufficiency that *raza* enjoyed for many hundreds and even thousands of years. These terms also serve as nutshells or encapsulations for the chain of events that have deprived *raza* of land and of the rural way of life. These are powerfully evocative terms; each stands for the whole, and the whole is the *rancho* economy: living on the land, self-sufficiency, roots. The *rancho* provides the setting for an emotional life in all its registers, from ecstasy to tragedy.[18] The *ranchera* encodes the full panoply of social roles played by men, women, children, and elders in relation to a higher power within the natural environment.

The "homeland" scenarios summoned by the *canción ranchera* function on various levels depending on the performance context. An urban context differently filters the *canción ranchera,* vesting "el rancho" with additional urban meanings, translations, knowledges, desires, dreams, and fantasies. For predominantly urban *raza* peoples of the late twentieth century in the United States, the *canción ranchera* is one complex pivot in the process of identity formation and negotiation. The images from the "homeland" can evoke a moment or movement of decolonial cultural consciousness, or what the cultural critic Juan Flores calls the "state of enchantment," in the face of otherwise oppressive and alienating social contexts. The *rancho* thus becomes a mythical fairy-tale realm, fueling that deep longing for a better place and relations that can translate into or accompany social movements.

Constructing an Auditory Collective/Community

The *canción ranchera* is a prominent oral tradition in constant circulation within the barrios. It performs and evokes collective memory and knowledge and remains one of the richest of *raza* archives and popular curricula. Ranchera music audibly expresses community memory and storyworld; it is a part of our social apprenticeship within Mexican communities. The *canción ranchera,* through Lydia Mendoza's voice and body, deterritorialized "Mexicanness" and reconstituted it into a non-national diasporic auditory community. Within the more intimate context of celebration and mourning, the *canción ranchera* opens up a cohesive space within communities, marking reunions, separations, kinship, and the experience and re-experience of manifold encounters, relationships, and solidarities (including bonds of enmity).

These songs circulate collectively and rise to prominence through the approbation of collectives who sing the songs and call out requests to performing singers. The close relationship between *ranchera* idols and their communities—and their mutual rootedness in traditional song—is evident at every performance. Throughout her career, Lydia Mendoza was an agent in the circulation of the beloved songs; she always took song requests: "Ya saben que aquí vengo en cuerpo y alma con mi guitarra a cantar lo que ustedes quieran. ¡Pídanme lo que quieran! ¿Cuál quieren oír?" (You already know I come with body and soul with my guitar, giving you what you want. Ask for what you want to hear, what do you want to hear?). She always sang from the collectively established repertoire of the oral tradition. Songworld is a collective auditory space and legacy that extends across generations and geographies. Beginning in the 1920s, the formidable collectivizing powers of music were augmented through the rise of the new sound technologies (film, radio, recordings, and later television), which enabled the growth of "mass culture" within which traditional roots music has managed to survive and thrive.[19]

Self-Processes/Strategies of Personhood

Taken as a body, love songs manifest a broad discursive range, serving (individually and collectively) as sounding boards for a diversity of social positionalities pertaining to gender relations, sexual relations, environmental relations, and the broader domain of human relations—for creating and recreating culture and subjectivities. The symbolic *ranchera* cultural archive serves up a heterogeneous vision of human possibilities and impossibilities. The singer and listeners of each song rehearse strategies of personhood or selfhood with multiple fractures, contradictions, maskings, differences, and affirmations; each song offers a shift in the articulation of identity. The range of possible moves is encyclopedic, and with each song you can take it or leave it. Everyone has favorite songs, and others they don't like. In any event, each love story unfolds in relation to the cultural matrix, providing the listener, the singer, and the community with a negotiation of personhood and identity vis-à-vis the song and each other. The song narratives together comprise an "art of operating" or a theory of life practices and behaviors. Songs continually replay real and symbolic enactments within everyday activities and contexts (see Certeau 1984:78) as well as imaginary contexts. Those who cultivate these songs are free to establish relationships between the domain of song and other lived domains. The body of songs thus presents and re-presents knowledge of behaviors and values from which listeners can negotiate and navigate the boundaries or boundlessness of collective and individual identities.[20] Songs are thus a social visioning process, a factor in constituting reality.

CHANGING TRADITIONS

Love songs circulate among *raza* in a rich variety of forms, including *ranchera* songs, *boleros, baladas,* lyrical love *corridos, huapangos, valses,* and *cumbias,* with innumerable themes and scenarios. Lydia Mendoza's repertory spans all forms and themes, yet her preference for the *canción ranchera* is undeniable. Her songs encompass "love" in a broad range of possibilities, including familial love (particularly for the mother figure, as in her classic "Amor de madre" [A mother's love]), love of place of origin ("Mexico lindo y querido" [Beloved beautiful Mexico]), love of the land or lost homeland ("Cuatro milpas" [Four cornfields]); the dispassionate love of old age ("Cuando estemos viejos" [When we are old]); romantic passion ("El lirio" [The lily]); romantic betrayal; unrequited love ("Celosa" [Jealousy]); happy adoration ("Amor bonito" [Beautiful love], which she authored); and aggrieved love due to death ("Cuando se pierde la madre" [When one loses one's mother]). Mendoza performed and recorded many of these songs throughout her career (e.g. "Mal hombre," "Cuatro milpas," "Amor de madre," "Besando la cruz," "El lirio"), and many of them are popularly

identified with her voice and person. These figured among the songs that
audiences always requested from her. I once witnessed a street concert in
San Antonio where Mendoza sang "Mal hombre" three times, by popular
demand. Love is constructed and sung in a broad range of musical vocabularies, poetic styles, and metaphoric languages—a rich universe that requires
its own extended study. Among those favored by Mendoza are the many
ranchera "bird" songs that reference the impassioned relationship through
bird imagery. One of her favorites is "Pajarito prisionero":

> Un lindo pajarito cierto día
> herido refugiose en mi ventana
> y yo lo recojí compadecida
> brindándole el amor que le faltaba.
>
> Pajarito, pajarito que en tu jaula vives prisionero
> yo también por un amor iqual que tú de pena muero.[21]
>
> [One day a beautiful wounded bird
> sought refuge in my window
> and I with pity took it in
> offering it the love it lacked.
>
> Little bird, little bird, living in your cage, prisoner
> I too because of love, just like you, die of sadness.]

Although many songs come down through the generations, Mendoza's
performance career within the memory arts and traditional Mexican music(s)
should not be construed as static and unchanging. Her changing relationship to music and to musical influences was a contradictory process, involving change within a dynamic continuity. "Tradition" means that diverse
tejano musics (which are diverse with regards to race/ethnicity, gender, class,
sexuality, and regionality) exist in a vital state of change and exchange.
Mendoza speaks to the dynamic qualities of a tradition that continually
reinvents itself through a steady process of appropriation, adaptation, innovation, maintenance, and resistance (Broyles-González 2001). Some might
imagine Mendoza's artistic constancy over the decades as a static "traditionalism." Of course, some elements of her music remained unchanged even
as she appropriated new elements. Yet change was also a constant. When
she did "foreign" songs, for example (like *milongas* or tangos), she transposed them into the *tejano/ranchera* vocabulary of the people for whom she
performed. Mendoza transposed many songs into *norteño*/polka rhythm.
There are numerous examples of songs originally composed in triple meter

that she converted into duple meter. One notable example is her interpretation and arrangement of the *corrido* "Delgadina."

Another example of her appropriation and innovation within tradition is her twelve-string guitar, which was not a standard *norteño* instrument. She refunctionalized the twelve-string guitar by tuning it to B, a perfect fourth lower than a regular guitar and a minor third lower than standard twelve-string tuning—a variation that was uniquely hers. (Regular guitar tuning is, starting from the first string: E, B, G, D, A, E; standard twelve-string is D, A, F, C, G, D; Mendoza's tuning was B, F#, D, A, E, B.) In essence, she adapted her twelve-string to emulate the double-course sound of the Texas *bajo sexto,* creating a guitar range between guitar and *bajo sexto.* She innovatively tuned her twelve-string in a pitch half-way between a regular twelve-string and a *bajo sexto* to achieve that booming bass sound that highlights and accompanies the expressiveness of her voice. In other words, she created a new space between the conventional boundaries of established instruments to fit her aesthetic needs.

Mendoza's process of appropriation and change within continuity always involved a double translation on her part: on the one hand, she translated all received songs into a collective regional musical vocabulary or recognizable *norteño/ranchera* mode of expression (with wide-ranging and fluctuating parameters); on the other hand, her appropriation of those received songs involved a transposition into her own personal aesthetics as a song stylist, arranger, and unmistakable voice. Lydia Mendoza's recognizable voice and twelve-string guitar combined to create her characteristic solo style of performance within the *norteño/ranchera* cultural matrix. Her voice came to be regarded as quintessentially expressive of the *norteño/tejano* collective musical vocabulary, its repertoire of songs and languages—those modes of expression that developed over time within the communities she sang for. Whatever instrumental ensemble she performed with, she articulated a *sentimiento* that resonated deeply within the realms of *raza* working-class experiences across geographies—in the Southwest, Midwest, and Northwest of the United States and throughout the Americas. Within her circle of song performance, her musical arrangements and her timbre, voice, body, and spirit enacted the space of a popular collective expression. The expressiveness of her voice encodes a sociocultural matrix far beyond the surface value of the notes; her voice generates a spirit. If audiences feel, think, and identify with the expressivity of her music it is because her music—her voice and repertoire—evokes the deep-rootedness of the people. Artistic modes of regional expression (like the *tejano/norteño*) are like mother tongues; just as you learn a mother tongue, you also absorb and understand a musical language with its own spectrum of *sentimiento*. From the cradle to the grave, we hear these songs, these sounds. In popular usage, *sentimiento* denotes sentience and cognition (consciousness) as much as an emotional quality or sentimentality; a shared music in the Texas of the first half of the twentieth century implies a shared consciousness, instinctual awareness, and structure of feeling. Mendoza's musical phrasing and style, her accentuations and nonaccentuations, resonate within the broader *norteño* borderland musical system that has evolved and spread in the last two centuries.

The expressivity of Mendoza's personal aesthetics is unmistakable and widely loved. It grew organically among the people, first by watching and hearing the women in her family and then by observing other musicians at work, by being among the people. As a self-trained singer, the mass appeal of Mendoza's voice had something to do with its lack of affectations and its clarity and strength. She never felt a need to go the route of various other popular singers, who attempted to attain a supposed polish by training operatically (Jorge Negrete and Pedro Infante are two examples). Mendoza had no bel canto ambitions and sang only with a minimum vibrato. Thus her vocal inflection and tone has a straightforward and almost speech-like quality. She articulated her musical phrasing in an economical style, close to the orational style (*declamadoras*), using the inflections from daily speech in her music. She typically avoided all the melismatic frills cultivated by singers who aimed to climb socially. Thus she represented all the rural and working-class qualities of voice and song, which later overtook the urban sphere as well.

During her long performance career—perhaps the longest of any American musician—Mendoza recorded and performed with various instrumental backups, yet her preferred mode was as a one-woman show, in some ways a throwback to the old itinerant *corridistas* and *cancioneras/os*. Her one-woman/one guitar configuration tends to ensure a high survival rate, due to the degree of independence from other musicians, flexibility, and mobility it offered. Unlike many contemporary *tejana* singers, Lydia Mendoza was not only a singer working with her voice; she was a musician who possessed musical skills beyond her voice. Her high level of musicianship involved original arrangements and the challenging artistry of making her voice work with the twelve-string guitar. Her musical phrasing and style, her accentuations and nonaccentuations, resonate with the larger *norteño* musical system. And yet she is unmistakable in the originality of her expression. She has referred to that expression as "el arte de sentirlo," or the innate "art of feeling," which she regards as a god-given gift. This "arte de sentirlo"—that enduring gift from her soul, of giving voice to *sentimiento*—is perhaps at the core of what has made her so beloved.

NOTES

I dedicate this essay to soulmate, Francisco González, whose "Cama de piedra" brought me home from exile. His voice, musicianship, and fine intellect have allowed me to better understand *la canción ranchera*. I thank María Elena Gaitán for encouragement. Before completing this essay I traveled by car to San Francisco with my mother (Julia Arana), Tía Tere, and Tía Fina. We sang many *rancheras* in the car, like we always did when we traveled together during my childhood. Their beautiful harmonies lent inspiration to this piece and to my life. *Gracias de todo corazón.*

1. All song translations by Norma E. Cantú.

2. The only sustained work in the area of *raza* popular musics (other than the *corrido*) is that by Manuel Peña. In his extensive studies on Texas *norteño* musics, Peña undertakes a socioeconomic analysis of the various *tejano* instrumental ensembles. The *canción ranchera* remains outside his analytical framework, although it figures squarely within the repertoire of the *conjunto* and *orquesta* styles he analyzes in *The Texas Mexican Conjunto: History of a Working-Class Music* (1985). I have not examined his more recent book, *The Mexican American Orquesta* (1999), published after this essay was written. Many popular books have been published on the *canción ranchera* in Mexico, some by *ranchera* composers themselves. One example is Juan S. Garrido's *Historia de la música popular en México 1896–1973* (1974). With regard to popular books on *raza* music in the United States, the tragic murder of the Chicana singer Selena Quintanilla Pérez occasioned a flood of books on her life and/or music (see Patoski 1996).

3. The term *raza* is short for *raza humana* (the people) and is used by indigenous peoples (in many different languages) to self-designate. I use it interchangeably with "Mexican Americans," "Native Americans," "native peoples," "indigenous peoples," *indias, indios, mexicanas, mexicanos,* and "Mexicans." It is a transnational term that (like *raza* cultures) transcends and blurs national boundaries and borders.

4. None of these singers has been the focus of any sustained study. Juan Gabriel has been the subject of one scholarly article (see Geirola 1993).

5. Most sources credit L. de J. F. Elizondo and M. de B. de J. García with composing this song.

6. In a book-length work in progress (tentatively titled "Norteño Borderlands"), I enter into a discussion of various overlapping yet distinguishable terms, such as *música ranchera, música norteña, canción ranchera, estilo ranchera*. For musicians from Texas (such as Lydia Mendoza) these terms also intersect, overlap, and diverge from terms such as *música tejana* (Tex-Mex). In this essay I use the terms *ranchera,*

norteño, and *tejano* interchangeably, although the terms *canción ranchera* and *música norteña* often overlap and the *canción ranchera* can be played in styles that are not "northern." Given the widespread migration and popularity of the "norteño" sound throughout the Americas, "música de acordeón" (the *norteño* button-accordion ensemble or "conjunto") has become something of a prototypical *ranchera* or rural sound—alongside the mariachi sound and the increasingly popular "banda" (wind ensembles) or "tambora."

7. Composer unknown. Lydia Mendoza recorded "Mal hombre" many times throughout her long career.

8. Composed by Daniel Garzés.

9. The only article on Mendoza to date, a brief generalist piece, was originally published in 1981 in an obscure journal (Gil 1997). This was followed by a short interview (Griffith 1982). *Lydia Mendoza: A Family Autobiography* was the first book-length oral history of Lydia Mendoza and her family (Strachwitz and Nicolopulos 1993). I review this book and its problematics in *Lydia Mendoza's Life in Music/La historia de Lydia Mendoza—Norteño Tejano Legacies* (2001).

10. The immensely broad musical domain of the *canción ranchera* cannot be adequately covered in one essay. I hope that this essay will occasion a reconsideration of the *canción ranchera,* which has been largely dismissed and even maligned in academia. There is virtually nothing written beyond two early articles on the *ranchera* composer José Alfredo Jiménez by Gradante (1982, 1983). One brief article sketches the domain known as *música norteña* (Bensusan 1985).

11. Phrases such as these abound in Bierhorst (1985:213 and 205).

12. Composed by J. López Alavés.

13. Against a narrow vision of what constitutes "the political," I want to suggest here that any working-class collective tradition of song is deeply political and that love songs are political in many ways.

14. "Monterrey," released on March 8, 1928, in San Antonio, Texas, on the OKeh Odeon label, no. 16314.

15. "México lindo" was written by Jesús "Chucho" Monge, one of the most prolific *ranchera* authors prior to José Alfredo Jiménez.

16. It has often been said that the United Farm Workers (UFW) and Chicano movement, for example, could not have made gains without music. Virtually all of the thousands of UFW marches were headed off by some form of musical expression using regional instruments associated with *ranchera* aesthetics and songs.

17. Many historians have reconstructed these dehumanizing social realities. See the work of Antonia Castañeda, Deena González, Emma Pérez, Vicki Ruiz, Rudy Acuña, Ramón Gutiérrez, George Sánchez, Arnoldo de León, and Ramón Ruiz, to name only a few. For a more focused account of the conditions faced by U.S. Mexicans from the turn of the century into the 1930s, see Rosales 1999; Valdés 1991; Vargas 1993; and Guerin-Gonzáles 1994.

18. Briggs analyzes the multifunctionality of triplex signs within oral historical discourse, while I apply that term here to my analyses of the *ranchera.* See chapter

3 of his pathbreaking book *Competence in Performance: The Creativity of Tradition in Mexicano Verbal Art* (1988).

19. For a fascinating account of Mexican music (mainly the *corrido*), the rise of mass culture in Los Angeles from the 1920s to the 1940s, and Chicana/o identity formation, see Sánchez 1993:171–87.

20. A handful of the prominent values that emerge in the *rancheras* composed by José Alfredo Jiménez are discussed in Gradante 1982, 1983.

21. Transcribed from the author's field notes.

WORKS CITED

Bakhtin, Mikhail M. 1984. *Rabelais and His World*. Trans. Hélène Iswolsky. Bloomington: Indiana University Press.

Bensusan, Guy. 1985. "A Consideration of Norteña and Chicano Music." *Studies in Latin American Popular Culture* 4:158–69.

Bierhorst, John, trans. 1985. *Cantares Mexicanos: Songs of the Aztecs of the 16th Century*. Stanford, Calif.: Stanford University Press.

Bonfil Batalla, Guillermo. 1996. *México profundo: Reclaiming a Civilization*. Trans. Philip A. Dennis. Austin: University of Texas Press.

Briggs, Charles L. 1988. *Competence in Performance: The Creativity of Tradition in Mexicano Verbal Art*. Philadelphia: University of Pennsylvania Press.

Broyles-González, Yolanda. 2001. *Lydia Mendoza's Life in Music/La historia de Lydia Mendoza—Norteño Tejano Legacies*. New York: Oxford University Press.

Certeau, Michel de. 1984. *The Practice of Everyday Life*. Trans. Steven Randall. Berkeley: University of California Press.

Garrido, Juan S. 1974. *Historia de la música popular en México, 1896–1973*. México, D.F.: Editorial Extemporaneos.

Geirola, Gustavo. 1993. "Juan Gabriel: Cultura popular y sexo de Los Angeles." *Latin American Music Review/Revista de Música Latinoamericana* 14 (2): 232–67.

Gil, Carlos B. 1997. "Lydia Mendoza, Houstonian and First Lady of Mexican American Song." In *Aztlán: Chicano Culture and Folklore, An Anthology*. Ed. José Villarino and Arturo Ramírez. 223–34. San Francisco, Calif.: McGraw Hill.

Gradante, William. 1982. "El Hijo del Pueblo: José Alfredo Jiménez and the Mexican *canción ranchera*." *Latin American Music Review* 3 (1): 36–59.

———. 1983. "Mexican Popular Music at Mid-Century: The Role of José Alfredo Jiménez and the *Canción Ranchera*." *Studies in Latin American Popular Culture* 2:99–114.

Griffith, Jim. 1982. "La Alondra de la Frontera" In *Ethnic Recordings in America*. 103–31. Washington, D.C.: American Folklife Center, Library of Congress.

Guerin-Gonzáles, Camille. 1994. *Mexican Workers and American Dreams: Immigration, Repatriation, and California Farm Labor, 1900–1939*. New Brunswick, N.J.: Rutgers University Press.

Lipsitz, George. 1994. *Dangerous Crossroads: Popular Music, Postmodernism, and the Poetics of Place*. London: Verso Press.

Patoski, Joe Nick. 1996. *Selena: Como la flor*. Boston, Mass.: Little Brown Press.

Peña, Manuel. 1985. *The Texas-Mexican Conjunto: History of a Working-Class Music*. Austin: University of Texas Press.

———. 1999. *The Mexican American Orquesta*. Austin: University of Texas Press.

Rosales, Francisco Arturo. 1999. *¡Pobre Raza! Violence, Justice, and Mobilization among México Lindo Immigrants, 1900–1936*. Austin: University of Texas Press.

Sánchez, George J. 1993. *Becoming Mexican American: Ethnicity, Culture, and Identity in Chicano Los Angeles, 1900–1945*. New York: Oxford University Press.

Strachwitz, Chris, with James Nicolopulos, comps. 1993. *Lydia Mendoza: A Family Autobiography*. Houston: Arte Público Press.

Valdés, Dennis Nodín. 1991. *Al Norte: Agricultural Workers in the Great Lakes Region, 1917–1970*. Austin: University of Texas Press.

Vargas, Zaragosa. 1993. *Proletarians of the North: Mexican Industrial Workers in Detroit and the Midwest, 1917–1933*. Berkeley: University of California Press.

MOUNTING TRADITIONS

THE ORIGIN AND EVOLUTION OF LA ESCARAMUZA CHARRA

OLGA NÁJERA-RAMÍREZ

This essay examines women's roles as they are constructed, reconfigured, and contested within the framework of the *charreada,* or Mexican rodeo, a traditional Mexican practice on both sides of the U.S.-Mexican border. While my primary concern is to explore women's active participation within the *charreada,* this essay also contributes to the larger theoretical scholarship on the "invention of tradition" by highlighting the knowledge, skill, and determination required to become an active participant in tradition making (Hobsbawm and Ranger 1983).[1] Specifically, I demonstrate that in the *charreada* women are aware that traditions are socially constructed: they understand the power and politics invested in creating traditions, and they have become important participants in tradition making.

My point is that although people create and constantly reshape traditions, they do not do so in completely arbitrary ways. Rather, I contend that traditions are created following a specific cultural logic. Therefore, altering traditions in a manner that is acceptable within a particular community requires an understanding of the cultural logic within which a given tradition exists. Viewed from this vantage point, the "invention" of tradition does not necessarily imply inauthenticity. Instead, it supports the idea that "authenticity" resides in a given cultural logic. Through an analysis of women's roles within the *charreada,* particularly the creation and evolution of the *escaramuza charra* (the all-female precision riding team), I show that only by understanding the cultural logic of a tradition can one become an effective participant in the power and politics of that tradition.

WOMEN IN THE CHARREADA

There's a popular saying among *charros* (Mexican cowboys): "un charro es un caballero dos veces." Literally, a Mexican cowboy is twice a "caballero"—a skilled horseman and a dignified gentleman (the term *caballero* means both). Neatly and concisely, this refrain summarizes men's prescribed role within the *charreada*.[2] But women's roles within the *charreada* present a more complicated case. Traditionally, women have participated in a *charreada* by managing the food booths, cheering in the stands as spectators, hosting visitors, and reigning as queens. More recently, a new role has been added to the repertoire: performing in an *escaramuza*[3] as members of an all-female precision riding team. The multiple roles women play within the *charreada* unquestionably attest to their numerous skills and abilities. Yet women have been primarily defined in relation to men, always as their subordinate counterparts or attachments, not as their equals. Commenting on gender roles and gender relations within *charrería*,[4] one scholar concludes, "they [women] rarely ponder the significance of their role in the gender iconography of Mexican culture, probably because their roles in *charrería* harmonize with their role expectation in the larger society" (Sands 1993:185). While I agree with Sands's latter point, my interviews with women in *charreadas* during more than five seasons of fieldwork suggest that these women do indeed engage in critical reflection on gender roles and relations.[5] Commenting on her own participation in the *charreada*, for example, one woman reported:

> I always come accompanied with my mother or my father, or just sometimes my father and I come, and it's very political. The fact that he knows a lot of the *presidentes*, a lot of the *charros*, that has helped me a lot. And they recognize me as his daughter. I cannot tell you they recognize me as me myself. I guarantee you half of them don't even know my name. But if they see me with my father they'll know who I am. So that has a lot to do with it. If I were to come here with, say, my boyfriend, and they knew he was my boyfriend—not a cousin, not a brother—they would probably not acknowledge me. So how they see you has to do with who you are with.[6]

Such comments reveal the heightened awareness some women have of their subordinate roles within the *charreada*. And this awareness, I argue, has compelled them to challenge this subordinate status in various ways. However, because men's dominance in *charrería* has been, in large part, sanctioned and protected by the authority implied by an "official national tradition," *charro* officials have successfully managed to maintain male dominance by constructing women's criticisms of the gender imbalance as "anti-Mexican" and by constructing women who dare to make such accusations as not only "un-Mexican" but "agringadas," a term that equates a feminist outlook with Anglo influences. Contesting women's subordination within *charrería*, therefore, is a sensitive matter that requires a great deal of courage, skill, cultural knowledge, persistence, and *una poca de gracia* (a bit of grace or diplomacy).

The development of the *escaramuza* provides one example of how women in *charrería* actively negotiate their own needs and desires even as they fulfill their prescribed roles as bearers of tradition. This negotiation requires that they understand the logic of the tradition ("the rules of the game") in order to introduce changes that others will accept as legitimate or at least consistent with the "rules of the game." Viewing the tradition of *charrería* as a "game" is consistent with the way cultural performances in general have been approached (Singer 1972; Geertz 1973; Bauman 1986; Stoeltje 1983; Abrahams 1977, 1981; Babcock 1978). Recently, however, Sherry Ortner has offered a way of understanding the complexity of gender roles and relations in games with her concept of "serious games," a model that recognizes "that social life is culturally organized and constructed, in terms of defining categories of actors, rules and goals of the game, and so forth; that social life is precisely social, consisting of webs of relationship and interaction between multiple, shiftingly interrelated subject positions, none of which can be extracted as autonomous 'agents'; and yet at the same time there is 'agency,' that is, actors play with skill, intention, wit, knowledge, intelligence" (1996:12). Ortner's model provides a useful framework for examining the development of the *escaramuza* precisely because it resists viewing women as either wholly passive or wholly resistant but rather seeks to capture the nuanced ways in which they negotiate their position. As women seeking to reform rather than eliminate a patriarchal tradition, the subtle ways in which they have institutionalized change have often gone unnoticed as a feminist project. Games have to be examined to uncover what kinds of subject positions they create and to what extent those positions impose themselves on the participants. Further, understanding how people negotiate these positions requires careful analysis of the cultural meanings and structural arrangements that construct and constrain their "agency." For this reason, I offer a brief account of the logic of gender as constructed in the *charreada*.[7]

GENDER ROLES IN THE CHARREADA

The *charreada,* a cultural event featuring a variety of riding and roping contests, emerged from the early Mexican cattle-ranching activities such as the *herraderos* (branding events) and *rodeos* (roundups to count and sort the livestock) (see Nájera-Ramírez 1994, 1996, 1997). During the Mexican postrevolutionary era, the *charreada* was refined and formalized as a romantic nationalist expression of *lo mexicano* (Mexicanness) by the urban elites—many of whom had been displaced from their haciendas during the Mexican Revolution. Consequently the formal *charreada* conspicuously embodied their aesthetic and ideological predilections, invoking a nostalgic, romanticized view of the patriarchal hacienda system of colonial Mexico.

Within the patriarchal hacienda system, "class, gender and ethnicity largely determined a person's place in society" (Nájera-Ramírez 1994:3). From an idealized perspective, however, the hacienda system neatly provided a social order in which everyone knew their place. In this romanticized view, men competed fairly in the world to achieve positions of status and prestige; therefore, those who achieved the highest positions deserved the respect of their social inferiors. Further, despite radical social differences within this rigid authoritarian social structure, a man could prove his moral worth by demonstrating his loyalty towards his family, his *patrones* (bosses), and his *patria* (nation). Explicitly designed to foster patriotism, promote Mexican customs and traditions, and nurture a sense of national unity, the *charreada* also helped naturalize a male-dominated social order by reproducing the patriarchal social structure of the family, the hacienda, and the nation.

Moreover, in the process of "upgrading" the *charreada* from a vernacular rural event to a national sport, the romantic nationalist urbanites imbued it with ideals of elegance, refinement, and respectability. Such gallant ideals, officially inscribed in the *charro* rule book, specified the proper way of performing, dressing, and behaving.[8] Contests emphasized grace and finesse, rather than speed, in handling the horse and the rope. The use of bright or loud colors was prohibited in costumes. And proper behavior meant that uneven relationships of power were cloaked with an aura of respectability. Thus emerged the popular saying that a *charro* should be a *caballero dos veces*—a skilled horseman and a *gentleman* who always comports himself with great dignity, especially with members of the "fairer" sex. Consistent with the celebratory view of patriarchy, women prove themselves worthy of the respectful, if paternalistic, treatment men accord them by remaining virtuous, upstanding, and loyal to their husbands, fathers, and brothers.

According to the gender logic inscribed within the *charreada,* men and women play distinct but complementary roles in promoting the ideals of family unity, patriotism, and Mexicanness. However, the distinction between men and women is not neutral in the patriarchal structure of the *charreada.* Therefore, both women and men must recognize the subordinate status of women within *charrería,* and they must do so graciously. However, the aura of respectability that permeates the social interactions also provides women the opportunity to make incisive, if polite, interventions. Since a gentleman must be courteous and attentive to women, women have opportunities to express their needs and desires. The key is knowing when, where, and how to do so most effectively. Understanding the logic upon which the *charreada* rests paradoxically allows women to negotiate changing gender roles and relations while behaving in culturally appropriate ways.

MOUNTING TRADITIONS: INVENTING THE ESCARAMUZA CHARRA

Now considered a fundamental component of the *charreada,* the *escaramuza* is a relatively new phenomenon and marks the greatest inroad women have made in this male-dominated sport. For years, only men enjoyed the privilege of performing and competing in the *charreadas,* while women functioned as "behind-the-scenes" organizers, hostesses, queens, and observers. But with the creation of the *escaramuza* in the 1950s, women gained the opportunity to perform publicly in the *charreadas.*

Prior to the existence of the *escaramuza charra,* the China Poblana held the position as the official partner for the *charro* (Rincón Gallardo 1993 [1939]). Dressed in an ankle-length silky red skirt trimmed with sequins, a short-sleeved colorfully embroidered scoop-necked peasant blouse, green pumps, and flesh-colored stockings, the China Poblana rarely rode a horse. D. Carlos Rincón Gallardo specifically notes that the costume is not appropriate for mounting; rather, it is to be used when going to ballrooms, attending the theater, or dancing the Jarabe tapatío (1993 [1939]: 271).[9] Hence, the first official partner of the *charro* was a decidedly nonequestrian woman. In fact, if she chose to ride on horseback, she was required to change into another costume (1993 [1939]: 271–72).

The earliest documentation of a woman displaying riding skills in a *charreada* was also recorded by Rincón Gallardo (1993 [1939]), who mentions that Conchita Cintrón requested that he teach her to perform the *charro suertes* (riding and roping acts). Noting that she was one of the best horsewomen he had ever met, he invited her to show off her newly acquired *charro* skills at a benefit fiesta *charra*. Dressed in *charro* pants and mounting astraddle for her debut, Conchita Cintrón was named an honorary member of the Asociación Nacional de Charros (Rincón Gallardo 1993 [1939]: 276–77). Since Rincón Gallardo makes no mention of any rules for women's participation in *charrería* except as Chinas Poblanas, Cintrón's participation was likely considered a "one-time-only" novelty act. Curiously, Rincón Gallardo openly lamented the fact that female riders were not sufficiently recognized in the *charreada*. Particularly significant is his observation that women who grew up around horses often acquired a special talent for riding and that they had a vernacular style of dress that was appropriate for mounting (1993 [1939]: 269). These horsewomen surely served as the precursors of the *escaramuzas*.

With the creation of the *escaramuza*, women finally gained the opportunity to publicly display their equestrian skills in the *charreadas*. Scholars credit the professional *charro* Luis Ortega with inventing the *escaramuza* tradition after witnessing a team of cowgirls and cowboys perform at a fair in Houston, Texas, in 1950 (Chávez Gómez 1991:90; Valero Silva 1987:107; Sands 1993:156).[10] Upon his return to Mexico, Ortega developed his own precision riding team composed of boys and girls and toured them throughout the country, thus inspiring the formation of subsequent *escaramuzas*.

Elsa López de Jiménez, the director of an *escaramuza* team in Tijuana and a writer for several *charro* magazines, has provided a slightly different version of the origins of the *escaramuza*. She reports that the *escaramuzas* began in the Rancho del Charro in Mexico City on March 22, 1952.[11] Nonetheless, she agrees that the *escaramuza* was established as an event that would integrate children in the *charreada* and that the original *escaramuza* consisted of three boys and three girls. As they traveled around Mexico, their popularity increased, and soon other *escaramuza* teams emerged. Considered "demasiado femenino" (too feminine) by some of the *charros*, boys were eventually eliminated from the event, and by 1958 the *escaramuza* was established as an all-female display event (Chávez Gómez 1991:90).

FROM SOLDADERA TO ESCARAMUZA

As a newly formed female tradition, the *escaramuza* required a rationale to explain its existence as a formal part of the *charreada*. The *soldaderas,* or women who accompanied, supported, and often fought alongside male war-riors, particularly during the Mexican Revolution of 1910, provided the im-portant rudimentary elements with which to justify the addition of the *es-caramuzas* as an appropriate counterpart to the *charro* in this national sport.[12] As a group, the *soldaderas* were considered brave, independent, patriotic, and, in many instances, skilled riders. Historically, however, they have also been depicted as lovers and even whores (Salas 1990). Clearly, a national tradi-tion could not embrace those qualities considered "immoral." Consequent-ly, the *escaramuza* emphasized selected qualities of the *soldaderas,* epitomized by the legendary Adelita, the lovely, brave, and skilled riding companion of Pancho Villa. As the "middle-ground" representation between the extremes of a fierce fighter and a base camp follower, Adelita is, as the historian Eliz-abeth Salas observes, "the 'sweetheart of the troops,' a woman who is val-iant, pretty, and a wonderful helpmate to the soldier" (1990:121).

Through song, dress, attitude, and equestrian skills, the *escaramuza* em-bodied the legendary spirit and qualities of Adelita. For example, the famous revolutionary *corrido* entitled "La Adelita" portrays her as an "uncut" flower, thereby emphasizing her status as a virgin, as evident in the follow-ing verse:

> Adelita se llama la joven
> a quien yo quiero y no puedo olvidar.
> En el mundo yo tengo una rosa,
> y con el tiempo la voy a cortar. (Jiménez 1995 [1986])

> [Adelita is the name of the young maiden
> whom I love and I cannot forget.
> In this world I have a rose,
> and in time I will cut this rose.] (my translation)

Adelita is also the name of the modest riding costume worn by the *escara-muza,* consisting of a high-necked long-sleeved dress with a long full skirt laced with ribbon, a white petticoat, white bloomers, and a *rebozo* (shawl) that often crisscrosses the chest.[13] By emphasizing the wholesome "Adelita" image, the *soldaderas* as represented by the *escaramuza* become sanitized and romanticized, thus appearing less threatening to the male-dominant gender relations in *charrería.* As a result, with regards to their appearance, the *escaramuzas* became more acceptable female counterparts for the *cha-rro* without seeming radical or controversial. Note, for example, how the *escaramuza* leader Diana Ozuna summarizes the history: "Adelita was one of the first women to ride back in the Civil War with Pancho Villa. The women started riding to the different camps to wash the men's clothes, feed them, and take care of them, but years after it became a sport where the women would go back into town and practice different crossings, and that's how the *escaramuza* started."[14]

Similarly, one judge explained, "the [tradition of the] Adelita comes from a lady that participated very strongly in the Mexican Revolution, so every woman tries to emulate the bravery and the energy of this legend."[15]

The Adelita image notwithstanding, the establishment of the *soldaderas* as the foundational origin of the *escaramuzas* allowed women the opportunity of emphasizing other, more controversial aspects of that history. "Las coronelas" (The female colonels),[16] a popular polka from the revolutionary period, provides a case in point. With its emphasis on women's status as military leaders and its invocation of the revolution, "Las coronelas" has quickly become the song most often selected for performances by the *escaramuzas*. Such choices allow for multiple readings; it is unclear whether *escaramuzas* select this song merely because it is one from the Revolutionary period or because it serves as a reminder that women have taken, and hence can continue to take, important leadership roles. No doubt it is this ambiguity that makes the song particularly attractive to women who want to push the gender boundaries without appearing confrontational.

NEGOTIATING BOUNDARIES

Another issue that has sparked great debate in shaping the *escaramuza* tradition concerns what particular skills women should be allowed to cultivate and display. For years, *charro* authorities vehemently regarded riding and roping skills as the domain of men despite historical evidence amply confirming that Mexican women rode horses and herded cattle throughout Mexico and the United States (Martin 1992; Ruíz 1992; Sánchez 1995; Salas 1990). Although the creation of the *escaramuza* provided women an opportunity to ride publicly, they still are not allowed to perform any roping skills. Moreover, officially required to ride sidesaddle at all times and dressed in full skirts, the young women continue to project an image of "daintiness" that deflects attention away from the rigorous riding skills (the ability to execute rapid turns, stops, and changes of speed) required to perform the choreographed patterns on horseback. One *escaramuza* director explains:

> It [the *escaramuza*] is very different from the *charro*: the *charro* rides like a cowboy, but they have a different style. These girls, the *escaramuzas,* ride side-saddle, and they work their horses with their legs by strength and the spur. If

you notice, they don't whip their horses very much—it's body movement more than anything. It's a lot of discipline. And you have watch your distances at all times . . . if you change speed it counts against you. If you don't keep the same trot, if you don't keep the same distance between horses, all of that is taken into consideration.[17]

Like the *charros,* the *escaramuzas* work year-round to perfect their equestrian skills. Knowing how to ride a horse is the obvious first step, but their work includes feeding, grooming, and training their horses. Many young women acquire the basic riding skills at home under the guidance of elder members of their family, but in some cases they can receive the necessary training from other *escaramuzas.* Performing as an *escaramuza* also requires that women learn to ride as members of a team, learn the choreographies, and learn to execute movements with the utmost precision. For that reason, team practice is strictly required of all participants.

The training cycle begins in the spring, when the members of the *escaramuza* begin practicing together to learn new choreographies under the leadership of their team captain. Usually, the team will practice for a minimum of two hours twice a week. Once the *charreada* season begins in May, the young women will also perform weekly at various *charreadas* and even in rodeos, parades, and fairs. These activities continue until late October, when the *charreada* season comes to a close. During the off-season, each member rides regularly on her own to further develop her technique as well as to enhance her knowledge of and control over her horse so that she will be even better prepared for the following season.

Despite the rigorous riding skills required to participate in an *escaramuza,* as an exhibit rather than a competitive event, it reinforced a view of women as objects of display, beauty, and adornment consistent with patriarchal notions promoted in the *charreada.* As a result, the *escaramuza* was first treated as an optional component of the *charreada* that could be eliminated at the whim of the *charros.* As one *escaramuza* reported in *Charrería patria y tradición,*

> Reducidas a nivel de artículo decorativo, asumíamos el lugar de un apéndice muchas veces molesto, siempre prescindible de la charrería: sin criterios unificados sobre la conservación del atuendo y los arreos, estos frecuentemente se veían distorcionados casi por completo; y puesto que no había un parámetro que diera cuenta con la habilidad, para muchas escaramuzas contaba mas la velocidad y el peligro inminente que la cadencia y la limpieza de los ejercicios. (Ramírez Barreto 1991:10)

[Reduced to a decorative element, we assumed a position as an often bother-some and always dispensable appendage of the *charrería*. Without a unified code to regulate dress and equipment, these were often quite irregular. And since there were no guidelines that accounted for skill, many *escaramuzas* emphasized speed and danger over cadence and well-executed movements.] (my translation)

Similarly, reflecting on the marginalized position of the *escaramuzas*, Luciana Ozuna complained: "They [the *charros*] say 'somos las flores de la charrería,' that we're the pretty flowers and we're there to be looked at, but we're not something that could be taken seriously. . . . There are certain times where they are saying, 'O.K., three minutes, two minutes, hurry up, let's get them [the *escaramuzas*] out, we have more important things to do.' And that is very offensive and very appalling to us because we work just as hard as they do."[18] Given the amount of time and dedication that *escaramuzas* invest in perfecting their skills throughout the year, it is no wonder that they want to be acknowledged as skilled riders and important participants in *charrería*.

Over the last decade or so, women on both sides of the U.S.-Mexican border have employed several different strategies to promote their cause. For example, in Mexico, during the late 1980s, the *escaramuzas* successfully organized an all-female competition called La Feria de Escaramuzas (the *escaramuza* fair) (Ruíz 1990). In the United States, however, this fair did not flourish. Nonetheless, in an effort to gain recognition for their riding and roping skills, in San Ysidro, California, a group of women in the late 1980s organized their own competition, in which they performed the *charro suertes* (riding and roping events) and rode astride (i.e., not sidesaddle). However, according to one informant, as soon as the authorities of the Federación Nacional de Charros found out about this event, they "completely tore those poor girls up and they were *castigadas* [punished]." Claiming that "this is not part of our tradition," the federation refused to sanction this event and even threatened to ban the participants from the federation if they continued that activity.

But that did not stop the women from searching for recognition and fighting for the right to define their own traditions. The thwarted women's competition in the United States and the successful Feria de Escaramuzas in Mexico made it clear that if women were not allowed to compete within the official *charro* events, they could establish competitions of their own, even if it meant dropping out of the association. However, this option was not the best alternative for either the men or the women, for it violated one of the fundamental principles of *charrería*—the promotion of family unity. As one *charro* judge told me, "The *charreada* is a means of getting the family together. This is not something that is done on Sunday by the *charro* and the family is left at home. . . . The family has to be and should be involved."[19] And, as another woman pointed out, "the *escaramuzas* are the ones *que jalan la gente* [who attract the people]. The people love to see the *escaramuzas*." To remain a vital national tradition, the institutionalized *charreada* had to find a way to accommodate women.

Seeking reform rather than separation, women began campaigning to change the *escaramuza* event from a display to a competition. Significantly, women recognized that in order to make a real difference, the negotiations to expand their participation within *charrería* had to take place on multiple fronts. First, women worked within their own families, exerting their influence as daughters, wives, and mothers. Since their husbands, fathers, and brothers often held voting rights, if not positions of authority within the associations, women could exert their influence on men to support their cause. For example, one woman reported to me that she established the *escaramuza* in her community when her husband became president of their association. She observed, "At first a lot of the fathers and all the *charros* resented the time that we took out of the *charreada* to do the presentation, but now they lend us horses, they saddle our horses, they watch us and everything!"[20]

Women also took advantage of regional, national, and international conferences to network and strategize with other women throughout Greater Mexico. For instance, at the 1991 U.S. *congreso nacional* (meeting), the U.S. queen of the Charro Federation strategized with the queen of the entire federation to share their networks and resources to give the *escaramuza* in both countries more recognition and rights within the sport.[21] And, finally, they established a national women's movement within *charrería*, El Movimiento Nacional de Escaramuzas (national *escaramuza* movement).

Knowing that if it was to remain a vital national tradition the institutionalized *charreada* could not ignore women altogether, the women framed their discontent within the discourse of *lo mexicano*, always emphasizing the concepts of patriotism, family unity, and respect. One of the most effective strategies for promoting their cause was the use of *charro* publications—such as *Charrería patria y tradición* or *Lienzo*—that circulate to practitioners of the sport on both sides of the U.S.-Mexican border. Consider the following excerpts from a letter written by Gloria García de González, a representative of the Movimiento Nacional de Escaramuzas:

Nosotras queremos a nuestro deporte y nos interesa fomentar nuestras raices y tradiciones mexicanas. Deseamos superarnos, superar a nuestros hijos e hijas y que se nos considere como verdaderas deportistas, no solo ser adorno o relleno que se puede mover de lugar como un objeto.

Deseamos fervientemente que se legitime nuestra participación deportiva para que cuando haya cambio de presidente nacional, no queden en saco roto todos los esfuerzos que se han realizado, pues detras de todo esto existe una entrega total de muchas madres y escaramuzas, que no han escatimado tiempo, dinero y esfuerzo para la realización de estos campeonatos. (1991:4)

[We love our sport, and we are interested in fostering our Mexican roots and traditions. We want to improve ourselves and our sons and daughters, and we want to be considered as true athletes, not merely as a decoration that can be moved out of place like an object.

We fervently desire that our participation in this sport be legitimized so that when there is a change of president our accomplishments won't be ignored, because many mothers and *escaramuzas* have given their total support to this cause and have not skimped on time, money, or effort to make the (female) competitions a reality.] (my translation)

Notice how skillfully García de González makes her points: first, she invokes their role as *mothers* responsible for raising *patriotic sons and daughters*. Second, she emphasizes their role as serious athletes, that is, individuals who train hard to participate in the sport. Finally, in mentioning their ability to contribute their own time and money, she presents women as active agents, not as victims. She suggests that to make the *charreada* (read: family and nation) a viable unit, the dedication, support, time, and energy of all its members is required. Therefore, all members are entitled to receive equal protection and treatment. Respectfully framed and using the rhetoric of patriotism and family unity, one of the underlying messages of the letter is that women could totally undermine the *charrería* if they chose to (or were forced to) withdraw their support.

After a period of voicing their discontent and opinions in public and private spheres in culturally savvy ways, the *escaramuzas* finally won the right to compete within the *charreada* in 1991. As a legitimate competition within a *charreada*, the *escaramuzas* could look forward to a uniform set of rules to regulate all aspects of the competition. Equally important, they were guaranteed a sanctioned time within which to perform, and they were guaranteed that qualified judges would evaluate their competitions. Officially implemented in the U.S. *congreso nacional* in 1992, the institutionalization of the *escaramuza* as a competitive event marked a great achievement for women in the *charreada*. Reflecting on this newly won right, Elsa Lopéz de Jiménez notes:

> La mujer en México pues ya ha logrado su lugar dentro de la charrería. Éramos el único deporte en el mundo en que la mujer no tenía derecho de competir. Y eso lo logramos a base de tenacidad, a base de diciplina y a base de que se nos ha exejido a nosotras mismas mucha perfección de movimientos. Y nos sentimos muy orgullosas de estar siendo pues las primeras escaramuzas que se califiquen y sabemos que vamos a dejarles a nuestras hijas una herencia de deporte y una herencia de respeto hacia lo nuestro.[22]

> [The woman in Mexico has finally achieved her place within *charrería*. Ours was the only sport in the world where women did not have a right to compete. We accomplished our goal on the basis of tenacity, discipline, and because we ourselves have insisted on perfecting our movements. And we are very proud to be the first *escaramuzas* to be judged, and we know we are endowing our daughters with this sport and with a respect for our traditions.] (my translation)

The advances women have made in *charrería*, however, have also elicited criticism, especially from those who fear that the women are refusing to "stay in their place." As one *charro* adamantly proclaimed, "In Mexico we respect women always, but they've got their place."[23] Another *charro* shared the following commentary on women's role in *charrería*:

> Pues la mujer es bonito porque, digo, que luzcan sus vestidos y en eso de la escaramuza, pero se ha mirado que en veces quieren jinetear, quieren andar con la reata y todo. . . . Y luego, digo, pues, esto viene haciendo como los trabajos de antes que hacían los abuelos. Era trabajo de agarrar ganado de meter los toros, curarlos, tumbarlos, y todo y antes las mujeres no andaban en eso. Pero ahora se estan metiendo sobre el deporte. Para mí estaría bueno que se queden no mas de puras escaramuzas y haciendo niños, y haciendo charros para el futuro.[24]

> [Well, it's wonderful for women to show off their dresses in the *escaramuzas*, but sometimes women have tried to ride and rope and everything! This (the *charreada*) is part of the work our grandfathers used to do. Their work involved roping cattle, medicating bulls, knocking them down and all that, and women were not involved in that. But now they are getting more involved in the sport events. For me, it would be better if women just stayed as *escaramuzas*, having babies and creating *charros* for the future! (breaks into laughter)] (my translation)

While this response was offered in a half-joking manner, both this and the previous comment reveal the kind of rocky terrain upon which discussions of gender occur. That is, while men do not repress their views on women's participation in the *charreada,* they sometimes frame them as a "playful rubbing" in order to state an admittedly "politically incorrect" view with which they identify.

Clearly, not everyone fully supports women's increased participation and visibility within *charrería.* However, the women cast their campaign so broadly and effectively that it has become virtually impossible to ignore their needs and desires. Framed as the desire to play a more active role in representing *lo mexicano,* their campaign could no longer be constructed as "anti-Mexicano." Significantly, it has become increasingly difficult to label supporters as *agringadas* because the campaign has united women and men across borders and from distinct classes, including members of some of the most distinguished and powerful *charro* families in Mexico. Only by understanding the rules of the game could women become effective participants in shaping the cultural traditions that had heretofore been exclusively dominated by men. While men still exercise more power than women within *charrería,* the changes that women have achieved within the *escaramuza* suggest that women can and will mobilize their knowledge of the tradition to protect their needs and desires.

In sum, cultural practices such as *charrería* are important places to examine how gender roles and relations become established as the transnational norm or ideal regarding what constitutes *lo mexicano.* Understanding cultural practices as sites of negotiation requires scholars and participants to acknowledge that traditions are socially constructed according to particular cultural logics. And, as the case of the *escaramuza* demonstrates, only by understanding the cultural logic of a tradition can one become an effective participant in changing the power and politics of that tradition.

NOTES

An earlier version of this essay was presented at the 1998 American Anthropological Association meeting in Philadelphia.

1. Jackson 1989 explores the politics encountered by anthropologists and "natives" in discussing the invention of culture. For a negative and quite insightful response to this question, see Briggs 1996.

2. For an analysis of gender in Anglo-American rodeo, see Stoeltje 1988.

3. The term *escaramuza* also refers to an individual member of the precision-riding team.

4. The term *charrería* refers to the ensemble of events related to Mexican rodeo, but in common usage, *charrería* and *charreada* are often used interchangeably.

5. Fieldwork for this project was conducted primarily in Sunol, California, but extended to various other cites in the United States and Mexico, including Las Cruces, New Mexico, and Toluca, Mexico.

6. Luciana Ozuna, interview with the author, Las Cruces, N.Mex., 1991.

7. For a detailed discussion of the evolution of the *charro* as a masculine national symbol, see Nájera-Ramírez 1994.

8. Each year, the Confederación Deportiva Mexicana, A.C., issues a new *charro* rule book, the *Reglamento oficial charro.*

9. According to the 1991 official *charro* rule book, the China Poblana costume is appropriate for parades, *concurso de presentación* (costume competitions), and social events (Confederación Deportiva Mexicana 1991). However, the *charro* federation can not exert its authority on nonmembers, such as filmmakers, who choose to ignore their rules.

10. These authors differ slightly in their accounts of the details.

11. Elsa López de Jiménez, interview with the author, Sunol, Calif., 1992.

12. For an in-depth study of the *soldaderas,* see Salas 1990.

13. Galarza Cruz demonstrates that the women's Jalisco costume originated in the clothing worn by *soldaderas* (1988:91).

14. Diana Ozuna, interview with the author, Las Cruces, N.Mex., 1991.

15. Armando Ledesma, interview with the author, Las Cruces, N.Mex., 1991.

16. The term *coronela* may also be used to refer to the colonel's wife (García-Pelayo y Gross 1994).

17. Patricia Rodríguez, interview with the author, Sunol, Calif., 1992.

18. Luciana Ozuna, interview with the author, Las Cruces, N.Mex., 1991. My translation.

19. Armando Ledesma, interview with the author, Las Cruces, N.Mex., 1991.

20. Patricia Rodríguez, interview with the author, Sunol, Calif., 1992.

21. From all accounts, it appears that the women encountered more resistance to fully incorporating the *escaramuza* as an official competition in the United States than in Mexico.

22. Elsa López de Jiménez, interview with the author, Sunol, Calif., 1992.

23. Arnoldo Bujanda, interview with the author, Las Cruces, N.Mex., 1991.

24. I have decided to withhold the name of this informant due to the controversial nature of his statement.

WORKS CITED

Abrahams, Roger D. 1977. "Toward an Enactment-Centered Theory of Folklore." In *Frontiers of Folklore.* Ed. William Bascom. 79–120. Boulder, Colo.: Westview Press for the AAAS.

————. 1981. "Shouting Match at the Border: The Folklore of Display Events." In *"And Other Neighborly Names": Social Process and Cultural Image in Texas Folklore*. Ed. Richard Bauman and Roger D. Abrahams. 303–21. Austin: University of Texas Press.

Babcock, Barbara. 1978. "Introduction." In *The Reversible World*. Ed. Barbara Babcock. 13–36. Ithaca, N.Y.: Cornell University Press.

Bauman, Richard. 1986. "Performance and Honor in 13th-Century Iceland." *Journal of American Folklore* 99:131–50.

Briggs, Charles. 1996. "The Politics of Discursive Authority in Research on the 'Invention of Tradition.'" *Cultural Anthropology* 11 (4): 435–69.

Chávez Gómez, Octavio. 1991. *La charrería: Tradición Mexicana*. Toluca, Mexico: Instituto Mexiquense de Cultura.

Confederación Deportiva Mexicana, A.C. 1991. *Reglamento oficial charro: Reglamento de las competencias, de los competidores, damas charras y escaramuzas*. México, D.F.: Comisión Nacional del Deporte.

Galarza Cruz, Guillermina. 1988. *Evolución del traje regional en Jalisco: Indumentaria de danzas, sones y jarabes de Jalisco*. Guadalajara, Mexico: Gobierno de Jalisco, Secretaria General, Unidad Editorial.

García de González, Gloria. 1991. "Tribuna charra." *Charrería patria y tradición* 3:3–4.

García-Pelayo y Gross, Ramón. 1994. *Pequeño Larousse Ilustrado 1994*. Mexico, D.F.: Ediciones Larousse.

Geertz, Clifford. 1973. "Deep Play: Notes on the Balinese Cockfight." In *Interpretation of Cultures*. Ed. Clifford Geertz. 412–53. New York: Basic Books.

Hobsbawm, Eric, and Terrance Ranger. 1983. *The Invention of Tradition*. New York: Cambridge University Press.

Jackson, Jean E. 1989. "Is There a Way to Talk about Making Culture without Making Enemies?" *Dialectical Anthropology* 14:127–43.

Jiménez, Armando, comp. 1995 [1986]. *Cancionero Mexicano*. 3d ed. México, D.F.: Editores Mexicanos Unidos, S.A.

Martin, Patricia Preciado. 1992. *Songs My Mother Sang to Me: An Oral History of Mexican American Women*. Tucson: University of Arizona Press.

Nájera-Ramírez, Olga. 1994. "Engendering Nationalism: Identity, Discourse, and the Mexican Charro." *Anthropological Quarterly* 67 (1): 1–14.

————. 1996. "The Racialization of a Debate: The Charreada as Tradition or Torture?" *American Anthropologist* 98 (3): 505–11.

————. 1997. *La Charreada! Rodeo a la Mexicana*. Videorecording. San Jose, Calif.: KTEH.

Ortner, Sherry. 1996. *Making Gender: The Politics and Erotics of Culture*. Boston: Beacon Press.

Ramírez Barreto, Ana Cristina. 1991. "Responsabilidad y Compromiso de las Damas Charras." *Charrería patria y tradición* 4:10–11.

Rincón Gallardo, D. Carlos. 1993 [1939]. *El libro del charro Méxicano*. Mexico, D.F: Editorial Porrua, S.A.

Ruíz, Marcela. 1990. "Mujer Charra." *Charrería patria y tradición* 2:14–15.

Ruíz, Vicki. 1992. "Foreword." In *Songs My Mother Sang to Me: An Oral History of Mexican American Women*, by Patricia Preciado Martin. xi-xvii. Tucson: University of Arizona Press.

Salas, Elizabeth. 1990. *Soldaderas in the Mexican Military: Myth and History*. Austin: University of Texas Press.

Sánchez, Rosaura. 1995. *Telling Identities: The Californio Testimonios*. Minneapolis: University of Minnesota Press.

Sands, Kathleen Mullen. 1993. *Charrería Mexicana: An Equestrian Folk Tradition*. Tucson: University of Arizona Press.

Singer, Milton. 1972. *When a Great Tradition Modernizes: An Anthropological Approach to Indian Civilization*. New York: Praeger.

Stoeltje, Beverly J. 1983. "Festival in America." In *Handbook of American Folklore*. Ed. Richard M. Dorson. 239–46. Bloomington: Indiana University Press.

———. 1988. "Gender Representation in Performance: The Cowgirl and the Hostess." *Journal of Folklore Research* 25 (3): 219–41.

Valero Silva, José. 1987. *El libro de la charrería*. México, D.F.: Ediciones Gacela. S.A.

12

CRUZANDO FRONTEJAS

REMAPPING SELENA'S TEJANO MUSIC "CROSSOVER"

DEBORAH R. VARGAS

> When we landed at the airport in El Salvador I remember the huge crowd and Selena saying, "I wonder who's here." We never imagined the crowd was for us.
> —Suzette Quintanilla, Corpus Christi, Texas, July 2000

THE POLITICS OF CROSSING/CRUZANDO AL OTRO LADO

For Texas Mexicans (Tejanas/os), like other *mexicanas/os* and Mexican Americans who reside in the United States, the notion of "crossing" (almost always linked with "border") consistently resides in our psyche as a metaphoric term for racialized "difference," no matter how many generations of one's family have resided in the United States. Inquiry: "When did your family cross over?" Newspaper headline: "Woman and Her Children Die While Crossing the Border." Conversation: "Vamos a cruzar al otro lado." Chicano humor: "Better have your papers in order or they might not let you cross back over." Chicano politics: "We didn't cross the border, the border crossed us."

The notion of crossing, whether within Chicano humor or linked to the extremely violent operations of U.S.-Mexico border policing, remains imbued with the historical telling of a population. The history of labor migration, the colonization process of mapping national and state boundaries, the unique manifestations of "border violence" inflicted on brown bodies, especially young women in *maquiladora* plants and by the INS border patrol, the racist politics of language against Spanish-speaking peoples, and the legacy of Jim Crow segregation imposed on Mexicans in Texas all discursively operate with the notion of "crossing over." Even so, the ideological ramifications of crossing over to that other place or land (*el norte*) imply moving toward something better: better job opportunities and better living conditions, perpetuated by American ideologies of success, democracy, and progress that mask the brutal exploitation of immigrant labor and the increasing gap between the haves and the have-nots. In relation to Latinas/os in the United States, and Mexican Americans in particular, within the arena of popular music, the conventions of music "crossover" offer similar discursive operations for analysis. As the sociologist Herman Gray reminds us, popular music is a critical social phenomenon through which major political debates, conflicts, and social expressions about identity, sexuality, community, place, history, gender, pleasure, and politics are staged and performed.[1]

Lipsitz asserts that music crossover reifies "the subject of Western popular music" (1994:61) and marks a linear pattern of success in terms of dominant codes of race and language. Thus, the concept of music crossover fails to capture the shifts and transformations in contemporary American popular culture, particularly as increased transnational movements of capital and culture impact Mexican-based music and cultural practices that have their origins *en este lado* on this side of the border. Conventional understandings of music crossover stifle the sociological complexity of such occurrences particularly at the end of the twentieth century. One such significant occurrence is the life and music of the Tejana singer, Selena.

The media, in their attempts to capture the social significance of Selena within the broader American public, often described her as having attained "crossover" status, crossing over from an ethnic music market to the U.S. pop music mainstream. This essay posits a different articulation of crossover that reflects the complications and contradictions of popular music. By placing characteristics of Selena's social location that directly relate to Tejano music and cultural production alongside a critique of the conventional construction of music crossover, we can better understand Selena's music and create more complex understandings of unique productions of Latina/o music in the United States.

The discursive operation of music crossover that frames Selena's career is linked to a notion of success embedded within a U.S. assimilationist narrative[2] The narrative within which Selena's life and music is cast is a familiar one, used to measure the significance of most racial/ethnic "success" within the broader U.S. context: working-class Mexican American girl lives out the American Dream by breaking in to U.S. pop music. As Lipsitz appropriately argues, because the model of assimilation posits the "existence of a discrete, homogeneous, and thoroughly unified center in any society [it] fails to describe the dynamism and complexity of contemporary culture" (1994:120).

Cruzando frontejas (crossing the Texas-Mexico border) offers a different way of understanding Selena's music moves, foregrounding what Chicana and Tejana feminist scholars have articulated as "third culture" or "third space,"[3] a geopolitical as well as discursive space symbolized by the socially constructed "in-between" territory north of the Rio Bravo (Anzaldúa 1987; Fregoso 1998; Pérez 1999; Saldívar-Hull 2000). The social navigation of Tejanas/os in this "third space," as with Selena and her music, engages the politics of cultural assimilation (particularly as linked to the politics of language), the racialization of Texas-Mexican music, and the impact of transnationality on this regional culture. Remapping Selena's Tejano music travels in this way highlights the intersections of history, race, music, sexuality, gender, class, language politics, and generation that are elided in conventional understandings of musical crossover.

One of the more significant accomplishments highlighted in Selena's *cruzando frontejas* was her success in Spanish-language markets south of the border. The success of her music in Latin America represents a metaphoric U-turn, wherein she travels along the north-south axis, reconfiguring the notion of success that has been equally advantageous for many Latina/o artists, especially Mexican Americans born and raised in the United States. Remapping Selena's crossover makes visible the operative "detours" and "signposts" of race, nationality, language, and the Texas-Mexico border that are embodied through Selena and her transcultural circulation of Tejano music.

NUESTRA SELENA Y LA ONDA TEJANA

On March 31, 1995, Latinos around the United States and abroad mourned the death of Selena Quintanilla Pérez, one of the most significant Mexican American figures in contemporary popular culture. For fans of Tejano music, who had followed Selena's growth within the music industry, her passing was especially difficult.[4] Selena was a significant figure within a Tejano music industry that began "booming" in the mid-1980s.[5] This music was particularly embraced by a unique "Tejano generation," a generation located somewhere between the post–Chicano civil rights era and the emerging pan-Hispanic identity formation of the mid-1980s. In the hearts of many Tejanas/os, Selena was someone familiar, someone whose social location defined their lives as well. The notion that "Selena was one of us"[6] resonated for many in terms of gender, color, language, social class, and a regional history and culture.

It is important to situate Selena within the context of Tejano music and the legacy of Tejana music artists.[7] Acknowledging this context allows us to better access the interplay of history, geopolitics, gender, and language in the transformations and travels unique to varied kinds of Latino music that often get lumped together as "Spanish-language" music. Unlike most varied styles of Latino music that currently circulate, *conjunto* music and by extension Tejano music has its developmental origins *en este lado,* within the borders (i.e., social structural processes) of the United States. For example, Juan Tejeda, the founder of the Tejano Conjunto Festival, states that, unlike *banda* music's direct migration from Mexico to the United States, the origins of *conjunto* music mark the unique cross-cultural dialogue between Mexicans and German and Polish immigrants within Texas. The roots of Tejano music are in the *conjunto* music that emerged in the Rio Grande Valley of Texas in the late 1800s, and although Texas-Mexican music encompasses several genres and styles, such as Tex-Mex, *conjunto, onda tejana,* and Tejano, "they all share one fundamental characteristic: they are all homegrown, and they all speak after their own fashion to the fundamental social processes shaping Texas-Mexican society" (Peña 1999:xi). Understanding the musical context in which Selena emerged offers us key insight into her music's engagement with questions of identity, language politics, transnationalism, and critical consideration of her crossing over into Mexico and Latin America.

Selena was introduced to the American public via mainstream press coverage of her tragic death. In some ways, the large outpouring of grief in urban Latino communities across the country symbolically called the attention of the American public to the "loss" felt within these communities. The extent of public grief in cities across the nation, including Chicago, Los Angeles, Miami, and all across Texas, was undeniable even to the mainstream press, who were immediately challenged to define "Tejano music" and the geographical whereabouts of a Texas coastal city called Corpus Christi. In this circulation of media coverage—ranging from Univision's *Primer Impacto* to VH-1's *Behind the Music*—Selena's life and music became discursively channeled through the narrative of American "success" as a Latina crossover artist. This discursive shift moved Selena from her accomplishments as a central figure within the Latina/o and especially Mexican American communities to a marginalized "young woman on the brink of success" who did not live to see the release of her "crossover" English-language CD.

Selena represented the forefront of Tejano music's contemporary boom, a genre in which women have had to be resilient in their desire to stay and succeed within the industry. Thus, Selena's unprecedented inroads into the "Latin international" market, in places like Puerto Rico and Central America,[8] can be understood as engendering a rare migration pattern for Tejano music.[9] Tejano music's transnational travels were embodied in Selena, a gendered relocation of Tejano music that made explicit the intricate connections between color, language, music, class, history, land, and migration. Selena's racialization as "Latina" in effect erased the music's crossover into the Latin American market, because there was no explicit racialized leap. Selena, as a singer of *cumbias* and *rancheras,* made sense in the racial register of mainstream America, unlike the hip-hop, freestyle, and disco influence that was often at the core of her singing style and musical sound. Yet, Selena was very much a social and cultural product of her generation and of *tejas.* After all, as a U.S.-born Latina and a third-generation Tejana, she grew up musically influenced by artists such as Kool and the Gang and Donna Summer.

The narrative of crossover worked to elide Selena's music accomplishments and the complexity of her representation within the broader U.S. Latino and Latin American community. As Garofalo (1993) suggests, the crossing-over of artists and audiences is extremely political, because the industry is set up around the racialization of musical genres and markets. These racialized operations, as well as the working-class representation of Tejano music, became explicit when Selena, a U.S.-born primarily English-speaking brown woman, crossed the border south in attempts to open new markets for Tejano music. Her accomplishments in new Latin American markets did not come easy. Larry Rohter of the *New York Times* reminds us that Selena was not an automatic sensation in Mexico, unlike what many believe, especially as the music began to make inroads into new class markets. Rohter stated, "South of the border, too, there was resistance at first to what Selena represented. In the upper-class neighborhoods of Mexico City, she was at first derided as *naco,* an ethnic and class slur meaning coarse or vulgar, because of her mestizo or mixed European and Indian features, which were a marked contrast to those of the typically fair-skinned and light-haired soap-opera stars" (Rohter 1997:39H).[10]

CRUZANDO IDIOMAS: ON THE POLITICS AND NEGOTIATIONS OF LANGUAGE

Cruzando frontejas allows us to make explicit the politics of language in *tejas* that is key to better understanding the complexity of the move of Selena's music southward.[11] Like other Tejanas/os several generations removed from Mexico, Selena's struggle with Spanish symbolized the legacy of violent language oppression over promoting Spanish-language use in Texas. Most likely raised on stories of parents and grandparents physically and institutionally punished for attempting to retain the Spanish language, Tejanas/os embraced Selena's struggles to communicate in Spanish in public interviews and Spanish-language television programs. This resonated with her public in *tejas,* whose fluency in Spanish was, at its best, some version of Tex-Mex Spanglish.

Selena's negotiations with the Spanish language were publicly played out within popular culture. As the San Antonio disc jockey Johnny Ramírez recalled, "[Selena's] first few brushes with the Spanish-speaking press were near disasters. In one of her early interviews, her Spanish was quite bad. In one of her last, it was eloquent" (Ramsey 1995:7). I recall my mother and I watching the *Johnny Canales Show* and witnessing the young performer struggle through one of her first television interviews with Canales in Spanish. Years later, an older and more mature Selena appeared on the *Cristina* show, much more fluent yet still quite *pocha*. She faltered here and there, often maintaining a flawless conversation in Spanish but almost always inserting Spanglish, just enough to make her Spanish-speaking audiences accountable to the existence of "third space subjectivities" in South Texas.

Selena made explicit the politics of language and the contradictions of its operation within an increasingly commodified Latino market. She often had to negotiate the problematic link between language and cultural authenticity on both sides of the border. One West Texas mother articulated the ineptness Tejanos often feel about connections between language, culture, and ethnicity: "Living in Lubbock, I worry that my children are losing their culture . . . [my] children never showed much interest in the language until they began singing [Selena's] songs."[12] Selena's public struggles with Spanish validated Tejanos' experiences with Spanish-language fluency. Moreover, Selena exemplified what Anzaldúa refers to as "linguistic terrorism" (1987:58) in third space culture, the burden of trying to maintain connections to culture and ethnicity through language within a legacy of violent and racist language policies, particularly in South Texas.

Yet, to acknowledge that Selena was meaningful to her Tejano public only because she resonated with their social experiences would be too simplistic. For she was also a keen marketer of herself (consider, for example, her entrepreneurial entrance into the clothing industry, Selena Inc.) who recognized the contemporary growth in the music market south of the border, farther south than northern Mexico, where Conjunto/Tejano music had found success before. One may certainly note the problematic nature of Latina/o artists participating in the increased capitalist exploitation of markets in Latin America, but it would be equally problematic to ignore the complex ways in which agency operates in the lives of working-class Chicanas/os and their justified desire to attain a more comfortable economic life. In this way, Selena's music map made explicit the high stakes for working-class Tejanas and Latinas who desire to make a living out of what they love doing, making records and singing and performing for the public.

Selena certainly represented a positive reclaiming of a key aspect of *mexicano* culture lost within a legacy of colonization and racial segregation in Texas. To many working-class Tejanos living in an era of post-NAFTA, she also represented how the acquisition of the Spanish language was a strategy for upward social mobility. Suzanne Gamboa, a writer for the *Austin-American Statesman,* described Selena's resonance with fans this way: "Although she will be considered by mainstream listeners as having been on the verge of success because she had not hit the English-language pop charts, to many Hispanics, Selena already had succeeded by choosing to sing in Spanish" (1995:A1).

Selena's negotiation with the Spanish language is an example of how language represents a contested terrain upon which Mexican Americans and Tejanos negotiate and reshape their relations to social, political, and cultural institutions. Exploring how language is connected to the racialization of U.S. Latinos makes explicit how the conventional conception of musical crossover limits the understanding of transformations and shifts in contemporary music, as different languages and cultural "dialogue" create new sounds and new discourses in popular music. Selena's musical influences, from disco and techno to freestyle and hip-hop, contributed to a kind of translation and fusion in Tejano music.

Songs such as "Techno-cumbia," "La tracalera," and "La carcacha" all became the auditory locators of this "place" represented in Tejano music. For example, "La tracalera" and "La carcacha" exemplified the negotiations of space, resources, social class, movement, and racialization—whether it's running from city to city in avoidance of debt and lovers or the reclamation of barely functioning old cars in the barrios as "smooth," these were negotiations of the everyday that working-class Tejanas/os could relate to. In particular, these songs and Selena's distinctive beat marked a "place" for Tejano urban ethnicity emerging in cities such as Houston, San Antonio, and Corpus Christi, which marked Selena's process of *cruzando frontejas*. "[I]n Selena, arguably the biggest star in Tejano music, a whole culture between the poles of Mexico and America had found a public face" (Watrous 1995:C15).

TRANS-FRONTERIZAS/TRANSNATIONAL CONSIDERATIONS

Cruzando frontejas, unlike the conventional conception of musical crossover, acknowledges the movement of Selena's music into new markets in Latin America.[13] Although several bands, such as La Mafia and Mazz, toured heavily in northern Mexico, most who follow the Tejano music industry agree that not since artists such as Rita Vidaurri, Chelo Silvia, and Eva Garza had a Tejana/o artist overcome barriers to Latin America until the success of Selena.

To be sure, Selena's Tejano music existed within a very unique context as well, in particular impacted by new modes of technology and the North American Free Trade Agreement (NAFTA) with its influence on cultural production on both sides of the border. NAFTA represents one of the most significant U.S.-Mexico public policies implemented in recent history, and its impact should not be underestimated. It is certainly a key contextual element for many analyses of contemporary Chicano popular culture. Lipsitz stresses that "As transnational corporations create integrated global markets and the nation-state recedes as a source of identity and identification, popular culture becomes an ever more important public sphere" (1994:5). As such, *cruzando frontejas* challenges the one-dimensional Mexico-to-U.S. linear travels of music and culture embedded in Selena's crossover narrative.

Cristina Castrellón, a spokesperson for Representaciones Artisticas Apodaca, noted Selena's significance within Tejano music and the broader landscape of the Latino and Latin American music market (Danini 1995). Castrellón stated that Selena was unlike most Tejano/Conjunto performers, in that she had taken this regionally based music beyond the northern Mexican region and "was one of the few performers to totally fill the Teatro del Pueblo in Monterey." Selena was making inroads into Central America, she played Guatemala in mid-1994, and there were plans for a tour of South America later in 1995 (Danini 1995). She even unseated Gloria Estefan when her 1994 single "Amor prohibido" went to number one on the Latin International Chart.

Cruzando frontejas marks the complications and contradictions of Selena's transnational movement into new Latino and Latin American music markets as well as her impact on the "place" of Tejano music. What is poignantly clear is that in her unique musical sound created within this process of *cruzando frontejas* there is a transformation of "place" represented by Tejano music, a new cultural politics of "making home" for Mexican Americans and the broader U.S. Latina/o public (Lipsitz 1994). In this circulation of Tejano music to Mexico, Central America, and Puerto Rico, Selena makes explicit the politics of language and race in popular music for U.S. Latinas/os and Mexican Americans. Selena pushed against the racial, linguistic, gender, and geopolitical borders that reify a monolithic notion of Tejano music and established a "place" for her multiply situated fan base to come "home" to.[14]

CLOSING REMARKS: THE POLITICS OF CRUZANDO

In the contemporary context of popular music, the term "crossover" is especially persistent in its attempt to "contain" music and performance within the construction of a particular genre. In terms of the Latino popular music scene, the notion of a one-dimensional music crossover does not capture the impact of an increasingly transnational capitalist economy on the cross-cultural dialogue occurring in music. The notion of crossover is also limited because it assumes a progressive move from lesser to better and, in particular for Chicanos, a discursive (and literal) move along the south-to-north axis. Juan Flores's scholarship is an example of a move to reconceptualize crossover with Latino popular music in mind. He argues that political and commercial spheres should be understood as vehicles that Latinos use to "create new cultural forms that cross over in both directions" (1993:215).

Selena's musical accomplishments propelled her to become the foremost representative of Tejano music at the end of the twentieth century, and her rise within the ranks disrupted the gendered institution of Texas-Mexican music, which had historically been represented by male figures. Selena introduced the music to wider audiences, circulating in Central American and Puerto Rican markets. Thus, Tejano music, embodied through Selena, validated a differently gendered working-class racialized aesthetic that uniquely represented Mexican Americans in Texas. What is important to note as well is that Selena's "node" of success was neither the Anglo "Hollywood dream-machine" market of Los Angeles nor the U.S. "Latin" media capital of Miami, but South Texas, the "home" of Tex-Mex music.[15]

If we consider that the familiar Chicano political statement "we didn't cross the border, the border crossed us" presents a discursive response to the hegemonic narratives of Mexican presence as "illegal aliens" and foreign invaders in the United States, then my deployment of the conceptual framework of *cruzando frontejas* similarly takes to task the discursive operations of crossover to elide the historical context required to comprehend and validate Selena's Tejano music and the loss her death represented within U.S. Latino popular culture. *Cruzando frontejas* offers a different process for mapping Selena's music and a better understanding of the relation between popular music and productions of multiply situated Latino racial and gender subjectivities. *Cruzando frontejas* not only offers a way of establishing a fuller understanding of Selena's Tejano music but perhaps motivates us as well to create new tools for analyzing the complexity of American popular music that U.S. Latino publics create.

NOTES

I would like to acknowledge the tremendous support and critical feedback I received from my brilliant colleagues at the University of California at Santa Cruz: Gloria Anzaldúa, Lynn Fujiwara, Sherrie Tucker, and especially Maylei Blackwell, who has consistently given me feedback on my various projects on Selena. I also thank my faculty mentors who heard and read various versions of this and other writing on Selena: Lionel Cantú, Angie Chabram-Dernersesian, Rosa Linda Fregoso, Herman Gray (my dissertation chair), Michelle Habell-Pállan, Emma Pérez, Dana Takagi, Norma Cantú, and Olga Nájera-Ramírez.

1. Gray's definition of popular music is taken from his course on popular music and cultural politics at the University of California at Santa Cruz.

2. For example, in Gregory Nava's *Selena: The Movie,* the opening scene introduces what is supposed to be Selena's career pinnacle at the Houston Rodeo. I agree that this concert was one of Selena's most significant performances, yet this opening scene of Selena singing an English-language disco medley sets up the assimilationist narrative reinforced throughout the movie. The viewer's first impression, Selena singing in English, reinscribes the idea that the pinnacle of her career was her "success" through an English-language crossover status.

3. I refer specifically to works by Chicana and Tejana feminist theorists because their theorizing of "third space" and "third space performative acts" speaks profoundly to the ways in which race, history, sexuality, language, geography, gender,

"place," and class uniquely converge on the literal (and discursive) landscape of South Texas, the Texas-Mexico border region, and, in particular, upon the bodies of Texas-Mexican women. See also Bhabha 1994 and Soja 1996.

4. This essay is dedicated to Kyra Y. Ioppolo and all of the young women of color who loved Selena. In our passionate conversations as fans of Selena's music, Kyra profoundly reminded me that my voice as a fan matters and that it does indeed have a place in this essay.

5. My dissertation discusses "the making of *tejas*" through third space cultural production, defined by those unique social and cultural processes shaping Texas-Mexican society. "Tejas" is a site where we may explore how Tejanas/os parody, contest, and reconstitute an Anglo-Texan colonial imaginary in negotiating their varied social relations through music and, by extension, Tex-Mex language, aesthetics, food, and *chisme* (gossip) as well as in public sites such as dance halls, radio stations, and print culture.

6. The mourning by Tejanos (as evident in comments in numerous South Texas newspapers) over Selena's death revealed the connections many felt based on similar aspects of their social location.

7. My larger dissertation work includes an analysis of Tejana singers and musicians throughout the twentieth century. To fully appreciate Selena's unique mark on the music, we must situate her within the legacy of other women who have made significant contributions to Texas-Mexican music. As early as the 1930s and well into the 1960s, Tejanas such as Lydia Mendoza, Ventura Alonzo, Rita Vidaurri, Eva Garza, Chelo Silva, and Beatriz Llamas, as well as Tejana duets such as Carmen y Laura and Las Hermanas Cantú, created the space for women's voices within Texas-Mexican music. Since the 1970s there have been women such as Laura Canales, Patsy Torres, Eva Ybarra, Elsa García, and Shelly Lares. By placing Selena within this rich legacy of Tejana singers, we validate a history of Tejana cultural production that Selena contributed to, provide a context that better informs an analysis of her cultural work, and disrupt the erasure of the histories of Tejanas in popular music.

8. Selena collaborated with the Puerto Rican (Nuyorican) hip-hop group the Barrio Boyz, producing the hit single "Donde quiera que estes." She also produced a duet hit single, "Buenos amigos," with the Salvadoran artist Alvaro Torres. The impact of Selena's death on the broader Latin American community is best exemplified through a CD released in her memory. Entitled *Recordando a Selena*, it includes recordings by a number of Puerto Rican artists, such as Celia Cruz, Tito Nieves, Manny Manuel, and Yolanda Duke. The CD is a collection of Selena's greatest hits re-produced into salsa and merengue tunes.

9. I acknowledge the need to elaborate on this point, in particular by drawing on scholarship pertaining to spatial feminist critiques and analyses of the relationships between space, cultural production, feminism, and geography. Soja 1996 discusses key feminist scholars in this area.

10. bell hooks further clarifies how race, gender, color, and sexuality combine to produce a unique subordination for darker-skinned women: "Just as whites now privilege lighter skin in movies and fashion magazines, particularly with female characters, folks with darker skin face a media that subordinates their image. Dark skin is stereotypically coded in the racist, sexist, or colonized imagination as masculine. Hence, a male's power is enhanced by darker looks while a female's dark looks diminish her femininity" (1994:180).

11. In an interview on the public radio program *Latino U.S.A.* (October 18, 1997), which featured a segment on Tejano writers and "third space culture," Sandra Cisneros provided an example of the kind of Tex-Mex language she's experienced in San Antonio, a language created from English terms that are Spanish-ized and vice-versa. For example, Cisneros recalls the statement, "Voy hacerle el try," used by a Tejana clerk she spoke with at a boot store.

12. Silvia Quirino, a nurse from Lubbock, interviewed by Phillip True (True 1995:4A).

13. This raises a possible and no less problematic strategy for U.S. Latinas/os to find success in Latin American Spanish-language music markets first before "reentering" the United States by marketing oneself as a "Latin" music singer within the current "Latin music boom." I thank Sherrie Tucker for reminding me of a similar occurrence in American jazz, when it traveled to Europe, finding recognition and validation it lacked, then returned to a more receptive white audience in the United States.

14. Selena also had an impact on women singers outside of Tejano music. In an interview on the popular talk show *Cristina,* the Nuyorican *salsera* India remarked that aside from Celia Cruz, Selena deserved credit for opening doors for young Latina music artists.

15. Special thanks to Lionel Cantú for contributing his key insight on this point.

WORKS CITED

Anzaldúa, Gloria. 1987. *Borderlands/La Frontera: The New Mestiza.* San Francisco: Aunt Lute.

Bhabha, Homi K. 1994. *The Location of Culture.* New York: Routledge Press.

Burnett, John. 1997. "Hispanic Heritage Month: Special Report on Tejano Writers." *Latino U.S.A.: Public Radio News Magazine.* October 18. Austin, Tex.

Danini, Carmina. 1995. "In Mexico Singer's Fans Mourn Loss." *San Antonio Express-News,* April 1, 12A.

Flores, Juan. 1993. "Living Borders/Buscando América: Languages of Latino Self-Formation." In *Divided Borders: Essays on Puerto Rican Identity.* Ed. George Yúdice and Juan Flores. 199–224. Houston: Arte Público Press.

Fregoso, Rosa Linda. 1998. "Recycling Colonialist Fantasies on the Texas Borderlands." In *Home, Exile, Homeland: Film, Media, and the Politics of Place*. Ed. Hamid Naficy. 169–92. New York: Routledge Press.

Gamboa, Suzanne. 1995. "Selena's Death Leaves Void in Hispanic Culture." *Austin-American Statesman*, April 3, A1.

Garofalo, Reebee. 1993. "Crossing Over: 1939–1992." In *Split Image: African Americans and the Mass Media*. Ed. Jannette L. Dates and William Barlow. 57–127. Washington, D.C.: Howard University Press.

hooks, bell. 1994. *Outlaw Culture: Resisting Representations*. New York: Routledge.

Lipsitz, George. 1994. *Dangerous Crossroads: Popular Music, Postmodernism, and the Poetics of Place*. London: Verso Press.

Peña, Manuel. 1999. *Música Tejana*. College Station: Texas A&M University Press.

Pérez, Emma. 1999. *The Decolonial Imaginary: Writing Chicanas into History*. Bloomington: Indiana University Press.

Ramsey, Bill. 1995. "The Ultimate Crossover: Selena, a Star and an Icon Is Born." *San Antonio Current*, November 1, 6–8.

Rohter, Larry. 1997. "A Legend Grows, and So Does an Industry." *New York Times*, January 12, 39H.

Saldívar-Hull, Sonia. 2000. *Feminism on the Border: Chicana Gender Politics and Literature*. Berkeley: University of California Press.

Soja, Edward W. 1996. *Thirdspace: Journeys to Los Angeles and Other Real-and-Imagined Places*. Cambridge: Blackwell Press.

True, Phillip. 1995. "Selena's Fans May Turn Her into a Folk Hero." *San Antonio Express-News*, April 17, 1A, 4A.

Watrous, Peter. 1995. "The Loss of a Star Who Gave a Face to a People's Hopes." *New York Times*, April 4, C15.

GOLDIE GARCIA

LA REINA DE SOUTH BROADWAY Y RASQUACHE

TEY MARIANNA NUNN

> To be *rasquache* is to posit a bawdy, spunky consciousness, to
> seek to subvert and turn ruling paradigms upside down. It is a
> witty, irreverent, and impertinent posture that recodes and moves
> out established boundaries.
> —Tomás Ybarra-Frausto, "Rasquachismo: A Chicano Sensibility"

> If I get run over by a car tomorrow, I'll die a happy woman be-
> cause Al Pacino bought my stuff.
> —Goldie Garcia, Albuquerque, New Mexico, June 30, 1999

This essay was inspired by a number of factors, including a personal appreciation of and attraction to the assemblage works of the Albuquerque, New
Mexico, artist Goldie Garcia[1] and my scholarly interest in the perceptions
of Latino, Chicano, Hispanic, Hispano, Mexican American, and Latin
American art as more "folk" than "fine." Garcia's art provides illustrative
examples of contemporary cultural expression and helps to collapse restrictive categories imposed by those who have failed to take the time to research,
learn, and understand. Not only that, her art sparkles.

I was attracted to the work of Goldie Garcia long before I met her. I first
saw her embellished bottle cap earrings, magnets, car medallions, pendants,
and button covers in a trendy gift store in Albuquerque's North Valley. Ever
since I was a small child, I have been drawn to things that glitter, glint, and
shine, things that are ornate and flashy but tastefully not overdone (at least
to my eye). One memorable episode illustrates my penchant towards gleam-
ing objects. I was about six years old when I needed my first pair of eyeglasses. My mother and I went to pick out some frames—any pair I want-

ed. Armed with such a guideline, I quickly selected what I thought to be the most exquisitely beautiful pair of "cat eyes." This particular pair was bedecked and bejeweled on the top rim and on the points. Upon learning of my choice, my mother replied, "No, you can't have those" and "I promise you will thank me when you are older." I ended up with a pair of little-girl baby-blue cat eyes and a neverending yearning for glitz. At times this desire has been so intense as to inspire me to explore it further as it relates to Mexican, Chicano, and Latino artistic expression.[2]

Goldie Garcia likes to call herself "The Queen of South Broadway." This title refers to the predominantly Mexican American or Hispano neighborhood situated south of Central Avenue and east of Interstate 25 in Albuquerque. Garcia spent the early part of her childhood witnessing both the flourishing and decline of the neighborhood, the barrio. The kitchen window of the Garcia family home directly faced Our Lady of Guadalupe Church, and Garcia remembers washing dishes and hearing sermons, weddings, and funerals. These church rituals and ceremonies were an integral cultural component of the South Broadway community. The decline of South Broadway's *mexicano* traditions, especially those celebrating December 12, the feast day for the Virgin of Guadalupe, are a source of reflection and some sadness for Garcia, who remembers processions, home *altares* (altars), and lots of decorations as components of these fiestas and celebrations. These memories permeate her art and provide the motivation behind all of her work. She once told me, "I remember South Broadway when things were nourished. Everyone used to participate in the fiestas, but many no longer do."[3]

Garcia has an intensely strong sense of self, of who she is. A few years ago, I curated a small contemporary art show featuring five Chicana/o, Hispana/o, and *mexicana/o* artists from the Albuquerque area, and Garcia was one of those featured. Upon my request for a brief biography to be included in the exhibition, Garcia quickly scanned what the other artists had written and provided me with the following information:

> GOLDIE GARCIA
> "QUEEN OF SOUTH BROADWAY"
> Education began @St. Francis Xavier, ABQ
> TVI (Technical Vocational Institute)—Shorthand Class
> UNM (University of New Mexico)—General Requirements
> Harvard University—Humanities
> "Yes, I'm a humanitarian! Watch Out!"

Her confidence in defying long lists of artistic accolades and honors and

Goldie Garcia in her Albuquerque studio, July 1999. Photo courtesy of Tey Diana Rebolledo.

taking pride instead in all of her education from shorthand to Harvard indicates her deep roots in her community, in her family, in her art, and in her own strong sense of identity.

Garcia's art encompasses many media and forms. She is a talented painter, photographer, and comedienne; but she is perhaps best known for her embellished bottle cap and jar lid art. She uses these recycled metal objects, as well as other items such as kitchen utensils, as her creative canvas. From these she makes bracelets, earrings, necklaces, pins, rings, magnets, money clips, button covers, and dog tags. She inserts printed images and other objects, which are then enhanced and decorated with glitter, sequins, beads, and foil stars (the kind grade schoolers receive on homework assignments). Each assemblage is then filled with Garcia's copyrighted and self-described "secret formula." When asked why she makes these smaller objects, Garcia replies, "I like to make small things that are affordable for women, especially working women . . . and Latinos . . . the working-class person. This way, then, everyone can afford a piece of art."

As mentioned previously, Garcia's art is heavily based in the *ephemera* created for religious festivals and home *altares* and *nichos* (niches), and she readily admits to utilizing such traditions. However, her adaptation of elements of *arte popular* (popular arts) and *ephemera* also pushes boundaries and has become emblematic of not only the artist but of the age-old scholarly discussion of what is "folk" and what is "fine" in the art world. A number of scholars have written on similar artistic expressions as they pertain to Chicano and Latino aesthetics and art. Kay Turner has specifically addressed the assemblage type art form in her research on the aesthetics of Mexican American women in Texas. Turner believes that the role of women engaged in creating *nichos* and *altares* is significant and all-encompassing. She writes:

> A woman's gathering of sacred and secular gifts at her altar—the arrangement she gives them, the embellishment she provides them, the meaning she assigns them—implicates the power of aesthetic productions to transcend the purely formalistic in favor of the strategically dialogic. The aesthetic of relationship improves the project of artistic practice by asserting the potency of objects to state and shape values that engage the maker in transforming and enhancing both her reality and the world's reality.[4] (Turner 1990:256)

I asked Garcia how she got started embellishing bottle caps, and she replied that it happened upon her return to New Mexico after receiving a degree in photography and women's studies from Harvard University. She had returned to Albuquerque with a degree from a prestigious school and could not find a job. At times the situation was so bad that she was literally going hungry. One day, during a backyard family gathering, she found a Budweiser bottle cap and began playing around with ideas on how to use it in art. She remembers viewing the bottle cap with a sense of irony. In her words, "Alcoholism and Catholicism hold our people down real bad." She says she used to be a proponent of people not drinking in her family, but now she tells them, "save all your bottle caps." The bottle cap, a small emblematic object, became a symbol for Garcia's work and inspired her to create ways to preserve values, traditions, and cultural expressions that she felt were disappearing rapidly from her culture.

When she was beginning her art, there was a time (before she discovered color Xerox!) that Garcia was unable to find enough religious prints small enough to fit inside the bottle caps. She tells the story of how she was so discouraged that she decided to give up on the idea of bottle cap saints and work on something else. About a half-hour after making this decision, she was on her way to work when she saw a garage sale. She pulled over, looked around the sale's offerings, and spied a box. She looked inside and found that the box was filled with hundreds of miniature religious prints. Garcia says, "I looked at the sky and I looked at the box . . . and I looked at the sky." For five dollars she bought the entire box, which was enough, she says, "to keep me going for a year." The previous owner had at one time owned a religious supply store. Garcia feels that finding the prints was definitely a "sign." She says she felt like Diego, referring to Juan Diego, who witnessed the apparition of the Virgin of Guadalupe at Tepeyac: "He [God] appeared to me in a box of holy cards!"

Garcia is drawn to all types of shimmering decorations for many reasons. "I've always loved glitter," she says. "When I was eighteen or nineteen, I had a dream of glitter falling from the sky." She still remembers when Valentine's Day cards had hand-applied glitter. "Today you can't find the same craftsmanship" because, according to Garcia, "nowadays, everything is made so fast." In her words; "Glitter takes us beyond black, white, Hispanic, racism, sexism, sexual harassment, sexual abuse. . . . You look at glitter and you just think of your childhood and how pure it [glitter] was the first time you saw it. . . . It's magical. . . . That's how I see it."

Goldie Garcia, earrings (bottle caps and conchas), with images of the Virgin of Guadalupe, ca. 1994. Private collection.

Garcia acknowledges her use of what are conventionally considered to be "folk" elements in her work, yet she dislikes being identified as a "folk artist." She feels that she is labeled a "folk artist" because she is Hispana and, if others were to engage in the same type of art that she creates, they would be thought of simply as artists. Garcia says "You know, if you are an ethnic person, they put you in folk art." She agrees that the use of assemblage and ephemeral elements in her work are a Latino or *mexicano* aesthetic, but she is quick to point out that "Maybe it's not just Latino . . . you know I was raised in the fifties where everybody saw that [glitter] and loved it. . . . That's why my product does so well . . . to me everybody identifies with that point of glitter because it is so pure to their life. Nowadays it's Latino art because we like shimmery stuff. . . . We like stuff that's way out there, you know."

Garcia displays an obvious preference toward images of the Mexican Marian representation of the Virgin of Guadalupe throughout her art. When asked what was her favorite image to use, she replied, "Guadalupe, because she is female first of all, and secondly, I grew up with her as my image." Garcia continued:

> And what I remember is going to St. Francis Xavier. . . . Did you ever attend Mother's Day events where they put the little crown on the statue? . . . Oh, it is so beautiful . . . then they have where you carry this little crown with little flowers on it . . . real pretty and they always get the smartest student in school . . . which wasn't me you know . . . and they march up and put it on the statue of the Virgin and it is so beautiful. . . . And that's what this all comes from. . . . This all comes from any ceremony I had in Catholic school. . . . This stuff [meaning her art] is just stuff that has grown out of that, but Guadalupe is my favorite. . . . Mainly because she's a woman. . . . You know . . . when I sit there and work and I look at the male saints . . . I think, oh they're okay, but it's the women saints . . . when I look at this, when I look at her she reminds me of when I was a little girl and all my hopes and dreams . . . I think she does that with a lot of people.

Garcia's prevalent use of Guadalupe throughout her art echoes the use of the image by many other Chicana, Latina, and Hispana artists and writers such as Yolanda López, Sandra Cisneros, and Denise Chávez, all of whom have reclaimed and transformed this icon of Mexico and Latin America, of femininity and motherhood. For many, Nuestra Señora de Guadalupe (our lady of Guadalupe) is a symbol of Mexicaness as well as Latina/o identity. Garcia looks upon her as something "permanent" and as a symbol of Hispanic and Latino peoples.

In addition to this Marian representation from the Americas, Garcia uses many other religious images in her art. Among them are the Santo Niño de Atocha, the Guardian Angel, Saint Christopher, San Martin de Porres, various versions of Jesus Christ, and many other representations of the Virgin. Sometimes she strategically places a sequin or mirror sticker so that the face of the saint or religious image is reflected in the ornament. She told me that this first happened by accident (with an image of Jesus, no less!). She was so pleased with the effect that she continues to do it, but not in every piece.

While religious images predominate her art, Garcia also incorporates personalities, celebrities, and other icons from popular culture such as Sor Juana Inéz de la Cruz, Frida Kahlo, Diego Rivera, Jackie Onassis, John F. Kennedy Jr., Elizabeth Taylor, Marilyn Monroe, Elvis and Priscilla Presley, Michael Jackson, Princess Diana, Kurt Cobain, Mickey and Minnie Mouse, Godzilla, Fabio (the romance-novel cover model), Madonna, Whoopi Goldberg, Dennis Hopper, James Dean, John Wayne, Frank Sinatra, Abbott and Costello, Barbie, Cher, the Beatles, *Star Trek*, Malcolm X, Carmen Miranda, and, of course, the Pope. She often uses images directly from newspaper headlines, current events, and trends. Some such examples include Tanya Harding and Nancy Kerrigen, John Wayne Bobbit, Martha Stewart, Agents Fox Mulder and Dana Scully from *The X-Files*, and more trendy phenom-

Goldie Garcia, Santo Niño de Atocha jar lid magnets, ca. 1994. Private collection.

ena such as the adolescent musical group Hanson, the Spice Girls, and Ricky Martin. Once these images are combined with ephemeral elements and sealed with Garcia's secret formula, they become enshrined as icons of popular culture, religious icons of everyday life. The secular and "rasquached" treatment gives the images a certain aura of religiosity, which also provides Garcia with a visual avenue for social and political commentary.

Garcia is actively involved with other media besides her bottle cap and jar lid pieces. She will often use her distinctive mixed media concept and apply it to other surfaces such as bottles, antique china, flower pots, light switch covers, and salt and pepper shakers. Garcia also paints with oils, acrylics, and watercolors. Among the titles of her paintings are *Barbie after Divorce, Home on the Mesa,* and *Tammy the Abused Woman. Barbie after Divorce* features a Barbie doll figure with long blond hair. The back of the figure faces the viewer, and her right hand is extended, holding a bra that she has obviously just removed as a symbol of independence. Images of women's experiences, not just that of Guadalupe, serve as recurring themes in Garcia's paintings. There is also her self-portrait, entitled *Fiesta Queen Runner Up,* which features a tiara-festooned Garcia as *la reina de la fiesta* . . . almost.

Goldie Garcia, *Kirk and Spock,* ca. 1994, bottle cap earrings. Private collection.

Goldie Garcia, Virgin of Guadalupe and Santo Niño de Atocha salt and pepper shakers, ca. 1993. Private collection.

Garcia finds another creative avenue in photography. One of the reasons she went to Harvard was to study this artistic medium. Saints and Catholic religiosity are again her focus in photographic images, only they are usually plaster statues of holy representations found in churches. Garcia takes these images and hand tints them or adds glitter sparingly. One of her photos is titled *Guadalupe for Sale*. Its shows a plaster statue of the Virgin, sitting on a shelf at a religious supply store, with a price tag around her neck. Many of her photographs are framed with beans. The bean frames, combined with saintly subject matter, send a strong message of Mexicanismo or Mexicaness. When asked why she uses beans, Garcia replies, "They represent Mexican culture and nourishment . . . beans gave me my life . . . they are a mainstay . . . beans should get some respect." Once again, she provides social commentary and empowerment through her art and the media she chooses to incorporate.

In the last few years, Garcia has been inspired to do larger works. The

Goldie Garcia, *Guadalupe,* 1995, tile and mixed media. Private collection.

results are mixed-media pieces that combine her distinctive embellishment techniques, on a much grander scale, with ceramic tiles, plaster, silk flowers, Christmas lights, ruffled foils, pennies, bottle caps, and marbles. The first of these pieces were inspired by a Mexican Christmas tree topper she saw at a party in Albuquerque. These larger works are reminiscent of yard art and *nichos,* larger assemblages meant for both private and public devotion. A recent work features La Virgen de Guadalupe with a crown made of computer parts and praying hands adorned with bright red false fingernails. Garcia views these larger pieces as extensions of her smaller bottle cap works.

In "Bits and Pieces: The Mexican American Folk Aesthetic," Suzanne Seriff and José Limón address the issue of the distinguishable aesthetic Garcia and others engage in. According to Seriff and Limón, this acknowledgment and utilization of "bits and pieces" connects the artist to identity and "becomes a marker of allegiance to a cultural "homeland" (1986:40). This aesthetic aids in differentiating oneself from the dominant culture: "the traditional art genres work together in Mexican American culture to form a complete aesthetic and this aesthetic helps create and define the concept of *mexicanismo*. . . . What makes this Mexican American aesthetic unique is the way in which 'bits and pieces' are creatively put together to form a coherent and meaningful whole" (1986:40).

More recently, the catalogue to the *CARA Chicano Art: Resistance and Affirmation* exhibition contained what has become an important, almost manifesto-like exploration of the Mexican American or Chicano aesthetic. If we are to apply this well-known definition of "rasquache" (quoted in part in the epigraph), written by Tomás Ybarra-Frausto, to the work of Goldie Garcia, it is quite evident that her artistic creations are replete with this Mexican American and Chicano artistic sensibility. In fact, her utilization of this aesthetic becomes a manifesto and declaration not only of who she is, but of who we are as a culture. As Ybarra-Frausto writes:

> Dressing (putting yourself together) with whatever is at hand does not make you *rasquache,* but it is a gesture in the right direction. In the realm of taste, to be *rasquache* is to be unfettered and unrestrained, to favor the elaborate over the simple, the flamboyant over the severe. Bright colors (*chillantes*) are preferred to sombre, high intensity to low, the shimmering and the sparkling to the muted and subdued. The *rasquache* inclination piles pattern on pattern, filling every available space with bold display. Ornamentation and elaboration prevail, joined to a delight for texture and sensuous surface. Witness the cumulative ensemble of home *altares* (which juxtapose plaster saints, plastic flowers, bric-a-brac, family photographs, and treasured talismans). The com-

posite organization has a sort of wild abandon yet is subtly controlled with precise repetitions, replications and oppositional orders of colors, patterns, and designs. (1991:157)

One more art form mastered by Garcia, and the media that perhaps best mirrors her bottle cap art, is her comedy. Garcia is a stand-up comedienne who performs on stage throughout the traveling comedy circuit. She has opened for other notable Chicano comedians such as Paul Rodríguez. Her comedy acts are filled with observations on (and bits and pieces of) Chicano, Hispano, and Latino culture. Much as she does in her art, Garcia addresses head-on issues of cultural identity, stereotypes, and other "hot" topics. Her act is filled with commentary on such things as typical Hispanic meals (bologna sandwiches) and cosmetics (Garcia worries that her car, a pink Karmen Ghia, will be mistaken as a Mary Kay "starter kit"). Throughout her act, she also addresses stereotypes that are thrust upon Latinos and Hispanics. She conveys her opinions through humor, as illustrated by her mantra, "Stop racism! Eat a burrito!"

Goldie Garcia, *Glow in the Dark Bizcochito*, ca. 1995, magnet. Private collection.

One of her characters that she doesn't use anymore is Rosarita. Garcia says, "Rosarita is funny. . . . She's like a Pee Wee Herman . . . only radical." As Rosarita, Garcia wore "fiesta-style" dresses and a rose behind her hair. She no longer uses Rosarita during her Albuquerque engagements because, in her words, "she feels so stereotypical." According to Garcia, her Rosarita character did very well, but too many Latinos complained, "Oh you make us look bad with that character." In response to their comments Garcia observed, "they're so self-destructive because they are so pressured to assimilate. I don't see why I have to get a little hair bob haircut and wear loafers to be successful. Why can't I wear my stiletto heals and red lipstick? . . . Let me be me."

Garcia's comedy is another example of the Mexican American and Latino aesthetic sense in the arts. She takes "bits and pieces" from her own life experience, current events, and cultural perceptions and combines them into yet another art form. She has no qualms about addressing social reality, and in doing so she reflects social reality. La Reina de Rasquache takes center stage and subverts the established system. She reclaims stereotypes and directly addresses others. Garcia relishes her role as a comedienne. In her own words, "I like comedy because it gives me more of a voice than I have in the everyday world." It is also a vehicle through which she can express and explore her identity as a Nuevomexicana, a Hispana, a Hispanic, a Chicana, and a Latina. As most comics do, she uses comedy to provide social commentary. As is the case for many persons of Hispanic and Latino descent, she identifies herself as either Hispanic or Latina, depending on the situation. She doesn't like the word "Hispanic," but feels she has to use it when she does comedy because the media has chosen to grasp it. Garcia says, "Sometimes I get mad when I have to use it because I feel much more Latina."

Through her art and her comedy, Garcia explores not only her own identity but the multiple identities of Nuevomexicana/o, Hispanic, Chicana/o, and Latina/o culture. She explores her own identity by setting the example and empowering herself and her family. As the oldest child, Garcia has provided an example for the rest of her siblings. Her sisters, Anita and Mona, have embarked on their own artistic careers using assemblage techniques to create their own individual styles of art. Another sister, May Ling, is one of the few people in the world who plays the glass harmonica, a musical instrument invented by Benjamin Franklin.

Goldie Garcia's art evokes feelings and memories of the ephemeral art of Mexican, Mexican American, Nuevomexicano, and Latino life and ritual. Celebration and community are captured in sequins and glitter. She takes the iconic, the sacred, and the popular and "rasquaches" them so they still function within traditional realms. Garcia says of her work: "What I do stems back to South Broadway." Regarding her art as a reflection of Hispanic, Chicano, Latino, and *mexicano* culture, she says, "I don't want to destroy it. . . . I want to bring it back. . . . I want to maintain it. . . . I want it to gain respect. . . . And that's what it is. . . . It's not even me. . . . It's reflecting the culture. . . . That's what I want. Deep inside my heart, all I want to do is empower my people." In true royal fashion, through her arts and her life, Goldie Garcia, The Queen of South Broadway y la Reina de Rasquache, is doing just that. She takes bits and pieces of Hispana/o, Chicana/o, and Latina/o everyday life and thought and creates brilliant shimmering reflections of her identity and her culture.

NOTES

1. At the request of the artist, her surname, Garcia, is not accented on the "i." Initial editorial corrections for this essay requested that the accent be included. When asked how she would feel if the author included the accent, Garcia replied that she had never spelled her name that way and requested that her identity not be changed. On an unrelated note, although she still stands by her 1997 statement regarding Al Pacino, since that time other celebrities, including Billy Bob Thorton, Laura Dern, and Julia Roberts, have purchased her "stuff."

2. I would like to thank my mother, Tey Diana Rebolledo, for saying "no" to the jeweled eyeglasses, thus inspiring scholarly avenues for art historical analysis and further research on sequins, Rasquachisma/o, and the Mexican-Latino aesthetic.

3. The quotes by Garcia throughout this essay are excerpted from a number of interviews conducted by the author with the artist since 1994.

4. Turner has conducted extensive research on Tejana/o and Mexican American aesthetic sensibilities.

WORKS CITED

Seriff, Suzanne, and José Limón. 1986. "Bits and Pieces: The Mexican American Folk Aesthetic." In *Arte entre Nosotros, Art among Us: Mexican American Folk Art of San Antonio.* Ed. Pat Jasper and Kay Turner. 40–48. San Antonio, Tex.: San Antonio Museum Association.

Turner, Kay Frances. 1990. "Mexican-American Women's Home Altars: The Art of Relationship." Ph.D. dissertation, University of Texas at Austin.

Ybarra-Frausto, Tomás. 1991. "Rasquachismo: A Chicano Sensibility." In *CARA Chicano Art: Resistance and Affirmation,* exhibition catalog. Ed. Richard Griswold del Castillo, Teresa McKenna, and Yvonne Yarbro-Bejarano. 155–62. Los Angeles: Wight Gallery, University of California.

SELECTED BIBLIOGRAPHY
OF CHICANA FOLKLORE

Alarcón, Norma. 1981. "Chicana's Feminist Literature: A Re-vision through Ma-lintzin; or, Malintzin: Putting Flesh Back on the Object." In *This Bridge Called My Back: Writings by Radical Women of Color.* Ed. Cherrie Moraga and Glo-ria Anzaldúa. 182–90. Watertown, Mass.: Persephone Press.

———. 1994. "Traddutora, Traditora: A Paradigmatic Figure of Chicana Femi-nism." In *Scattered Hegemonies: Postmodernity and Transnational Feminist Practices.* Ed. Inderpal Grewal and Karen Kaplan. 110–33. Minneapolis: Uni-versity of Minnesota Press.

Barakat, Robert A. 1965. "Aztec Motifs in 'La Llorona.'" *Southern Folklore Quar-terly* 29 (4): 288–96.

Barker, Ruth Laughlin. 1965 [1932]. "New Mexico Witch Tales." In *Tone the Bell Easy.* Ed. J. Frank Dobie. 62–70. Dallas, Tex.: Southern Methodist University Press.

Braddy, Haldeen. 1962. "Queens of the Bullring." *Southern Folklore Quarterly* 26: 107–21.

Brown, Mary Helen de la Peña. 1981. "Una Tamalada: The Special Event." *West-ern Folklore* 40 (1): 64–71.

Broyles-González, Yolanda. 1986. "Women in El Teatro Campesino: ¿Apoco Estaba Molacha La Virgen de Guadalupe?" In *Chicana Voices: Intersections of Class, Race, and Gender.* Ed. Teresa Cordova et al. 162–87. Austin: Center for Mexi-can American Studies, University of Texas Press.

———. 2001. *Lydia Mendoza's Life in Music: La historia de Lydia Mendoza—Norteño Tejano Legacies.* New York: Oxford University Press.

Buss, Fran Leeper. 1980. *La Partera: Story of a Midwife.* Ann Arbor: University of Michigan Press.

Cabeza de Baca Gilbert, Fabiola. 1994 [1954]. *We Fed Them Cactus.* Albuquerque: University of New Mexico Press.

————. 1993. "The Herb Woman." In *Infinite Divisions: An Anthology of Chicana Literature*. Ed. Tey Diana Rebolledo and Eliana S. Rivero. 52–56. Tucson: University of Arizona.

Cantú, Norma E. 1982. "The Offering and the Offerers: A Generic Illocation of a Laredo Pastorela in the Tradition of Shepherds' Plays." Ph.D. dissertation, University of Nebraska.

————. 1992a. "Costume as Cultural Resistance and Affirmation: The Case of a South Texas Community." In *Hecho en Texas*. Ed. Joe Graham. 117–30. Denton: University of North Texas Press.

————. 1992b. "Los Matachines de la Santa Cruz: Un acto de resistencia cultural." In *Entre la magia y la historia: Tradiciones, mitos, y leyendas de la frontera*. Ed. José Manuel Valenzuela Arce. 167–73. Tijuana, Mexico: Colegio de la Frontera Norte.

————. 1995. "Los Matachines de la Santa Cruz de la Ladrillera: Notes toward a Socio-Literary Analysis." In *Feasts and Celebrations in North American Ethnic Communities*. Ed. Ramón A. Gutiérrez and Geneviève Fabre. 57–67. Albuquerque: University of New Mexico Press.

————. 1996. "La Virgen de Guadalupe: Symbol of Faith and Devotion." In *Familia, Fe, y Fiestas/Family, Faith, and Fiestas: Mexican American Celebrations of the Holiday Season*. 15–20. ArteAmericas and Fresno Arts Council, December.

————. 1999. "Quinceañeras: Towards an Ethnography of a Life-Cycle Ritual." *Southern Folklore* 56 (1): 73–101.

Cantú, Norma, and Ofelia Zapata Vela. 1991. "The Mexican-American Quilting Traditions of Laredo, San Ygnacio and Zapata." In *Hecho en Tejas*. Ed. Joe Graham. 77–92. Denton: University of North Texas Press.

Cardozo-Freeman, Inéz. 1975. "Games Mexican Girls Play." *Journal of American Folklore* 88:12–24.

Carpenter, Ann. 1974. "Scratches on the Bedpost: Vestiges of La Lechuza." In *The Folklore of Texan Cultures*. Ed. Frances Edward Abernethy. 75–78. Austin, Tex.: Encino Press.

Carrasco, Sara M. Campos. 1984. "Mexican American Folk Medicine: A Descriptive Study of the Different Curanderismo Techniques Practiced by Curanderos or Curanderas and Used by Patients in the Laredo, Texas, Area." Ph.D. dissertation, Texas Woman's University.

Dávalos, Karen Mary. 1996. "*La Quinceañera*: Making Gender and Ethnic Identities." *Frontiers: A Journal of Women's Studies* 16 (2–3): 101–27.

Del Castillo, Adelaida R. 1974. "Malintzin Tenepal: A Preliminary Look into a New Perspective." *Encuentro Femenil* 1 (2): 58–77.

Erevia, Angela. 1980. *Quinceañera*. San Antonio, Tex.: Mexican American Cultural Center.

Espin, Oliva M. 1988. "Spiritual Power and the Mundane World: Hispanic Female Healers in Urban U.S. Communities." *Women's Studies Quarterly* 16 (3): 33–47.

Espinosa, Carmen Gertrudis. 1970. *Shawls, Crinolines, Filigree: The Dress and Adornment of Women of New Mexico, 1737–1900.* El Paso: Texas Western Press.

Gallardo, Ernesto. 1973. "'*Curanderas*': A Story of Mexican Folklore." *El Chicano* 7 (38): 5–6.

García, Rogelia O. 1970. *Dolores, Revilla, and Laredo (Three Sister Settlements).* Waco, Tex.: Texian Press.

Garza, Humberto. 1961. "Owl-Bewitchment in the Lower Rio Grande Valley." In *Singers and Storytellers.* Ed. Mody C. Boatright, Wilson M. Hudson, and Allen Maxwell. 218–25. Dallas, Tex.: Southern Methodist University Press.

Gil, Carlos B. 1997. "Lydia Mendoza, Houstonian and First Lady of Mexican American Song." In *Aztlán: Chicano Culture and Folklore, An Anthology.* Ed. José Villarino and Arturo Ramírez. 223–34. San Francisco, Calif.: McGraw Hill.

Glazer, Mark. 1984. "La Llorona in South Texas: Tradition and Modernity in a Mexican American Legend." In *Plenary Papers: The Eighth Congress for the International Society for Folk Narrative Research, Bergen, June 12–17, 1984.* 205–12. Bergen, Norway: International Society for Folk Narrative Research.

Goldkind, Victor. 1959. "A Comparison of Folk Health Beliefs and Practices between *Ladino* Women of Denver, Colorado, and Saginaw, Michigan." M.A. thesis, Michigan State University.

González, Alicia María. 1988. "'Guess How Doughnuts Are Made': Verbal and Nonverbal Aspects of the Panadero and His Stereotype." *Perspectives in Mexican American Studies* 1 (1988): 89–107.

González, María del Refugio. 1952. "The Spanish Folklore of Webb and Zapata Counties." M.A. thesis, University of Texas.

González, Rosalinda. 1962. "Work and Play on a Border Ranch." In *The Golden Log.* Ed. Mody C. Boatright, Wilson M. Hudson, and Allen Maxwell. 141–55. Dallas, Tex.: Southern Methodist University Press.

Guerra, Fermina. 1941. "Mexican and Spanish Folklore and Incidents in Southeast Texas." M.A. thesis, University of Texas.

———. 1967a [1941]. "Rancho Buena Vista: Its Ways of Life and Traditions." In *Texian Stomping Grounds.* Ed. J. Frank Dobie, Mody C. Boatright, and Harry H. Ransom. 59–77. Dallas, Tex.: Southern Methodist University Press.

———. 1967b [1943]. "Mexican Animal Tales." In *Backwoods to Border.* Ed. Mody C. Boatright and Donald Day. 188–94. Dallas, Tex.: Southern Methodist University Press.

Harpham, Lois Bartlett. 1950. "Witches and Witchcraft in the Hispanic Folklore of New Mexico." M.A. thesis, University of New Mexico.

Hawes, Bess Lomax. 1968. "La Llorona in Juvenile Hall." *Western Folklore* 27 (4): 153–70.

Herrera-Sobek, María. 1982a. "The Acculturation Process of the Chicana in the Corrido." *De Colores* 6 (1–2): 7–16.

———. 1982b. "The Treacherous Woman Archetype: A Structuring Agent in the Corrido." *Aztlán* 13 (1–2): 135–48.

———. 1986. "'La Delgadina': Incest and Patriarchal Structure in a Spanish/Chicano Romance-Corrido." *Studies in Latin American Popular Culture* 5:90–107.

———. 1987. "The Discourse of Love and Despecho: Representations of Women in the Chicano Decima." *Aztlán* 18 (1): 69–82.

———. 1990. *The Mexican Corrido: A Feminist Analysis.* Bloomington: Indiana University Press.

———. 1991. "'Rosita Alvirez': Gender Conflict and the Medieval Exemplum in the Corrido." *Centro de Estudios Puertorriqueños Bulletin* 3 (2): 105–10.

———. 1992. "The Treacherous Woman Archetype: A Structuring Agent in the Corrido." In *Chicano Border Culture and Folklore.* Ed. José Villarino and Arturo Ramírez. 129–43. San Diego, Calif.: Marin Publications.

———. 1993. "The Representation of Mexican Immigrant Women Workers in Ballad and Film: Issues of Ideology and Nationalism." Paper presented at the History of Latina Working Women Conference, George Meany Memorial Archives, Silver Spring, Md.

Jaramillo, Cleofas M. 1939a. *Cuentos del Hogar* (Spanish fairy stories). El Campo, Tex.: Citizen Press.

———. 1939b. *The Genuine New Mexico Tasty Recipes: Pajajes Sabrosos.* Santa Fe, N.Mex.: Seton Village Press.

———. 1941. *Shadows of the Past/Sombras del Pasado.* Santa Fe, N.Mex.: Seton Village Press.

———. 1945. *Romance of a Little Village Girl.* San Antonio, Tex.: Naylor Co.

Jones, Pamela. 1988. "'There Was a Woman': La Llorona in Oregon." *Western Folklore* 47 (3): 195–211.

Jordan, Rosan A. 1975a. "Ethnic Identity and the Lore of the Supernatural." *Journal of American Folklore* 88:370–82.

———. 1975b. "The Folklore and Ethnic Identity of a Mexican American Woman." Ph.D. dissertation, Indiana University.

———. 1985. "The Vaginal Serpent and Other Themes from Mexican Women's Lore." In *Women's Folklore, Women's Culture.* Ed. Rosan A. Jordan and Susan J. Kalcik. 26–44. Philadelphia: University of Pennsylvania Press.

Kay, Margarita Artschwager. 1972. "Health and Illness in the Barrio: Women's Point of View." Ph.D. dissertation, University of Arizona.

Kearney, Michael. 1969. "La Llorona as a Social Symbol." *Western Folklore* 28 (3): 199–206.

Kirtley, Bacil F. 1960. "'La Llorona' and Related Themes." *Western Folklore* 19 (3): 155–168.

Kraul, Edward García, and Judith Beatty, comps. and eds. 1988. *The Weeping Woman: Encounters with La Llorona.* Santa Fe, N.Mex.: Word Process.

La Manita. 1973. *From Envidia to La Llorona . . . A Few Reflections.* Denver, Colo.: Southwest Clearing House for Minority Publications.

Leddy, Betty. 1948. "La Llorona in Southern Arizona." *Western Folklore* 7 (3): 272–77.

———. 1950. "La Llorona Again." *Western Folklore* 9 (4): 363–65.

Limón, José. 1980. "La Vieja Inéz, A Mexican Children's Game: A Research Note." In *Twice a Minority: Mexican American Women.* Ed. Margarita Melville. 88–94. St. Louis, Mo.: Mosby.

———. 1986. "La Llorona, the Third Legend of Greater Mexico: Cultural Symbols, Women, and the Political Unconscious." *Renato Rosaldo Lecture Series Monograph* 2:59–93.

———. 1997. "Tex-Sex-Mex: American Identities, Lone Stars, and the Politics of Racialized Sexuality." *American Literary History* 9 (3): 598–617.

Lomas Garza, Carmen. 1976. "Altares: Arte espiritual del hogar." *Hojas* 1976:105–11.

Lucero-White Lea, Aurora. 1941. *The Folklore of New Mexico.* Vol. 1: *Romances, Corridos, Cuentos, Proverbios, Dichos, Adivinanzas.* Santa Fe, N.Mex.: Seton Press.

———. 1947. *Los Hispanos.* Denver, Colo.: Sage Books.

———. 1953. *Literary Folklore of the Hispanic Southwest.* San Antonio, Tex.: Naylor Co.

Macklin, June. 1980. "'All the Good and Bad in This World': Women, Traditional Medicine, and Mexican American Culture." In *Twice a Minority: Mexican American Women.* Ed. Margarita Melville. 127–48. St. Louis: Mosby.

Márquez, Mary, and Consuelo Pacheco. 1964. "Midwivery Lore in New Mexico." *American Journal of Nursing* 64 (9): 81–84.

Martin, Patricia Preciado. 1992. *Songs My Mother Sang to Me: An Oral History of Mexican American Women.* Tucson: University of Arizona Press.

Mason, Terry. 1980. "Symbolic Strategies for Change: A Discussion of the Chicana Women's Movement." In *Twice a Minority: Mexican American Women.* Ed. Margarita Melville. 95–108. St. Louis: Mosby.

Melville, Margarita. 1994. "'Hispanic' Ethnicity, Race, and Class." In *Handbook of Hispanic Cultures in the United States.* Ed. Francisco Lomelí and Thomas Weaver. 85–106. Houston, Tex.: Arte Público Press.

———, ed. 1980. *Twice a Minority: Mexican American Women.* St. Louis: Mosby.

Mikhail, Blanche I. 1994. "Hispanic Mother's Beliefs and Practices Regarding Selected Children's Health Problems." *Western Journal of Nursing Research* 16 (6): 623–38.

Nájera-Ramírez, Olga. 1994. "Engendering Nationalism: Identity, Discourse, and the Mexican Charro." *Anthropological Quarterly* 67 (1): 1–14.

———. 1997. *La Charreada! Rodeo a la Mexicana.* Videorecording. San Jose, Calif.: KTEH.

———. 1999. "Of Fieldwork, Folklore, and Festival: Personal Encounters." *Journal of American Folklore* 112:183–99.

————. Forthcoming. "Unruly Passions: Poetics, Performance, and Gender in the Ranchera Song." In *Chicana Feminisms: Disruptions in Dialogue*. Ed. Aida Hurtado, Norma Klahn, Olga Nájera-Ramírez, and Patricia Zavella. Durham, N.C.: Duke University Press.

O'Grady, Ingrid Poschmann. 1973. "Childbearing Practices of Mexican-American Women of Tucson, Arizona." M.A. thesis, University of Arizona.

Otero-Warren, Adelina (Nina). 1936. *Old Spain in Our Southwest*. New York: Harcourt Brace and Co.

Oyler, Margaret M. 1952. "Denver Tries a Witch." *Western Folklore* 11 (2): 114–17.

Palacios, Mónica. 1991. "La Llorona Loca: The Other Side." In *Chicana Lesbians: The Girls Our Mothers Warned Us About*. Ed. Carla Trujillo. 49–51. Berkeley, Calif.: Third Woman Press.

Peña, Manuel. 1991. "Class, Gender, and Machismo: The 'Treacherous-Woman' Folklore of Mexican Male Workers." *Gender and Society* 5 (1): 30–47.

Perales, Alonso M. 1972. *La Lechuza: Cuentos de mi Barrio*. San Antonio, Tex.: Naylor Co.

————. 1974. "Violeta and the Owls." In *The Folklore of Texas Cultures*. Ed. Francis Edward Abernethy. 78–81. Austin, Tex.: Encino Press.

Pérez, Soledad. 1949. "Mexican Folklore in Austin." M.A. thesis, University of Texas.

————. 1951. "Mexican Folklore from Austin, Texas." In *The Healer of Los Olmos and Other Mexican Lore*. Ed. Wilson Mathis Hudson. 71–127. Dallas, Tex.: Southern Methodist University Press.

————. 1954. "The Weeping Woman." In *The Best of Texas Folk and Folklore*. Ed. Mody C. Boatright, Wilson M. Hudson, and Allen Maxwell. 127–30. Denton: University of North Texas Press.

Ramírez, Arturo. 1997. "La Llorona: Structure and Archetype." In *Aztlán: Chicano Culture and Folklore, an Anthology*. Ed. José Villarino and Arturo Ramírez. 21–27. San Francisco, Calif.: McGraw Hill.

Rebolledo, Tey Diana. 1995. "From Coatlicue to La Llorona: Literary Myths and Archetypes." In *Women Singing in the Snow: A Cultural Analysis of Chicana Literature*. 49–81. Tucson: University of Arizona Press.

Romano-V., Octavio Ignacio. 1965. "Charismatic Medicine, Folk-Healing, and Folk-Sainthood." *American Anthropologist* 67 (5): 1151–71.

Sánchez Mayers, Raymond. 1989. "Use of Folk Medicine by Elderly Mexican-American Women." *Journal of Drug Issues* 19 (2): 283–95.

Sands, Kathleen Mullen. 1993. *Charrería Mexicana: An Equestrian Folk Tradition*. Tucson: University of Arizona Press.

Sedillo Brewster, Mela. 1935. "New Mexico Weaving and the Practical Vegetable Dyes from Colonial Times." M.A. thesis, University of New Mexico.

Simmons, Marc. 1974. *Witchcraft in the Southwest: Spanish and Indian Supernaturalism on the Rio Grande*. Flagstaff, Ariz.: Northland Press.

Soto, Shirlene Ann. 1986. "Tres modelos culturales: La Virgen de Guadalupe, la Malinche, y la Llorona." *FEM* 10 (48): 13–14.

Turner, Kay. 1982. "Mexican American Home Altars: Toward Their Interpretation." *Aztlán* 13 (1–2): 309–26.

———. 1986. "Home Altars and the Art of Devotion." In *Chicano Expressions: A New View in American Art*. Ed. Inverna Lockpez. 40–47. New York: INTAR Latin American Gallery.

Velasquez Treviño, Gloria. 1988. "Jovita Gonzáles, una voz de resistencia cultural en la temprana narrativa chicana." In *Mujer y Literatura Mexicana y Chicana: Culturas en Contacto*. Ed. Aralia López-González, Amelia Malagamba, and Elena Urrutia. 77–83. Tijuana, Mexico: Colegio de la Frontera Norte.

Walrich, William Jones. 1950. "Five Bruja Tales from the San Luis Valley." *Western Folklore* 9 (1): 359–62.

———. 1994. "The Weeping Woman (La Llorona)." In *The Corn Woman: Stories and Legends of the Hispanic Southwest*. Trans. Jennifer Audrey Lowell and Juan Francisco Marin. 11–13. Englewood, Colo.: Libraries Unlimited.

Weigle, Marta, ed. 1987. *Two Guadalupes: Hispanic Legends and Magic Tales from Northern New Mexico*. Santa Fe, N.Mex.: Ancient City Press.

Williams, Brett. 1984. "Why Migrant Women Feed Their Husbands Tamales: Foodways as a Basis for a Revisionist View of Tejano Family Life." In *Ethnic and Regional Foodways in the United States: The Performance of Group Identity*. Ed. Linda Keller Brown and Kay Mussell. 113–26. Knoxville: University of Tennessee Press.

Wolf, Eric R. 1958. "The Virgin of Guadalupe, A Mexican National Symbol." *Journal of American Folklore* 71:34–39.

Zamora O'Shea, Elena. 2000 [1935]. *Mesquite: A Story of the Early Spanish Settlements between the Nueces and the Rio Grande as Told by "La Posta del Palo Alto."* College Station: Texas A&M University Press.

CONTRIBUTORS

YOLANDA BROYLES-GONZÁLEZ, a native of the Arizona/Sonora borderlands, received her Ph.D. from Stanford University. Currently she is a professor of Chicana studies and German studies at the University of California at Santa Barbara. She is the author of *El Teatro Campesino: Theater in the Chicano Movement* and *Lydia Mendoza's Life in Music/La historia de Lydia Mendoza: Norteño Tejano Legacies*. She also edited *Re-emerging Native Women of the Americas: Native Chicana Latina Women's Studies*.

NORMA E. CANTÚ received her Ph.D. from the University of Nebraska and is currently a professor of English at the University of Texas at San Antonio. Her book, *Canícula: Snapshots of a Girlhood en la frontera*, a fictionalized autobioethnography, was awarded the Premio Aztlán in 1996. She is completing *Soldiers of the Cross: Los Matachines de la Santa Cruz* and a second novel, *Hair Matters*.

MARÍA HERRERA-SOBEK received her Ph.D. from the University of California at Los Angeles. She holds the Luis Leal Endowed Chair in Chicano Studies at the University of California at Santa Barbara. Among her numerous publications are *The Bracero Experience: Elite Lore versus Folklore* and *The Mexican Corrido: A Feminist Analysis*. She is featured in the poetry anthology *Three Times a Woman*.

CÁNDIDA F. JÁQUEZ, an assistant professor in the Department of Folklore at Indiana University in Bloomington, completed her Ph.D. at the University of Michigan at Ann Arbor. She is the director and founder of Mariachi de la Flor and coeditor, with Frances Aparicio, of the forthcoming book *Musical Migrations: Transnationalism and Cultural Hybridity in Latin(o) America.*

HELEN R. LUCERO, the director of visual arts at the National Hispanic Cultural Center, received her Ph.D. from the University of New Mexico. With Susan Baizerman she coauthored *Chimayó Weaving: The Transformation of a Tradition.* She worked on the major traveling exhibition *Arte Latino: Treasures from the Smithsonian American Art Museum* and on the exhibition *Familia y Fe* at the Museum of International Folk Art in Santa Fe.

OLGA NÁJERA-RAMÍREZ, an associate professor of anthropology at the University of California at Santa Cruz, received her Ph.D. from the University of Texas in Austin. Author of *La Fiesta de los Tastoanes: Critical Perspectives in a Mexican Festival Performance,* she also produced the award-winning video *La Charreada: Rodeo a la Mexicana.* Forthcoming is her coedited volume, *Chicana Feminisms: Disruptions in Dialogue.*

TEY MARIANNA NUNN is curator of the Contemporary Hispano and Latino Collection at the Museum of International Folk Art in Santa Fe, New Mexico. She is the author of *Sin Nombre: Hispana and Hispano Artists of the New Deal Era.* She received her Ph.D. from the University of New Mexico in Albuquerque.

DOMINO RENEE PÉREZ, an assistant professor of ethnic literatures and cultural studies at the University of North Texas, received her Ph.D. in English from the University of Nebraska at Lincoln.

LEONOR XÓCHITL PÉREZ received her Ph.D. in education research from the University of California at Los Angeles. Among her publications is the award-winning coauthored article, "College Rankings: Democratized College Knowledge for Whom?" Currently, she performs with Mariachi Mujer 2000, the only all-female mariachi group in the United States directed by a woman.

BRENDA M. ROMERO, an associate professor of ethnomusicology at the University of Colorado in Boulder, received her Ph.D. from the University of California at Los Angeles. She has published articles on the Matachines dance tradition and has edited and contributed to a forthcoming ethnomusicology and world music textbook. She performs the old folk music of the Southwest, including the *inditas.*

DEBORAH R. VARGAS is a Ph.D. candidate in the Department of Sociology at the University of California at Santa Cruz. She is completing her dissertation, "Las Tracaleras: Tejanas and Tex-Mex Music in the 'Making of *Tejas*,'" a feminist cultural studies exploration of Tejanas in music throughout the twentieth century. She was the recipient of the Latino Studies Pre-Doctoral Fellowship at the Smithsonian Institution, National Museum of American History, and is currently a dissertation fellow in Chicana/Latina studies at the University of California at Davis. Born and raised on the west side of San Antonio, she is a researcher and interviewer with the Latino Music Oral History Program at the Alameda Museum in San Antonio.

CYNTHIA L. VIDAURRI, a curator at the Smithsonian Institution, is an expert on U.S.-Mexico borderlands culture. She coproduced *Taquachito Nights: Conjunto Music from South Texas* and co-curated *El Río: Culture and Environment in the Río Grande/Río Bravo Basin* with Olivia Cadaval for the Smithsonian Folklife Festival.

INDEX

The University of Illinois Press
is a founding member of the
Association of American University Presses.

Composed in 10/13 Sabon
with Fajita Mild and Gill Sans display
by Jim Proefrock
at the University of Illinois Press
Designed by Dennis Roberts
Manufactured by Thomson-Shore, Inc.

University of Illinois Press
1325 South Oak Street
Champaign, IL 61820-6903
www.press.uillinois.edu